Supporting

Refugee

Children

Supporting Refugee Children

Strategies for Educators

Jan Stewart

UNIVERSITY OF TORONTO PRESS

Library and Archives Canada Cataloguing in Publication

Stewart, Jan, 1967–
        Supporting refugee children : strategies for educators / Jan Stewart.

Includes bibliographical references and index.
Also issued in electronic format.
ISBN 978-1-4426-0030-0

        1. Refugee children—Education—Canada. 2. Refugee children—Canada— Social conditions. 3. Children and war—Psychological aspects. I. Title.

LC3665.C3S74 2011   371.826'9140971   C2011-901752-0

We welcome comments and suggestions regarding any aspect of our publications—please feel free to contact us at news@utphighereducation.com or visit our Internet site at www.utppublishing.com.

NORTH AMERICA   UK, IRELAND, AND CONTINENTAL EUROPE
5201 Dufferin Street   NBN International
North York, Ontario, Canada, M3H 5T8   Estover Road, Plymouth, PL6 7PY, UK
                                   ORDERS PHONE: 44 (0) 1752 202301
2250 Military Road   ORDERS FAX: 44 (0) 1752 202333
Tonawanda, New York, USA, 14150   ORDERS E-MAIL: enquiries@nbninternational.com

ORDERS PHONE: 1-800-565-9523
ORDERS FAX: 1-800-221-9985
ORDERS E-MAIL: utpbooks@utpress.utoronto.ca

The University of Toronto Press acknowledges the financial support for its publishing activities of the Government of Canada through the Canada Book Fund.

Printed in Canada

For Hana

Contents

PART TWO
PRAXIS

Illustrations

TABLES

Foreword

CANADA IS ONE OF THE WORLD'S LEADERS in resettling individuals flee-ing persecution or oppression in their homelands or those displaced by wars and small-scale, intrastate conflicts around the world. Canada's immigration policies and the work it has done to support refugees have received high praises; therefore, the certain fact is that Canadian educa-tors will find refugee children sitting in their classrooms. Through no fault of their own, children from conflict zones have become heads of family, orphans, or, in some cases, soldiers bearing arms. These involun-tary experiences follow them to their new homes in North America. Are educators ready? Jan Stewart's *Supporting Refugee Children: Strategies for Educators* is an essential resource to help educators take on the chal-lenges associated with teaching war-affected refugee children. While multiculturalism is promoted and celebrated, Stewart emphasizes how it has taken on a new meaning when most orphaned or displaced children and former child soldiers enter the Canadian classroom. Most often, these children are reluctant to share their stories because they are filled with such violence and horror that it makes one marvel at their personal strength.

In *Supporting Refugee Children: Strategies for Educators*, Stewart procures stories from refugee children—sometimes the unbearable truths of their lives—and does so in such a way that their stories become their histories devoid of the sensationalization that is too often viewed in movies and other media. By sharing their stories, Stewart offers them hope in a time of disparity, confusion, and grief. She skilfully links theory and research with practical strategies and lessons. Stewart eloquently weaves together her fieldwork and research with teachers and children in sub-Saharan Africa, her involvement with the Child Soldier Initiative, and her teaching and counselling experiences with refugee children in Canada to provide readers with the most comprehensive knowledge for supporting refugee children. The book's most immediate merit resides in supporting the reader to better understand how refugee children and youth have unique challenges and obstacles, and through careful intervention in the educational system, a teacher can prevent valuable talent loss. The concrete lessons presented in this book are timely, practical and useful examples of what teachers can utilize right now to provide effective programming.

Canadian teachers are expected to, first and foremost, teach core values of respect, responsibility, and care for human life and the environment. A refugee child may come into the classroom after witnessing the most inhumane acts of violence and be expected to follow along with the lessons—to do as the others do. But this is unrealistic. One must not immediately expect the same outcomes from children affected by war and conflict, and Stewart stresses how a better understanding of the children's stories can make a significant difference in how to teach them without lowering the expectations. Relocated children of war, who often arrive by circuitous and dangerous means, may be inclined to regard the unfamiliarity of North American schools with caution. Once in their new environments, children feel lonely, fearful, and essentially defenceless against what may emerge from the unfamiliar surroundings. Some children risk invitations into a life of unscrupulous entrepreneurship by gang members, who may also be former victims of war. What can rescue them from this harmful prospect are, most often, their resourcefulness, their resilience, their caring teachers, and a strong connection with the educational community.

Rooted in both theory and praxis, in a language made for the classroom, this book is an indispensable tool for anyone working with children affected by war. The strategies provided herein can lead children of war on a journey of self-discovery, healing, and hope. This timely, perceptive summary, full of practical teaching strategies, is for novice and master teachers, for social workers and counsellors, for administrators and policy makers. The theoretical framework and lesson guides will become the go-to book for providing authentic teaching strategies in the classroom and for gaining a deeper understanding of the complexities of refugee children.

No reader of this book can fail to note its infusion of enthusiastic promise. My hope is for the messages in this book to reach all those who care about the plight of refugee children in the North American classroom and who want to make a difference in their lives.

Lieutenant-General Roméo Dallaire (Retired)
Ottawa, Ontario

Sokut's Story

THE FOLLOWING STORY WAS WRITTEN BY SOKUT, who was a participant in a study that examined the needs and challenges of children affected by war. Edited by Jan Stewart.

They told us to run. If you hear the horses, run as fast as you can. You never know when the Janjaweeds will attack, and when they do, they will kill or capture everyone they find.

I was five. I was visiting my uncle. My family was in my home village, which is a day's walk away. The soldiers came. I was holding my uncle's hand when the bullet hit him. He fell to the ground, I knew he was dead. I didn't know where to run. I hid in the bush. Women were attacked and raped in front of me.

I saw my own sister. It is very hard to talk about. I try not to remember.

I ran with the other boys, they were running in all directions. For about 100 days we walked through the bush. No shoes, no clothes, no water or food. We ate dead animals. I had to drink my own urine. We had no choice, we would die. Sometimes there was fruit or bark from the trees that we ate. Some of the berries were poisonous and children would die. We knew to be careful, but it was hard to resist; we were so hungry. Someone said that there was food in Dimma, Ethiopia. We walked for two months. There were 20,000 boys and no parents. Most of the girls were captured, but some walked with us. Many of us were taken by insects or by sickness. We had to bury them. I worried that I would go too. I knew that I would never see my family again. Some of the children were too tired to walk—they sat down. They would die of starvation or the wild animals would get them. It was hard to keep going.

I was in Dimma Camp for three years. We had to cook by ourselves and sleep by ourselves. We drank water from the river, but it was not clean. It made our stomachs hurt. The UN gave us maize, beans, and sometimes sugar, oil, and salt. We soaked the rice overnight before we cooked it. The camp was hot and dirty, but we had food.

In 1997, the Ethiopian government was overthrown and the rebels chased us with guns. They gave us one week to leave. We didn't move fast enough. They shot at us. Many children were killed; we were just young children. Coming to Ethiopia was hard, but going back to Sudan was worse. We had to cross the Gilo River. Many more died. I couldn't swim. I held on to the dead bodies in the water to cross. The crocodiles ate some children.

The Sudanese government didn't want us; they thought we would fight them. By the time we got to Sudan, 4,000 boys had died. The Red Cross said we must go to the Kenyan and Sudanese border. It took one month to get there. There was no grass, rivers, or trees—it was a desert. We had to walk at night. We started at 4:00 pm. If we walked in the day, we were shot and killed. The UN dropped food, but sometimes the animals ate it.

I was in a camp at the Kenya-Sudanese border. We had to go to another camp when the Sudanese captured Keapore, which was two hours away. They would come and get us, so they moved us to Kakuma in 1998. I was about nine.

In Kakuma, we were put into groups. There were 16,000 of us and we had to live in groups of five. A school was opened. For grades 1 to 4, we studied under the tree. When I reached grade 5, I studied in the school building. In August 2000, I was moved to Ifo Camp in Dadaab. People in my settlement were moved so that there would be more security.

Ifo Refugee Camp was a hard life for me. The UN told me to go back to Kakuma, but I refused. They told me that I would not get any more food rations if I stayed. I walked to Dadaab town and I cleaned clothes for money and I cut trees in the bush to sell. I was captured by child rebels, but I was not hurt. They didn't want me to take the trees. They said they would kill me if they caught me cutting more trees. I had to keep cutting trees or I would die. In 2001, I went back to Kakuma because the UN adjusted the rule to give everyone food rations.

I was rejected by the Canadian Embassy in 2001 because I was younger than 18. I spent more than two years in a refugee camp in Kenya. I was really 15, but I increased my age to 21. It was not my choice to come to Canada, it was the UN's choice to send me. I lived in Winnipeg with three other boys from Sudan. Two boys were 16 and one was 17. We lived like adults. I have never really been a child … I have had no childhood.

I have been in Canada since 2003. I enjoy being in high school; it is the best part about being in Canada. I came here to have a peaceful life, but my life is not peaceful. It is still hard and I hope that it will change someday. When I came here I thought life would be like heaven. That is what I thought life was like in North America. But it is not. I am still a refugee. It is not safe for me here. I have been threatened and beat up. Other kids attack us because we are African and they think we are gang members. I don't have money for food. There are the same problems for me in Canada that I had in Africa.

Some kids find the street life. They don't have food and they want what Canadian kids have, but they don't have any money. We need more support because sometimes we have to leave school to make money. Schoolwork is hard for us. It takes us longer to do the work and there is no one to help us. I want to educate myself and change my life so that it is better than before. I want to finish my high school. Unless I die, nothing will get in my way.

A total of 40 million people have fled their homes because of armed conflict or human rights violations. It is estimated that 20 million of these displaced people are children (Machel, 2001).

PART ONE

Theory
and
Research

CHAPTER ONE

Children

and Armed Conflict

More and more of the world is being sucked into a desolate moral vacuum. This is a space devoid of the most basic human values; a space in which children are slaughtered, raped, and maimed; a space in which children are exploited as soldiers; a space in which children are starved and exposed to extreme brutality. (Machel, 2001, p. 5)

THE IMPACT OF WAR ON CHILDREN

THROUGHOUT HISTORY, children have been affected by war; however, the nature of war has changed dramatically. In today's conflicts, children assume the roles of casualties of war, soldiers of war, and survivors of war. In August 1996, the secretary-general of the United Nations (UN) released Graça Machel's groundbreaking report entitled *Impact of Armed Conflict on Children*, which revealed that in the past 10 years, as a result of armed conflicts, about 2 million children have been killed, more than 6 million have been disabled, 1 million have been left orphaned, and about 12 million left homeless. It is estimated that in 2001 there were 20 million children who had been uprooted from their homes. Many of these children are internally displaced within their country or they are refugees seeking asylum in another country (Machel, 2001). More than half of all victims of worldwide armed conflict are children, and their experiences with conflict have serious consequences for various aspects of their development (Garbarino & Zurenda, 2008). The United Nations International Children's Fund (UNICEF) estimates that more than 1 billion children live in countries or territories affected by armed conflict and approximately 300 million of these are children under the age of five (United Nations International Children's Fund [UNICEF], 2007).

More than 10 million children have been psychologically scarred by the trauma of abduction, detention, sexual assault, and the brutal murder of family members (Canadian International Development Agency, 2005). Today's warfare often entails horrific levels of violence and brutality aimed specifically at children (Knudson, 2004). The United Nations claims that 10 per cent of the casualties of World War I were civilians and this percentage grew to 45 per cent in World War II. It is estimated that in today's warfare, 90 per cent of the casualties are civilians (UNICEF, 2004). "War undermines the very foundation of children's lives, destroying their homes, splintering their communities and shattering their trust in adults" (Machel, 2001, p. 80).

While there are citizens around the world who have a moral and ethical disposition to promote peace education, human rights, multiculturalism, and diversity, there are others who continue to engage in human rights violations, war crimes, and crimes against humanity. Murder, abduction, torture, rape, and the military use of children are ubiquitous to the wars occurring in approximately 30 countries. The United Nations reports that there are 57 parties in situations of armed conflict that have committed "grave violations against children" (UN General Assembly, 2008, p. 2). Armed conflict refers to a much broader spectrum of violence than war; however, these forms of conflict have created additional direct and devastating effects on children, including "unlawful recruitment, sexual violence, displacement, killing and maiming, separation from family, trafficking and illegal detention" (UNICEF, 2007, p. 1). These consequences are exacerbated by the numerous indirect effects such as loss of basic services, health and education, and a rise of poverty, malnutrition, and disease.

While exemplary programs and services to support children after war do exist, these are at best a piecemeal approach to solving a widespread problem that if not addressed has serious consequences for this generation of children. For years the gap between the Global South and the North (or "the rich and the poor") has continued to widen, while very few citizens of the North appeared to notice and even less of them demonstrated that they cared. Evidence of genocides and eliminationism persist while most of the world does little to understand why they occur. Powerful countries with tremendous wealth, access to technology, and sophisticated communication systems neglect to intervene despite knowledge of mass slaughter and human suffering (Goldhagen, 2009). UN Security Resolutions concerning children and armed conflict, such as 1612 (2005) and 1882 (2009), exist on paper (UN Security Council, 2010), but limited evidence suggests that these concepts or policies are enacted to the point that they were intended. For a full discussion on Security Council Resolutions on Children in Armed Conflict, see Chapter 4 of *Children and Armed Conflict* by the International Bureau for Children's Rights (IBCR) (2010). Despite reports of some progress, the UN Security Council reports they are

> *deeply concerned* that children continue to account for a considerable number of casualties resulting from killing and maiming in armed conflicts including as a result of deliberate targeting, indiscriminate and excessive use of force, indiscriminate use of landmines, cluster munitions and other weapons and use of children as human shields and *equally deeply concerned* about the high incidence and appalling levels of brutality of rape and other forms of sexual violence committed against children, in the context of and associated with armed conflict including the use or commissioning of rape and other forms of sexual violence in some situations as a tactic of war. (UN Security Council, 2009, p. 2)

It has been more than 10 years since Graça Machel's report and children continue to be killed, maimed, trafficked, and raped with little concern from the international community. More recent tactics in conflict include using children as suicide bombers and human shields (IBCR,

2010). The protection of children will require an ecologically based, multisectoral approach that includes discussion and action from social welfare, education, health, law enforcement, and justice (UNICEF, 2007). Monitoring, reporting, and adhering to legislations and plans of action will be an integral part of providing children the protection in which they are entitled. Understanding better how children are affected by conflict holds important information that can make significant progress in how we educate and support children after war.

Literature related to refugees has typically focused on political, medical, social, and linguistic issues pertaining largely to adult populations. Less research has been conducted on the issues concerning refugee children, and there is a paucity of literature related to the unique issues of refugee children who have been affected by armed conflict. There is insufficient knowledge about the effects of conflict, the displacement of children, and the types of interventions that are needed to help children who have emigrated from countries affected by war. Because of the significant between-group differences between cultural groups and the diverse circumstances affecting refugees, it is difficult to determine commonalities and similarities between children's learning and development across the different contexts and settings in which they live (Anderson, Hamilton, Moore, Loewen, & Frater-Mathieson, 2004). As such, general guiding principles for the development and assessment of instructional interventions for refugee children must be more clearly defined and educational policy should be developed to ensure that the needs of these children are addressed with the necessary support systems.

Children and adolescents who have been exposed to war and are now attending schools in Canada represent a particularly vulnerable group of students. Their experiences have been diverse and many have suffered from severe personal trauma, violence, and loss. It is argued that the current system is not meeting the unique social and psychological needs of these students and they are not provided with an appropriate education. When students' needs are not being met by the system, students often leave it, either reluctantly or voluntarily. This often results in the exacerbation of social issues and the further marginalization of the individual.

EDUCATIONAL ISSUES

It is expected that the number of students coming to Canada from war-affected countries will increase significantly over the next decade (Statistics Canada, 2007), and this will likely compound many of the current issues we already see in schools and in the community. School leaders and educators need to learn about the issues related to war-affected children so that they are able to understand how they might best meet the needs of these students. This process requires working with these students, their families, and the communities in which they live to acquire cultural understandings, shared values, and pragmatic solutions for a more socially just school system. Educators must critically examine and reflect on current practice and then use this knowledge to transform future practice. The Canadian school system is in a unique position to provide educational interventions and psychosocial support to refugee children. Moreover, the educational system must become more prepared and knowledgeable about the experiences and needs of refugee students to more adequately address their learning needs.

WHERE TO START

In September 2005, Winnipeg hosted a conference on war-affected children that included representatives from the United Nations, World Vision, War Child, Canadian Foreign Affairs, as well as national and international scholars. The key recommendation from this conference was the need to educate teachers and school leaders on the issues of war-affected children and youth and to develop practical strategies for helping these students. Considering the increasing number of refugee children coming to Canada, it is timely to review existing literature, explore approaches for helping war-affected children, and suggest future directions for research, practice, and policy.

Although some students adjust quite well into Canadian schools, others do not (MacKay & Tavares, 2005). Little empirical evidence is available to examine the factors that contribute to the successful adjustment of these students into Canadian schools, and information on the effects of different types of interventions remains sparse. The context of the school environment is crucial to the pro-social development and the acculturation of the war-affected child (Boothby, Strang, & Wessells, 2006; Hamilton & Moore, 2004; McBrien, 2004; Rutter, 2003, 2006; Rutter & Jones, 1998). Having said this, little information is available on the most suitable educational context and the most appropriate support mechanisms for the student.

The trajectories of these youth hinge on our ability to provide the most appropriate educational program that meets their diverse learning needs. By "our" I refer to the local, divisional, provincial, and national educational communities across Canada. For far too long the majority of the educational community has had a taken-for-granted notion that refugee students should be treated "just like every other student" and they should readily assimilate into our classrooms and schools. It is now imperative that educational communities adjust to the changing landscape of Canada and that they work diligently to address the needs of refugee children.

While some meritorious programs and services do exist in pockets across the country, the reality is that schools are, for the most part, failing these children and contributing to their marginalization in society. A growing number of advocates strongly criticize the educational community for their lack of attention to the needs of refugee children. This generation of youth will be the parents and workers in the next decade, and it is imperative that the present school system responds to their immediate needs. School is arguably one of the most influential social systems—it has the ability to significantly affect our lives, both in how we think and how we conduct ourselves as individuals and as a collective society. As such, most would agree that theory and practice should support the type of system that liberates rather than marginalizes; few offer pragmatic ways to make this occur.

The stories of war and the harrowing atrocities that children and adults have endured are a burgeoning topic in literature, film, and speaking events as many more people "tell their story" to the world. The realities of these stories are played out in classrooms throughout the world. How do we teach a former child soldier? How do you teach calculus to a student who has not learned to write his or her name? Where do you start with a 15-year-old student who has never been to school? How do we help students to feel safe in our classrooms and school hallways?

Host countries such as Canada, the United States, the United Kingdom, and Australia permit a predetermined annual quota of immigrants and refugees into their respective countries. Collectively, these countries fall short on the support and assistance that is needed to ensure that these people are given a fair shot at fulfilling their dreams and making a successful transition to a new culture (Boyden & de Berry, 2004; Hamilton & Moore, 2004; McBrien, 2009; Stewart, 2007). As Sokot, the young man in the prologue, articulates, "I am still a refugee." Although the food that he eats and the clothes he wears are different, he is, in his mind, still a refugee. This is a compelling statement that should mobilize the local and international communities to act. Perhaps we need to ask ourselves as a collective society if we are "okay" with our newest citizens feeling this way. Moreover, when we hear statements from newcomer parents such as "I would be better off going home" or "My children are not safe in Canada," we know that there is work to do in the area of supporting new Canadians.

While the aforementioned discourse sounds bleak, one overarching positive factor has the potential to make a tremendous difference in the lives of refugee children. Education is a catalyst to change and schools are where most students want to be. The role of educators does not need to be overly complicated. In most cases, it does not require a large-scale school reform movement or a new cutting-edge method of teaching. Before building elaborate programs and services that have not been empirically tested to be effective or helpful, we must first recognize the existing barriers to student success. As the following chapters will elaborate, there are broad systemic issues underlying the challenges facing refugee children, and the first steps to addressing a problem are to recognize it, understand its complexities within a larger systemic context, and make a conscious decision to do something about it.

Book Overview

The following chapters will examine some of the experiences of children who have been affected by war and are now living in Canada. Some of the key educational challenges for these students will be outlined, and the systems, structures, or programs that assist with the process of adjustment for refugee students will also be investigated. To do this, various ecological systems that interact with one another to influence student development will be explored. An ecological model will be woven through the following chapters as a means to connect the conversations and to link the research to educational practice.

This book examines the personal, social, and academic needs of refugee students who are now living in Canada. The motivation for writing this book was to address the challenges and obstacles that refugee children and youth encounter while living in Canada and to discuss factors that contribute to students dropping out or being pushed out of the school system. By doing this, I hope to provide educators with a more thorough understanding of the issues refugee children encounter throughout the three phases of migration. This book will also provide numerous practical recommendations and activities to support refugee students and keep them connected to school and the community.

The focus will be on students at the secondary level as there appears to be a paucity of programs and services available in high schools and this is typically the time when students, who are not having success, leave the school system. A significant section of this book will be devoted to outlining ways that policies and practices could better support refugee children. Specific recommendations and practical lessons are included to provide educators with activities and strategies to support refugee children. Not intending to be a "how to" model, the purpose of providing lessons is to suggest some practical strategies that have been developed to support children after war. The lessons have been developed in collaboration with non-government agencies who work with refugee children, school teachers, education faculty members, and teachers from northern Uganda.

This book is designed for pre-service and practising teachers, administrators, counsellors, special education teachers, English as an Additional Language (EAL, formerly known as English as a Second Language [ESL]) teachers, and resource teachers. It is also an excellent resource for education policy makers and administrators, social workers, mental health practitioners, and agency workers who are involved in issues related to the improvement of services and programs for refugee children.

Contents in this book are drawn from a qualitative study conducted in Winnipeg, Manitoba (2007) and a similar study conducted in Uganda (2008). To protect the names of the participants and the research locations, pseudonyms are used and fictional names have been given to the schools, organizations, and community agencies discussed throughout the book. Additional data are derived from an ongoing research project, starting in 2009 among the University of Winnipeg, the University of South Florida, Kenyatta University in Kenya, Kigali Institute of Education in Rwanda, and Makerere University in Uganda. Observations and anecdotal notes have also been collected over the past six years while I have worked as the director of the Institute for Children Affected by War at the Global College, affiliated with the University of Winnipeg, and over the past two decades of working as a teacher and counsellor in the public school system. Having the opportunity to teach both undergraduate- and graduate-level courses for educators on the topic of teaching and counselling children who have been affected by war has contributed significantly to the practical activities and the suggested teaching strategies that are offered in this book. Working with the newcomer community has encouraged me to examine critically the ways in which we educate refugee children and the means by which we support their families. I hope that this book provides practising educators and pre-service educators with a greater understanding of the issues related to refugee children as well as concrete and practical suggestions and lessons to assist with their educational programs.

I have organized this book into two main parts that systematically build on each other to provide readers with a balance of the theory, research, and recommendations for practice. While it would be logical to begin with an overview of the related literature to provide a context for the issues discussed herein, I have chosen to begin with the stories and voices of the people who I believe are the "experts" in the field. I have endeavoured to bring forth the voices of the participants from the study whenever possible. This narrative approach was purposefully chosen to bring the reader as close to the stories and events as possible and to allow for the opportunity to make inferences and to analyze the data independently. The risk in doing this is to sensationalize the stories and to contribute to the marginalization of the individuals who have entrusted me with their stories. This is not my intent; rather, I have chosen to weave together the stories to create a composite picture of the numerous experiences and complex challenges that children have endured before and after coming to Canada. As the researcher and writer, I feel a tremendous responsibility to the participants to be accurate, honest, and true to the events that they discussed. I have been told these stories with the purpose of understanding their personal issues. With this, I hope that these stories are heard by the people who craft policies and who create change in organizations that will improve the lives of children who have been affected by war.

PHILOSOPHICAL FOUNDATION

Originating from the fundamental principles put forth by critical theorists, the purpose of this book is to identify how current educational systems respond to the needs of children who have been affected by war, to discuss some of the inadequacies that have been identified in both the related literature and research, and to suggest recommendations and strategies to better meet the needs of these students. To do this, it is important that the reader be informed of the philosophical orientation and overarching lens of the author so that the discussion is appropriately framed and the context is clearly defined.

The philosophical underpinnings herein originate in critical theory, post-colonial theory, work in educational administration and leadership, and literature in multiculturalism, diversity, critical race theory, social justice, and citizenship.

Critical Social Theory

Stemming from Plato and from the modern Marxist and anti-colonialist thinkers were the contributions of Brazilian-born philosopher Paulo Freire. In his seminal work, *Pedagogy of the Oppressed* (1970), Freire criticizes the top-down "banking model" of education. According to Freire, the banking concept of education considers the teacher as the authority of knowledge who deposits information upon those considered to know nothing. Freire asserts that the process of dialogue is what positions the needs, wants, and interests of marginalized people at the centre of their learning and what frees them from oppression. Liberating the oppressed requires "... the action and reflection of men and women upon their world in order to transform it" (Freire, 1970, p. 79). The fundamental goal of the dialogical process is to create a process of learning where the oppressed are positioned at the centre of the process. Freire states, "It is absolutely essential that the oppressed participate in the revolutionary process with an increasingly critical awareness of their role as Subjects of the transformation" (p. 127).

Freire's arguments are particularly relevant to the assumptions underlying my work with refugee populations. Although Freire argues that the oppressed must be actively engaged in their own liberation, leadership or active facilitation of the process is still necessary. If researchers do not assume the role of facilitators of liberation or, worse, if they continue to promulgate the ideological characteristics of oppressors, little progress will be made toward social justice. Educational researchers must look for and expose the inequities they find in the school system; to do this, researchers must engage in dialogue with marginalized populations in an attempt to find strategies for the problems they discover. While pre-service teachers and practising teachers may not view themselves as educational leaders or school administrators, the critical discourse stemming from this field provides essential background and scholarship to support a solid argument about what kind of changes are needed and what type of thinking is necessary if we hope to transform schools so that they are culturally relevant and socially just for all children.

Post-Colonial Theory

Post-colonial theory emerged as a major critical theory in the humanities while at the same time globalization emerged in the social sciences. It is an effort by academics to question and explore power, politics, international relations, and, most importantly, knowledge after colonialism began, as opposed to after colonialism ended. Post-colonialism seeks to gain theoretical knowledge from the past. Because a generally accepted definition of colonialism or post-colonial theory is not clear, much of the writing generated under these terms is rather diffuse. Post-colonialism includes the period of time marking the beginning, continuance, and aftermath of colonial rule. The term *post-colonialism* is not meant to be understood literally as the time after colonialism; however, understanding the concepts of colonialism and imperialism are necessary to understand contemporary meanings and implications for post-colonial theory.

Post-colonialism refers to the "multiple political, economic, cultural and philosophical responses to colonialism from its inauguration to the present day ..." (Hiddleston, 2009, p. 1). Post-colonial is used to describe experiences in different geographical places, a specific time period, the relationship between space and time and specific events, in addition to a critique of oppression and subjugation (Lunga, 2008). Considering the intersections of the past and the present with much of the post-colonial discourse, an examination of both imperialism and colonialism helps to inform the current discussions and debates surrounding this theory. Colonialism is generally agreed upon as a deliberate act of conquest and exploitation, whereas *imperialism* is a broader term related to domination and authority. Post-colonial thinkers hope to deconstruct and analyze the assumptions made during and after colonialism by destabilizing the dominant discourse and bringing forth the voices of the "marginalized" or "subaltern" in an effort to equalize power and to establish mutual respect.

The long-term consequences of colonialism and how these have informed current-day thinking are the essence of post-colonial critique. Post-colonial theory involves critical thinking and questioning about identity, race, gender, ethnicity, racism, language, place, history, and globalization. It is the epistemological and ontological investigation into power and resistance, knowledge and identity, and how this is used by the colonized and the colonizers, by the developing and the developed. How knowledge is legitimized and shared to satisfy imperial interests is a central construct of post-colonial theory. This theory is self-reflexive and theorists are continually questioning their own assumptions and personal self-interests. Spivak (1985) posits it is impossible to challenge that which one intimately inhabits. Speaking for and representing others cannot be separated from power inequalities.

The representations of the following narratives contained in this book are implicated by my own epistemological and ontological constructs of position and power of which I cannot be separated. I also acknowledge these stories will be influenced by my own perspectives because of the place that I hold as a citizen of the western world. Parker (1998) refers to the potential for problems associated with researchers studying African-American communities. He argues that the process can lead to subject exploitation, the misuse of power, and the failure to self-question the nature of university status and privilege. That said, the use of qualitative research and the techniques of storytelling and the general theme of "voice" are regarded by numerous researchers as being highly effective in challenging racial policies and providing the contextual background to positivist perspectives (Delgado & Stefancic, 2000; Dixson & Rousseau, 2005; Ladson-Billings, 1998; Ladson-Billings & Tate, 1995; Stovall, 2005, 2006). While I have framed and woven together the narratives from the students, I have constructed this discussion without adopting an expert opinion and with conscious thought about my position as a western researcher. In doing so, I have attempted to bring the voices of the participants to the forefront of this discourse without imposing intellectual rhetoric and perpetuating homogeneous assumptions and classifications of people. The use of the term *voice* does not suggest that one common experience is shared by all refugees. For further reading on post-colonial theory, see Bhabha (1994), Gandhi (1998), Memmi (1967), Said (1978, 1993), Spivak (1985), and Young (2001). For edited books and collections of various post-colonial theorists, see Ashcroft & Ahluwalia (1999), Brydon (v. 1–5) (2000), Castle (2001), and Williams & Chrisman (1994).

THEORETICAL FRAMEWORK
Urie Bronfenbrenner's Bioecological Model

The theoretical framework utilized in the discussion in the following chapters originated from three distinct models. Urie Bronfenbrenner's bioecological model (Bronfenbrenner & Morris, 1999) provided the framework for the investigation into the psychosocial and educational needs of war-affected children. The model of refugee adaptation and development (Anderson et al., 2004) was amalgamated with

Bronfenbrenner's model to examine the points of potential disruption for refugee students and to also consider the typical points of major developmental changes in adolescence. The theory of segmented assimilation (Portes & Zhou, 1993) provided the initial framework on which to understand the process by which refugee children adjust to or assimilate into the school culture in Canada.

Bronfenbrenner's seminal work in 1979, entitled *The Ecology of Human Development*, made significant contributions to the field of developmental psychology. The ecological model investigates the role of the environment in shaping human development through the life course (Bronfenbrenner, 1979). Bronfenbrenner believes that human development occurs in contexts or environments that are ever-changing. His theory purports that humans do not develop in isolation; rather, they develop in relation to the various contexts or systems to which they belong throughout their life. Two important distinctions of Bronfenbrenner's theory are that the person is both a producer and a product of development. Moreover, the individual and the environment are in a reciprocal relationship whereby the person is both influenced by the environment and also influences that environment. Secondly, the environment is not a single entity; rather, it is the compilation of several multilevel environments and the interconnections between them (Bronfenbrenner, 1979).

Bronfenbrenner's most recent model makes a clear distinction between environment and process (Bronfenbrenner, 1999), and as such it is now called the bioecological model. Bronfenbrenner and Morris (1999) note that the bioecological model is a "more complex reciprocal interaction between an active, evolving biopsychological human organism and the persons, objects, and symbols in its immediate external environment" (p. 996). Bronfenbrenner intentionally expands and differentiates the original conceptualizations in an effort to illustrate the practical application of his theory. Although the basic tenets of the theory remain unchanged, evidence suggests that the model has become more complex and multifaceted through the years.

One of the key criticisms of Bronfenbrenner's theory is the lack of developmental stages, which for the purposes of this conversation is seen as its most valued attribute. Uncertainty, turmoil, and crisis are ubiquitous in the lives of children who have come from countries of war.

The investigation into their personal experiences and their educational needs requires a framework that is multidimensional and comprehensive so that it includes the many factors that could potentially impact the developmental stages of the child. Trauma, stress, and change disrupt the development of children, and a model to investigate these events must be flexible and adaptable enough to capture the appropriate data.

Anderson et al. (2004) adapted Bronfenbrenner's ecological model to include three phases of migration: pre-migration, trans-migration, and post-migration, which acknowledge the disruptions in the individual's life in addition to the other developmental or ecological changes (e.g., puberty, starting a new school year). Anderson et al. state, "The development of the refugee child is influenced by the ever-changing ecologies that surround and interact with the child, for the refugee child, the potential for major changes in the ecologies can occur due to pre-migration, trans-migration and post-migration factors" (p. 8). In addition to these phases of migration, normal developmental changes will be occurring simultaneously that will also need to be considered.

ENVIRONMENTAL SYSTEMS

Bronfenbrenner (1999) conceptualizes the ecological environment "as a set of nested systems ranging from the 'micro' to the 'macro'" (p. 11). Five environmental systems, ranging from the individual's family to the broader culture of society, provide a framework for the model. At the centre of the model are the individual and the specific characteristics that influence and shape the course of his or her development (see Figure 1.1). Bronfenbrenner refers to the five systems as the microsystem, mesosystem, exosystem, macrosystem, and chronosystem. These five systems are examined in relation to the refugee youths and their process of adjustment to Canadian society. Because of the interconnectedness of the model, it would be remiss to study the individual through only one system, specifically the school, in an effort to determine the educational interventions that would foster the psychosocial development of the refugee student. Not only did this model provide an organizational structure to the investigations, but it also provided insight into what systems needed to be involved and what interventions needed to occur in order to provide both short-term and long-term assistance to these students.

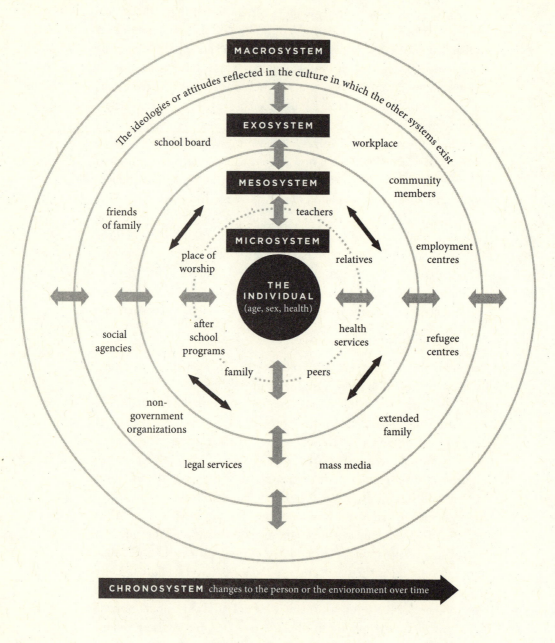

FIGURE 1.1 *Bioecological Model*

As the following discussion reveals, educational support will include the interactions of numerous systems that, to some degree, all influence the development of the individual. The following pages will define the five systems that comprise the bioecological model put forth by Bronfenbrenner and Morris (1999) and will discuss the importance of examining these systems to better understand the issues related to refugee children.

MICROSYSTEM. The microsystem represents the closest and most inner circle of relationships that the individual has with people, objects, or symbols in his or her immediate environment. "A microsystem is a pattern of activities, social roles, and interpersonal relations experienced by the developing person in a given face-to-face setting with particular physical, social, and symbolic features that invite, permit, or inhibit, engagement in sustained, progressively more complex interaction with, and activity in, the immediate environment" (Bronfenbrenner, 1994, p. 1645). The microsystem is the immediate environment in which the individual lives and it includes the close interpersonal relations with the person's family, relatives, peers, teachers, or others who participate in the life of the developing person on a fairly regular basis over extended periods of time (Bronfenbrenner & Morris, 1999).

MESOSYSTEM. The mesosystem refers to the linkages or connections among the various microsystems, or contexts. Examples might include the linkages between the school experiences and the family, or the family and the peer group. Bronfenbrenner (1979) states, "A mesosystem comprises the interrelations among two or more settings in which the developing person actively participates (such as, for the child, the relations among home, school, and neighbourhood peer group; for an adult, among family, work, and social life)" (p. 25). A mesosystem is formed whenever the individual moves into a new setting. The linkages or interconnections may take on a variety of forms, both formal and informal. Experiences in one microsystem can have an effect on another microsystem.

EXOSYSTEM. The exosystem represents the events that occur in more distant systems that indirectly affect the experiences in the immediate context. The exosystem might be comprised of friends of the family, community members, social agencies, or neighbours. What occurs in these more distant systems can indirectly influence the individual. For example, school board members have an integral role in determining the priorities for the school division, which indirectly affects the programs and services offered to children in the school. These programs could hinder or assist with the refugee child's development.

MACROSYSTEM. The macrosystem represents the ideologies or attitudes reflected in the culture in which the other systems exist. This system includes the values, customs, and laws of the society. In essence, the macrosystem refers to the homogeneity found within the same culture, such as the roles and relations in the particular settings, the types and kinds of settings, and the organization and content of activities in the settings.

CHRONOSYSTEM. The chronosystem refers to the changes in an environment that occur over the time that the individual lives. These developmental changes are triggered by life events or experiences that occur both internally, within the individual (e.g., puberty), or externally, in the environment (e.g., birth of a sibling) (Bronfenbrenner, 1992). "Whatever their origin, the critical feature of such events is that they alter the existing relation between person and environment, thus creating a dynamic that may instigate developmental change" (Bronfenbrenner, 1992, p. 201). The most notable of environmental changes for refugee children is most certainly the transition to a new country. The move to a new country will likely be accompanied by changes in the child's social class, family structure, and system of education. Long-term changes will also occur with the individual as he or she adjusts to a new culture. These changes could quite possibly occur throughout the rest of his or her life (e.g., career, marriage, changing family dynamics).

Because of the vast array of experiences that characterize the lives of refugee children, and the significance of the pre-migration, trans-migration, and post-migration events and circumstances, the bioecological model provided a framework that supported the investigation of the individual within his or her ecosystem. The model supported the investigation of the individual and the examination of the factors that influenced his or her life as the individual moved from one country to another. Because the pre-migration experiences that children and youth have had prior to coming to Canada are so unique, and in many cases traumatic, understanding the individual from this perspective was paramount to the research. For most individuals, environmental changes occur gradually over time, but for the refugee, these changes are more sudden and occur at all levels of the individual's environments, ranging from micro to macro.

Changes for some refugee children, in particular children who are affected by war, occur in almost all aspects of their lives: family structure, schooling, community, friends, culture, and the overarching society in which they live. Bronfenbrenner's model provides a framework in which to examine all of the environments that affect the individual as well as how these environments are connected to, and influence, each other. The basic premise of the bioecological model is that "development is a function of the forces emanating from multiple settings and from the relations between these settings" (Bronfenbrenner, 1999, p. 17). Combining this framework with the three phases of a refugee's migration to a host country (Anderson et al., 2004) provides the most comprehensive illustration of the unique experiences of these students as well as insight into their psychosocial and educational needs. The knowledge derived from the investigations provide insight into how best to assist these students using an integrative systems approach at all three phases of migration.

Segmented Assimilation

The concept of segmented assimilation was first introduced by Portes and Zhou (1993) and then further expanded as a result of data that were collected by the Children of Immigrants Longitudinal Study (CILS) conducted by Portes and Zhou (1993) during the 1990s on both coasts of the United States. More than 5,200 youths from several different nationalities were followed throughout their high school years. Portes and Zhou discovered that there were many contingencies and too many variables to suggest a straightforward path to assimilation. Zhou (1997) asserts, "Segmented assimilation theory offers a theoretical framework for understanding the process by which the new second generation—the

**FOUR FACTORS CONTRIBUTING TO
ASSIMILATION PATTERNS**

1 The situation of first generation that immigrates
2 The pace at which parents and children acculturate
3 Cultural and economic barriers confronted by
   immigrant youth (race, location, mobility ladders)
4 Resources (family and community) available to
   manage the barriers

**STRAIGHT-
LINE
THEORY**

(Consonant
acculturation)

**DOWNWARD
SPIRAL**

(Dissonant
acculturation)

**UPWARD
MOBILITY
AND ETHNIC
SOLIDARITY**

(Selective
acculturation)

**PARALLEL
INTEGRATION
INTO WHITE
MIDDLE CLASS**

Direct family
support
•
Parental guidance
and family resources
•
Mostly upward
assimilation;
blocked at times by
discrimination

**ASSIMILATION
INTO THE
UNDERCLASS**

Drop out of school
•
Gang involvement
•
Racialized
•
Permanently
impoverished
•
Drug involvement
•
Criminal activity
•
Imprisonment

**RAPID ECONOMIC
ADVANCEMENT
WITH DELIBERATE
PRESERVATION OF
COMMUNITY'S
VALUES AND TIGHT
SOLIDARITY**

Family and community
support filtered through
ethnic networks
•
Upward assimilation with
biculturalism
•
Little or no
intergenerational conflict

FIGURE 1.2 *Segmented Assimilation Model*

children of contemporary immigrants—becomes incorporated into the system of stratification in the host society and the different outcomes of this process" (p. 975).

Three major challenges to educational achievement and career success of children of immigrants have been delineated by several authors: (1) the persistence of racial discrimination, (2) the bifurcation of the American labour market, and (3) the consolidation of marginalized people in the inner city (Portes, Fernandez-Kelly, & Haller, 2005; Portes & Rumbaut, 2001; Portes & Zhou, 1993). Together, these factors contribute to the educational achievement and ultimately the pattern of assimilation for the immigrant child.

Using Portes and Zhou's (1993) conceptualizations of the three forms of assimilation and the factors that influence adaptation into American society provides an initial framework for the purpose of analyzing the data pertaining to refugee children. The theory of segmented assimilation is also supported by extensive empirical support from their longitudinal study as well as studies conducted by other researchers, who have confirmed many of their assertions (Gibson, 1998; Hirschman, 2001; McBrien, 2005; Nunez, 2004).

The theoretical framework proposed by Portes and Zhou (1993) includes three possible patterns of assimilation: straight-line theory, upward mobility, or downward spiral (see Figure 1.2).

Straight-line theory refers to the pattern in which immigrants assimilate into the white middle-class majority (Portes & Zhou, 1993; Zhou, 1997). This pattern is one of growing acculturation and paralleled integration into the white middle class. Examples used to illustrate this concept are the European immigrants who arrived in America post–World War II. Straight-line theory is also referred to as "consonant acculturation" (Rumbaut & Portes, 2001). The second path is that of upward mobility and ethnic solidarity, which is associated with "rapid economic advancement with deliberate preservation of the immigrant community's values and tight solidarity" (Portes & Zhou, 1993, p. 82). This second path is referred to as "selective acculturation" (Rumbaut & Portes, 2001).

The last pattern of adaptation, the downward spiral, leads to "permanent poverty and assimilation into the underclass" (Portes & Zhou,

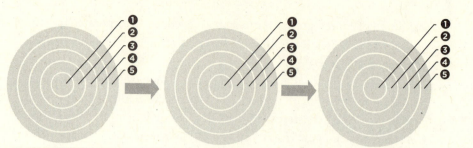

1. Individual 2. Microsystem 3. Mesosystem 4. Exosystem 5. Macrosystem

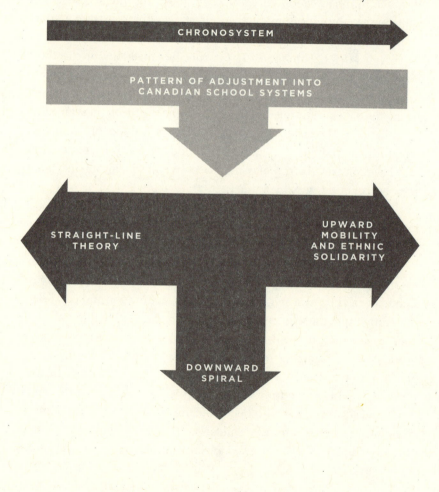

FIGURE 1.3 *Conceptual Framework*

1993, p. 82). This unsuccessful pattern is associated with cultural dissonance. Children associated with this pattern of assimilation often acquire language skills much faster than their parents, join oppositional peer groups consisting of other marginalized peers, and often reject the culture of their parents as they adopt more North American values. Family conflicts increase as the values of the parents differ from those of their child. This pattern is also referred to as "dissonant acculturation" (Portes & Rumbaut, 2001).

Knowing what leads to the pattern of a downward spiral of assimilation may assist with the development of programs, services, or support networks that can help to prevent or limit this occurrence. While most refugees aspire to the lifestyles of the upper middle class (Portes et al., 2005), it is clear that not everyone will achieve this outcome "... at the opposite end of society, there is a very unenviable scenario of youth gangs, drug-dictated lifestyles, premature childbearing, imprisonment, and early death" (Portes et al., 2005, p. 1004).

The overarching framework for the major study informing much of this book included the tenets of the bioecological model (as illustrated in Figure 1.1) combined with the three phases of migration (as outlined in the model of refugee adaptation and development by Anderson et al. [2004]), as well as the theory of segmented assimilation (Portes & Zhou, 1993, 1997) (see Figure 1.3). For a more detailed explanation of these three theories, see Stewart (2007), *Children Affected by War: A Bioecological Investigation into Their Psychosocial and Educational Needs.*

CHAPTER TWO

Pre-Migration, Trans-Migration, and Post-Migration

A RESEARCH STUDY WAS CONDUCTED in Winnipeg, Manitoba that investigated the educational needs and challenges of children from war-affected backgrounds. More than 50 participants were interviewed from various ecological systems as a means to examine some critical issues for refugee children and the people who work with them. For a more detailed description of the research study, see Stewart (2007). I will weave together the stories from the students and the participants from the various ecological systems to construct a narrative account of the educational and psychosocial needs of children who have come from war-affected countries. In the following chapters I will discuss some of their challenges and successes, their problems and suggestions, as well as the programs, services, and systems that are needed to support their adjustment to Canada.

PRE-MIGRATION EXPERIENCES

For the purpose of this discussion, the period of pre-migration is the time that the student spent in his or her country of origin. Trans-migration is the time spent fleeing war (travelling within the same continent) or the time spent living in a refugee camp. Trans-migration also includes the time spent travelling to Canada. Post-migration experiences are those that occur in Canada. This chapter will focus on more of the short-term post-migration experiences and the following chapter will outline the long-term post-migration experiences.

All student interviews began with a question about their experiences prior to coming to Canada. It became apparent that these experiences could not possibly be generalized into a set of characteristics that would adequately describe the pre-migration or trans-migration experiences. Combined with the information obtained from the participants in the microsystem, the pre-migration and trans-migration phases were highly varied and ranged in almost every possible characteristic. It was also difficult to discern all of the details in the various stories and to sort out all of the events that occurred.

Many student comments about their past experiences were somewhat rushed and some students hesitated before providing an answer. However, later in the interview, more details were provided. The tentativeness at the beginning of the interview was most likely a result of the students and me both becoming more comfortable with each other. Although specific information was divulged, often subtle hints led me to think that there was more information than what the participants shared. Anna asked me midway through the interview if I wanted to know about her circumstances because it would take more of my time. She then disclosed a very personal story, uninterrupted, for the next hour.

The following quote from Akot illustrates both the initial tentativeness in answering the question as well as the seemingly matter-of-fact statement that both of his parents were murdered. This was later discussed in more detail. The interview with Akot began with the researcher asking him about his experiences in Sierra Leone.

> It's kind of hard to ... well, there is not enough food. And the shelter, the shelter is different, like there is no place to sleep at all.

I used to live with my uncle ... I'm thankful that I am in Canada now.

My parents are dead already. I didn't know them at all [pause].

They made a mistake on my age. I am 18 right now, but I came with a different age. My age on paper is 21. I am 18.

At times it was almost as if some of the students were asking permission to go into more detail before they explained what their life was like in their country of origin or in the refugee camp. I found that when I told them I knew very little about the area where they came from and that I needed help understanding what it was like for them, they felt more at ease.

The references to suffering, loss, and pain were evident in all of the student interviews. What became interesting was the seemingly matter-of-fact manner in which many of the students told their stories or parts of their stories to me. Some of the students looked away when they talked about loss or witnessing violence, and some of their voices became quiet or they became emotional (watery eyes, cracking voices) while they were speaking, and I noticed that they often changed the topic quickly or stopped talking altogether. I sensed a distance between their current lives and their pre-migration experiences, yet I also sensed an emotional connection. Although most of the students did not go into detail about their experiences, they did state numerous times how "dangerous," "scary," or "horrible" their situations were.

Bango talks about the rebels attacking his village. He recalls both the brutality of the violence as well as the indiscriminant abduction of youth to serve as child soldiers.

My house got burnt. Rebels, they don't pick anyone—they kill everyone. They kill kids. All years, middle age, old age. They don't pick, no. They chop kids' hands, eight-month-old babies they chop their hands down. We do see kids like them, they chop hands down. Heartless people. And if you asked them what is the reason you're doing this fighting? And it's like nothing, they don't even know what they're fighting for. I don't understand. When they cut you, they will grab a few young youths. And after that they will train them to the force. They will start giving them things like drugs and things like that to help them adapt to that life. And you do things beyond your imagination. They do things beyond your thinking, as long as you are being drugged.

I know a lot who were captured. Now, they will tell you that it's just because of the drugs that make them do all this horrible things. And after everything is over, they appear to people for forgiveness. It is so hard.

I asked Helen to tell me a little about herself to start the interview. She begins with the following statement:

I'm coming from Rwanda. I was born there. I left that country when I was 17. Then I went to Uganda, which was my refugee country, and I lived there for three years. It wasn't easy for me though because my mom was sick, and she passed away. And all the money we had we spent at the hospital. And I lived with my dad, and there was no security, and there was a kind of suffering, sickness. There was sickness, and no money for going to the hospital. We have a life and we had 10 kids in the house. And our family, two of them passed away. They were kidnapped and they poisoned them. Two of the children were kidnapped, and they took them away and poisoned them and then they passed away, and we buried them where my mom was laying down. And then we had to come to Canada. Our life is not easy. It's just been three years. People don't know because to get here, you are having a good life. If they see you looking fine and feeling a good life, they think that everything was fine in the past. And you don't have the chance to talk to them because they don't come and ask you. You don't have somebody to talk to and tell them your feelings. You can't get any help for your heart inside. Because nobody's talking to you. I feel that way.

Helen's comments toward the end of this quote imply that she believes that people think everything is fine with her and she has put the past behind her because she looks fine on the outside. What she points out is that people do not really know her feelings because she is not provided an opportunity to talk about herself. This statement proved to be a point of departure for my thinking about how the students' pre-migration experiences influence their post-migration lives. Do we simply think that these children or young adults are fine because they look fine on the outside? Is the fact that they are not talking openly about their past lives mean that they are no longer affected by their experiences? Are the memories too painful to talk about? It could also be that the students would rather keep their past to themselves. I questioned whether people were attempting to talk to these children about their experiences. I continued to ask myself these questions as I interviewed more students and participants from the microsystem and the exosystem. The importance of body language, tone, and how the students spoke was equally as important as the words they used.

It was also difficult at times to really understand how much the students remembered or what they were told about an event. I began to question whether the student simply wished that someone was alive or whether the person really was alive. At the beginning of an interview, Anna stated that her mother was dead. Later in the interview she stated that she had talked with her on the phone. When I tried to clarify whether her mother was alive, she explained,

> Yeah, she died, she was shot, but she made it and she came back to herself. They shot her, but it was on the other arm and she was just lying down. And my aunt told me that my mom died. I was with my mom when she was shot. I was upstairs in my room and I came down and she was lying on the floor. I thought she was sleeping, and I saw a lot of blood. And she wasn't breathing, my aunt said, "Just go." Everybody was just shooting and shooting and they said, "Run, just go and save your life." And we scattered, we went to different places. Now my aunt says that my mom is not dead and that I can talk with her on the phone.

Whether Anna's explanation was factual was irrelevant, as the purpose of this study was not to uncover the actual facts; rather, it was to more fully understand the experiences of these students. It appeared that Anna had endured a memorable and frightening event and her recollection of the actual event was not altogether clear. There could be many factors that might affect her recollection of the events, such as her age, the events leading up to the event, or a defence mechanism that has helped her suppress a painful memory. When the same statement is examined within the context of the rest of the interview it provides insight into her overall mental status at the time of the interview. This will be discussed further when examining the effects of trauma and the debate surrounding trauma discourse.

Mike, an executive director of a reception centre for refugees in Winnipeg, indicated that the people from the refugee community tell the families to solve their own problems and not to ask for help because it shows that you are weak. He suggests that this may be a reason why people do not reach out to agencies for help. This way of thinking may have also influenced the youth; as such, they may believe that it is inappropriate to talk about the past or to suggest that they may need help. Some of the teachers reported that students' stories often emerge in less obvious means, such as in an assignment, during a discussion, or in personal writing.

Sandra, an English teacher at Walter Duncan School in Winnipeg, states that stories often come out in the students' writing. She asked her class to write about a safe and an unsafe time in their lives. One of the girls wrote that an unsafe time was when she remembered running from village to village as she saw her friends' hands get chopped off and she saw people who were burned to death in their homes. When students disclose these situations in an assignment, Sandra will talk to them individually about what they have written and she will refer them for further assistance if needed.

Personal Stories: Hints and Glimpses

What emerged from the pre-migration data is that there are only a select few individuals who really get to know the specific circumstances of the refugee students. Moreover, even these individuals receive, at the very best, only bits and pieces of a total experience.

Paul, the vice-principal of Walter Duncan School, refers to a sense of loss he feels as a result of not knowing the stories of his students. He also shares his concern for the students, who he knows have tremendous burdens to bear. He frequently refers to "hints and glimpses" of what he learns about the pre-migration experiences of his students.

> I feel at a loss because I don't know their stories. They don't talk a lot about what happened. For example, one student I know came from Sierra Leone.... He smiled all the time. I asked him why he was always so cheerful? And he said, "Because I'm here, Mr. B." I did not know this until later that he was one of the few that survived in his family. He had survived because people had fallen over him when they died in the massacre. And he was underneath everybody in a mass grave. And then when people left, he was able to pick himself up and walk to the refugee camp. And I don't think you ever really will hear the full story until these young men and women and people have had at least a generation to absorb and to distance themselves and to heal the wounds and give them perspectives. So there is tremendous pain there. So pre-migration really comes down to hints and glimpses of the pain and the tremendous suffering and flashes of anger as well. And sometimes depression in terms of the experiences that they have gone through.

Taylor, a coordinator of a work education program and also the student services coordinator, admits that it was not until he met the families after some time that the reality of his students' lives really hit him. He states,

> I had two girls who had a brother and their mother just had a baby and they were living by themselves in a very dilapidated house and they were having some difficulties. I went to visit the home and I noticed that the mother who had just had a baby—the father was murdered in front of the daughters' eyes but the mother was left for dead. She had a very large machete mark on her face. That was the

realization for me, the machete mark. I've heard the stories about what life is like in the camps. And I knew what camps they had been in and how long they had been on the move and the risks they had, especially for the girls. The boys, for the most part, were secure in the camps and coming here. I don't know how they managed to get lucky enough to come here, to come to Canada.

Taylor also expresses his discontent with how little information he receives about the students.

About pre-migration there is generally very little or no information, unless you get it verbatim from the family. And whenever I take a new student into the school, I want to know where they were. I want to talk to the parents, I want to talk to the sending school and get a history of where they came from. And I want to deal with what their issues are. And I don't get any of that with the EAL kids.

A common theme was the lack of information that school staff received about the child and the difficulties they had with getting information from the various agencies that were supporting the child.

Age Discrepancies

In many cases, students have had to construct their own life stories to gain entry into the country. Many of the children have had to lie about their ages and the details of their lives to get legitimacy for their claim to come to Canada. Other students simply do not know their age because there is no one alive that can attest to when they were born. When they were in refugee camps they knew that they had to be 18 to come to Canada, so they increased their age. In a conversation with Imran, I asked him how old he was when he was in Kakuma Refugee Camp.

I don't really know. Now I am 19.

When I came here, I used a different age to come here. Because when you are underage, they will not let you come to Canada. You have to increase your age if you want to come here. I increased my age two to three years. I was 15 when I came to Canada.

Most of the students referred to two ages: "my real age" and "my age on paper." The age discrepancy was problematic because the school officials would place the students in an age-appropriate classroom based on their paper age as opposed to their developmental level. As Sokut states,

> The age that I came with said that I was too old to go to high school. And the teachers and the counsellors have to understand the position that I am in. I want to go to high school, but they said I was too old to go. Other students are in the same position; I am 25 on my papers. But that is not exactly the age that we are. I had to explain a lot to everybody to make them understand the position that I am in. They were really helpful, all of the people in my high school. Even if they're not high school age they have to be allowed to go to high school. So I was allowed to go to high school, and I started in grade 10.

Sokut also stated that when he first came to Canada, he was tested and the school said that he had to go to an adult education centre because of his age.

> And they said I had to go to 900 Smith, by the hospital, but that was for old people and I'm not an old person. I went to my counsellor and I said this is not the level I am supposed to be in. It is an adult education centre and this is for old people and I cannot share with the older people. I want to go to high school.

In another conversation, a student indicates that most of the Sudanese young people came with a fake age. I asked what he meant by a fake age and he responds,

> Everybody is born in January. On January 1, everyone from Sudan has the same birthday.

Why is that?

Well they just give you a birthdate by the Canadian Embassy and for me, I was just given a date. So, actually, they had to increase my age so that I could come to Canada. I think I am 23.

And how old are you really?

18.

So you came when you were 16?

Yes, and people don't believe we are not that age because the government issues the papers. Everybody works on what the government says on the papers. It is hard to change your age. Some people come with a different name. Some people just picked any name, and they didn't even know what they were doing. Whatever name came to them they just put it down.

What is clearly problematic about the three students mentioned in the preceding quotes is that these Sudanese boys indicated that they were 17, 16, and 15 when they travelled, unaccompanied, to Canada. They were then housed with one other 17-year-old boy, also from Sudan, in a house in what would be considered one of the poorest socioeconomic areas in the city. They were placed in a classroom that was clearly not suited to their "real age" or ability level. Had they not advocated so strongly on their own behalf to be in a high school setting, they would never have had the opportunity to attend Walter Duncan School. Now these same students have had to advocate to remain in school because their paper age says they are 22 and are considered "mature students" and should be attending an adult education centre.

Based on data obtained from participants in the exosystem and the microsystem, the challenge to acquire background information about the pre-migration experiences of the students was a difficult task. After the initial interviews with the students, I was able to more fully understand some of their pre-migration experiences; however, much of this information was quite sparse. The lack of information provided during the interview might be entirely attributed to the developmental stage of the students or it could have been limited because of language or cultural issues.

One of the student interview questions was intended to identify potential participants who were a part of the students' microsystem and whom I had not previously considered interviewing. As it turned out, the two people most frequently mentioned were two teachers in the school, whom I then arranged to interview. Based on the interviews with the participants in the microsystem, who had a much closer relationship with many of the students, I was able to acquire substantially more information regarding the students' experiences. I was also able to understand the overall response of the microsystem and the pivotal role that the school has in assisting refugee children.

TRANS-MIGRATION EXPERIENCES
Refugee Life: Displacement, Distrust, and Danger

Both the students and the participants in the microsystem commented about what life was like as a refugee. The four boys from Sudan referred to themselves as "the Lost Boys." The term was adopted from *Peter Pan* and is widely used to describe the boys who walked on foot, without any adults, to flee the massacres of Sudan's civil war. When I interviewed James, I told him that I did not know much about the Lost Boys and he readily offered to tell me the history. What I found particularly interesting was his closing statement, "Now you can go ahead with your questions." It was almost like he wanted this story out of the way, or to have it out in the open, before I proceeded with the interview. He states,

> The history of the Lost Boys is ... at the time that the war started in 1983 there was, let me say, a disagreement between the rebels in Sudan in the South and the government in the North. They did not want to power share. That is the problem why they fight. Rebels, they fight the government. The people who are living in the south are Christians and the people in the north are Muslims. And people just fight between the Christians and the Muslims and they are all involved in the

politics and they fight. The government attacks the people who were living in the south. They destroyed their houses and killed their people and tortured people and everything they set fire. And they killed their kids. And the people who were against the government, the rebels they talked to the government of Ethiopia and they take the young men now. The Lost Boys, and the young boys. They took them away from parents and some of the Lost Boys, their parents have been killed during the war, and the young boys started to run away from their places and went to the neighbouring countries. Ethiopia, it is one of the neighbouring countries of Sudan in the East. So they walk to Ethiopia, and they stayed there for about four years. And then the government of Ethiopia was overthrown by the new government. The new government don't want refugees living in a country. They shove them away. The Lost Boys … they run away from there and they move to Kenya, where other lost boys are living right now. This is where I was living. There are other people coming there who are from other countries neighbouring countries where there are wars going on. There are several nations of refugees from seven countries living in one refugee camp. Kakuma, that's a refugee camp, where I was living and where Sokut was living before they moved to the other camp. At the time that we moved, there were about 35,000 Lost Boys. From 1983 to 1990s, and then from when they walk from Sudan to Ethiopia for about 10 days without enough food to eat on the way.… And they walked again from Ethiopia to Kenya, and during that time many people died on the way. Some of the people died by hunger, some of the people were lost in the forest. Some of them were eaten by the wild animals, like the hyena. And the survivors of the Lost Boys, they arrived in 1992. There were about 10,000 from 35,000. And I was one of those people. Still, it is in my mind.

[looking uncomfortable, looking down, visibly getting upset.]

It's kind of difficult, you know. But why that people have the life like me is that because what is going on or what the government is doing to us. We see that it is not good. We are supposed to finish our school. And the other kids now, they don't have a chance to go to school; there is no school. There is no school now where those children can go, and the Lost Boys; they are trying to be able to get what they want for their people like to be educated to be able to change the course of the government.... That is why we want to do it, we made that decision even though it is hard decision to leave our parents, to come here by ourselves, to live without talking to our parents. And we hope that one day, one time, we will see our parents again. Okay, you can go ahead with your questions.

James's words depict several key themes found in many of the students' stories: their exposure to conflict, the fear they experienced, the treatment they received from neighbouring countries and their subsequent relocation to another country, the lack of basic necessities, the lack of trust, and the loss of family and friends. What surfaced for all of these students was the importance and the priority they placed on receiving an education. This theme emerged in all of the students' interviews and was further reinforced by all of the members of the microsystem. The desire to get an education outweighed their other needs, including basic necessities and the reunification with their families.

The overriding importance of getting an education is brought forth in James's comments. James recounts,

Sometimes there is other people that attacked the refugee camp, and they kill you in the night. People are scared for their security. There is insecurity in the camp. There are many people living in the refugee camp, and also what is sometimes called people fighting between other nations, other refugees with other refugees in the camp.

So even in the camp, you have to worry that someone is going to kill you throughout the night.

Yeah. It's not good or secure.

We have three or four in one room. In the camp. But the camp
is better than back home because there is school to go.

The importance of education to the students will be discussed
further in the following chapter, particularly as it relates to their educational experiences in Canada. Numerous references were made by
various participants to what life was like in a refugee camp: food was
sparse, personal security was compromised, and the living conditions
were "miserable."

Imran, one of the Lost Boys from Sudan, explains what life was like for
him when he lived in Kakuma Refugee Camp. All four boys commented
about how they feared they would be killed when they slept or that their
food or other supplies would be stolen. Both James and Imran talked
about how difficult it was for them to recount their stories. Imran states,

The government gives us food and we keep it in our tent. The
rebels can come to you anytime during the night. If they need
food, and if you don't give them what they need, they will kill
you. So we moved from Kakuma to Dadaab Camp. We stayed
there for some years. When we moved there, we didn't have our
ration card so they would have to give you a ration card so that
you can eat. You have to show it when you go to get the food.
They would punch it for you when you went to get the food, but
we did not have that. So what we did is we just went to look for
the other refugees like us in order to get the food. We did this
until the UN was going to let us get a card. So we had to do this
for a few months until the UN allowed us to get a ration card.

How old were you when you were in Kakuma?
I don't really know. Now I am 19. I was with another boy.

*So you were one of the Lost Boys? The two of you walked to
another country?*
No, somebody carried me.

PP

I still have actually a lot of memories, but sometimes to express
some is hard. Sometimes it's hard to talk to close friends.
Refugee life was like you know in Kakuma, it is hard. You know,
the temperature is around 40° or something. And there is a
lot of people. Kakuma was a really big mix of a lot of different
people. The same in Dadaab too. There is a big mix of different
people, different countries. My family is not here. They are in
Sudan. I don't have any parents; I have brothers and sisters.

Bango explains that life in the camp is miserable and that he lived
without hope. He recalls how little food there was and how the resources
or food supplies would be temporarily cut off. He states, "Hope in the
sense that, you know, like your day-to-day living, is just kind of ... it is
miserable. The expectation is that low; what are you expecting from the
government or the NGOs. There is just not a lot."

Helen discusses the insecurity, poverty, and violence within the
camp and the government's response to people leaving Rwanda.

Yes, because there is a lot of kidnappings and poisons. The
people came from my country to the refugee camp. And maybe
right now the government is not happy because people are
leaving and who are you going to lure? Understand? So you feel
kind of uncomfortable, and so you come and you kidnap some
refugees. Sometimes you hear that people are killed before
they come to Canada. And so when you are there, you never
tell people when you are going to go to Canada. And you don't
have to say that you are going to Canada because you do not
know who is your friend and who is your enemy. Because some
people are kidnapped when it is their time to come here. And
people say, where did those people go, and they say they kidnapped them. Sometimes they killed him, and sometimes they
just torture them by beating them or not giving them any food.

Living in a refugee camp was accompanied by feelings of insecurity, despair, fear, loneliness, and uncertainty about the future. Many
of the students commented about being frequently displaced and about

the loss of family members, as well as a breakdown of their social networks. Only two out of the thirteen students live with both parents; all other students had at least one parent who was killed during the various conflicts or who died from illness and a lack of medical care. Six of the students currently live alone or with another family member who is not their parent. As no formal schools existed in the camps, much of the schooling was conducted outdoors, usually under a tree or in a tent.

There was also the fear that the United Nations or the hosting country would take the people from the camps back to their country of origin if the fighting ceased. Rassan stated, "They would randomly pick people to send back to the border and there are cases where people are shot right at the border when they are handed back." This uncertainty about displacement and the fear of being returned also contributed to the distrust among the people in the camps, toward the agencies that were trying to assist them, and toward the governments from which they were fleeing.

Some students have been in refugee camps in excess of 10 years before coming to Canada. As Bill, a member of the Sudanese community, indicates, some of the students, who were not part of this study, were born in refugee camps. This instability and movement is the result of continuing civil wars accompanied by horrific violence targeted toward children and civilians. The children have been affected by war, which elicits an entirely different dimension to the pre-migration and trans-migration experiences. With war comes violence and with violence there is loss.

Loss and Loneliness

Two of the most frequently occurring themes related to the personal experiences of the students were loneliness and loss. Twenty-four different participants cited 32 different references to loss. Loneliness was the second most commonly cited reference. Although many researchers would argue that qualitative data should not be quantitatively expressed (Miles & Huberman, 1994), the frequency of references related to loss and loneliness was certainly indicative of an important theme that was worthy of discussion.

For many of the students, this loss has been a family member, a close friend, a parent, or a schoolmate. There was loss of a way of life, the loss of a home, school, and social and family networks, as well as the loss of languages and customs. Children have lost their childhoods, and parents have lost their pride. Loss is ubiquitous to war and loneliness is quite often the result.

Donna, the principal of Walter Duncan School, expresses the extent and magnitude of some of the students' losses.

> Some have come with ... well, they've lost their families completely. They have witnessed torture, they have been tortured, they have witnessed their own family being killed. A couple of them have been forced to kill. Some of them have body scars. We have a little girl who has bullet wounds in her stomach and she has had many operations here.... They have seen babies thrown into the fires. You cannot even begin to comprehend what they have been through. They have had to flee for their lives, they have lost their possessions.

In some cases, the students witnessed the violent killing of their family members. Bev, the EAL teacher at Walter Duncan, indicates that some of the Afghani girls' fathers were teachers and they were shot in their home or shot at school in front of the children. She further explains that the loss of the father leaves the family at a more serious disadvantage in terms of negotiating for basic needs or for navigating the family through the process of seeking a refugee claim.

For some of the students, the losses they have endured or the uncertainty of whether their parents are alive has exacted a toll on their lives in Canada. Laurie, Walter Duncan's school counsellor, was called to a math room last year to assist a teacher, and she noticed a girl who was surrounded by other female students. She saw the girl was visibly upset and the other girls were trying to comfort her. When she asked what was wrong, the girl indicated that she did not know how to do the math. Laurie empathically stated her own math frustrations and said "maybe we could figure it out together." She then proceeded to put her hand on the girl's back in an endearing manner, in what she referred to as acting like a "mom" as she does with her own children. Laurie remembers the girl's response,

> And she just collapsed. Just collapsed. And she was sobbing, sobbing, sobbing. So, I took her out and I said, "Let's go for a walk."... Well, she tells me that she hasn't seen her mother in three years because when she was leaving she ran into the bush. She described the scene, which to me was exactly the scene of this movie *The Constant Gardener* where they come in on a horse and everybody scatters. Everybody scatters in the village, and they run off. She went with an auntie and her mom went with her sister. One went one way and one went the other, and they never saw each other again. To this day, she still doesn't know whether her mother is alive. And this woman ended up being the auntie and I'm sure you've probably heard of this already. They just grab a child because it gets them on the plane. So they take two children with them and off they go. So they end up living with people that they didn't even know that are not their real parents. But they might become guardians of them. I could tell you about some older students that I have right now. They are really struggling with that because discipline is very difficult at home because this person is not my mom but on paper she is. But this one little girl, one kind word, just brought her to pieces. I'd say that war is affecting her. It is not that she can't do her math, I don't think so. The issue is that she can't even think straight, because she doesn't even know if her mom is alive or not. That is what is affecting her at school.

Sokut discusses the loneliness he feels and his desire to be with a family. Despite his current feelings, he remains positive and hopeful that things will change.

> If I go now, my father may not notice me because I have grown up. I was four years old when I left my parents. My village was attacked, and I was not with my parents. I was with my uncle and he was killed and I had to run on my own. It was extremely bad and I have no power, so that I can go to see them.

Especially this year it was very hard, because I have no money
to go. I have no papers, I have nothing. This is how life goes;
after some years it will change.

Sokut also tells me that Christmas is a hard time for him and his
friends. "We had to spend it in our apartments, but others with families, they spend it together with other families because they are families
and they stay together." He suggests that young people who are alone
should be integrated with other families instead of "putting us alone
and suffering." Although there was a difference between the loneliness expressed from the students who were with family members as
opposed to those who were alone, the theme was common to both circumstances. Many of the students who were with parents also talked
about never seeing their parents because their parents worked two jobs
or they worked evening shifts, or the students themselves were working
to support the family.

Working Toward Relocation

Most of the students have been to several countries prior to coming to
Canada. When they fled the war in their home countries, most were
relocated to refugee camps. In the camps they had to follow a process to
register to be relocated to another country, usually the United Kingdom,
Canada, or the United States. Individuals would go to an embassy to fill
out application forms and they would have to go through a full medical
check and a criminal records check. An interview would also be conducted by officials from the United Nations. This process could take years
to complete. Bill, a community and school liaison worker who was also a
refugee from Sudan, explained that this time is a period of interruption
and only a few are "lucky to go through the process and be successful to
migrate to another country." Bill's statement is particularly important
because it infers that the students who do end up getting into Canada
have been through an intensely demanding period of time that appeared
to him to be driven more by happenstance than anything else. It also provides insight into the kind of person who might get through this process
and how it might contribute to his or her overall personal agency.

It is essential to keep in mind the tremendous and often life-threatening experiences that many of the refugees have undergone just to get to a host country. The personal agency and human capacity demonstrated by the students and their families is noted by the aforementioned quotations. As the pre-migration information tells us, many of these individuals have overcome remarkable adversity, personal loss, and hardship. This, combined with the fact that some of these students have not had any family support, illustrates just how resilient many of these young people are to be able to get through the pre-migration and trans-migration phases.

Many of the students' hopes for relocation were quickly dashed by disappointments and rejections, accompanied by little explanation from the officials. Securing relocation in another country was a difficult and lengthy process that appeared on the surface to be more of a game of luck and chance than an officially governed procedure. The trans-migration experience was occasionally referred to as a period of uncertainty, lost hopes, and then disbelief about actually coming to Canada. It became obvious why one student noted that he never actually believed it would happen until he was on the plane.

Relocating to Canada: Hope and Happiness

Although the indiscriminate phases of the pre-migration and the trans-migration experiences have been noted, the following discussion will centre on the experiences the students had once they knew they were coming to Canada. For many of the students, this period was distinctly different from the feelings and experiences described in the pre-migration phase. The latter phase of trans-migration for the students was a period of in their lives that represented hope, happiness, and a chance to believe that the dreams they had always envisioned could now come true. It was an escape from poverty, a chance to go to school, and an opportunity to start a new life. Although this meant leaving people they loved and losing friends who had become their only family, it was felt to be worth the sacrifice.

Bango recalls,

It was one of the fantastic things in my life, the thing that I can remember in my life, ever since I knew we got approved. It was so good when I boarded the plane to here. It was like, finally, I have a chance. This is the time for me to make life better, for my life to be better for myself. When I boarded the plane, I was not sure. Even though we had been approved, but I was not. I couldn't get that excited, unless I am aboard the plane. It was good and always really good because everybody knows that Canada is a free country.

Trans-migration experiences ranged from as little as one or two years to in excess of 10 years. Fleeing war meant leaving home and living in a refugee camp or being relocated to a neighbouring country. Some of the neighbouring countries were not accepting of refugees, and many of the governments in these countries prohibited refugees to work or to go to school. The separation or loss of both family members and friends was common. The latter phase of trans-migration represented a time with happiness and hope, yet also some tentativeness and fear. Coming to Canada was exciting, but it was coupled with numerous uncertainties and cultural adjustments that posed substantial challenges and significant barriers for the students.

POST-MIGRATION EXPERIENCES
First Impressions

Many of the students recounted the difficulties that they had when they first arrived in Canada with acclimatizing and learning enough English so that they could navigate their way through the city. Most of the students suggested that adjusting to a new place and figuring out the various systems were enormous tasks. Some of them recounted their stories, laughing about some of their misunderstandings about Canadian culture and the environment.

Afem recalls his first few memories of arriving in Canada, smiling and laughing about the first time he saw snow. He also remembers the first housing placement he was in and the difficulties he had getting to school. Housing placement arises in almost all of the students' interviews, as many of the students have had to relocate in the city several times due to numerous factors, including personal safety, difficulties with landlords, or the unsuitability of the dwelling.

> When I come to Canada, it was new for me. The first thing you do is come to reception place, and it was the winter. So, I never met winter in my life. When I came, I thought at first it was sugar on the ground. I went to reception centre. I got a counsellor, who was an African who had been here for a while already. So she was giving me a lot of ideas how to go to school and how to adapt to life in Canada. Our first house was on Alberta Avenue. It was not good. It was too horrible. It was too dirty, and it was too far from school, and they said we need a place that's near to school so that we have time to come. And so we went to another one on Southside.

Even a subtle cultural difference, such as greeting people on the street, was an adjustment. Aran states,

> And another one was the communications. In the culture I came from, it's like when you walk around, you just go around and say hi to everyone and say, How are you. It is kind of a regular thing to just walk around and say "hi" to everyone you know. When I'm walking and I see people, even when don't know them, I have to say "hi," it is kind of like a tradition in Sudan. And then when I was walking here, I was saying "hi" to everybody and they just looked at me and said, "What?" And sometimes they don't even answer and then one friend told me you don't do that here, and then I'm, like, "Okay."

Levia also recalls a time when the fire alarm went off in the temporary residence at the reception centre. When they heard the alarm they walked out in the winter in their bare feet, thinking that they were going to burn. She said that she started crying from being so cold.

For most of the students, post-migration meant a bombardment of absolute different cultural practices, nutrition, housing, education, peer groups, and even family dynamics. Essentially, there was a complete shift and a dramatic change in all of their ecological systems. The words of Aran and Afem are a reminder that even some of the seemingly smaller adjustments that the students made were also personally significant and should also be considered as important factors related to adjustment.

Most students made reference to the reception centre that provided initial support to them when they first arrived in Canada. Someone from the centre met them at the airport and made arrangements for housing and basic necessities. While this support was acknowledged, students reported that the centre did not provide continuing support. As Mike, the executive director of the centre, indicated, the federal government is going to need to increase the amount of funding to provide services beyond primary settlement.

When newcomer students first arrive at the receiving school, the typical process of registration is followed; the student fills out a registration form and presents his or her school record if it is available. The counsellor or teacher works with the student to develop a timetable that best fits his or her academic level. In some select schools, there are fairly sophisticated English as an Additional Language (EAL) programs and in others the EAL program is non-existent. When I asked Bev what schools do when a specialized EAL program is not in place, she said, "They just go right into the regular classes and they hope for the best. Most of those kids just fail or drop out."

Understanding the Experiences

Len, who works in a counselling clinic for refugees, argues that families and children and all members of the refugee community go through phases, and each phase brings a new challenge. He indicates that different overlapping phases were quite overwhelming. He has seen families get quite distraught about not knowing where to start and how to handle some of the stressors. Len suggests that the stress could be related to the past, the present, an immediate danger, or a combination thereof. To explain this cultural adjustment, he uses the analogy of being thrown into the middle of an ocean. The adjustment is often related to basic needs or to past trauma, and he reinforces the urgency in dealing with these stressors immediately when people arrive in Canada. Rob, a minister in a local Sudanese church, states that he witnesses a pattern of soaring and crashing with new refugees in the community. He states, "... You have to work with that and it's wonderful when they soar and your heart breaks when they crash." Jill Rutter also notes, "Children go up and down and they crash" (personal communication, November 28, 2006). Sokut also states, "Things settle, then they don't go my way ... then they settle again, and then not go my way again ... my life keeps going like that."

Rassan, who is also a former refugee, articulates the importance of the school system recognizing the previous experiences the students have had and considering this when they receive new refugees into their school. Throughout the interview with Rassan, he argues that teachers must strive to first create a relationship with each student and then to proceed with assessment and more formal educational activities. Without this relationship, he argues, you have nothing. The people in the ecological systems who appear to know more about the experiences of the students are those people who state that they have taken the time to foster and nurture a close interpersonal relationship with the students. Although the complete stories might take years to tell, the students have clearly selected individuals whom they trust and to whom they are willing to talk.

Carrying on with Life

After the initial excitement of coming to Canada, the realities of starting a new life were accompanied with some disappointment, frustration, and regret. Students indicated that they were frustrated with trying to keep up with the schoolwork and they did not know if they were going to ever be able to achieve what they wanted. Some of the participants from the microsystem indicated that people have incorrectly assumed that bringing refugees to Canada will be all they need to give them a better life. During the student interviews, five different students hinted that they would be better off being back at home. Sokut illustrates this point:

> I was in a refugee camp all my life. I still consider myself a refu-
> gee. There is nothing here. Maybe there are clothes, the food
> that I eat, the place that I sleep, but I'm still a refugee. I don't
> see anything changing. Why I say that because life in the camp
> is the same as life like here. The same food I eat. The only thing
> that changes is the school, because I go to school everyday, but
> life is the same. When I was living in the camp, it was better
> than here, because I worked by myself. I had a nice house, I built
> my own house. It was comfortable. It was my home.

Carrying on with life in Canada was accompanied by numerous continuing challenges that were often associated with moments of regret about having come to Canada. These challenges will be more thoroughly discussed in the following chapter.

SUMMARY AND CONCLUSION

All 13 students lived during intense periods of brutal civil war. Afghanistan had been at war since 1970, and Sudan, Liberia, and Sierra Leone had been at war since the late 1980s or early 1990s. Rwanda's genocide in 1994 resulted in an estimated 800,000 deaths. These various civil wars were often accompanied by government coups, strict regimes, genocide, and endemic poverty. Two of the students reported that they attended school regularly, and the remaining 11 students indicated that their schooling had been disrupted because of the war and their forced migration.

Evidence supported that students' pre-migration experiences included loss, starvation, abuse, persecution, danger, displacement, distrust, and exposure to violence. Eight of the thirteen students indicated that one or both of their parents had been killed, and three students were not sure whether their parents or siblings were alive. Only two indicated that they currently had a mother and a father. Twelve of the thirteen students indicated that they were separated from family members when they had to flee their homes. Some have not heard from any family members since they left their homes. One student witnessed the violent sexual assault of her mother and her subsequent shooting.

All 13 students have witnessed high-intensity violence in which a family member, friend, or a community member was brutally murdered. One student indicated that he witnessed rebels chopping the arms off of children and adults as a means to intimidate the community. One of the female participants indicated that girls were not safe, and she lived in fear that the men would sexually assault her. The four Lost Boys of Sudan witnessed the starvation and subsequent death of countless children as they travelled from one country to another. Some of the students witnessed the destruction of their own homes, and others fled their homes when rebels invaded their communities.

The initial conceptual framework used to start this discussion depicted a distinct and sequential progression from pre-migration, trans-migration, and post-migration phases. The evidence provided by the students' stories suggests that the phases are much less defined than originally assumed. Several students made comments about the emotional connection they still had to friends and family who were still living in their former countries. War is only a phone call away. Family members are suspended in pre-migration or trans-migration phases that still very much influence the post-migration phases of the students in Canada. Students worry about whether their parents are alive or whether they would even recognize them if they were to go home. Memories of violence and coping with loss continue to affect the students.

The reality of war and violence is still very close to the lives of the students. A complication that arose for people within the school system is that they are not fully aware of the pre-migration and trans-migration experiences of these students. Piecing together a composite of the experiences that an individual has had may take years to accomplish, and school staff suggested that this compromised their ability to provide the most appropriate programs and services to these students. Experiences during pre-migration were also discussed positively. Students talked about going to school, being with friends and family, and carrying on with daily tasks, despite the insecurity they felt.

The pre-migration experiences of the students culminated with a forced movement from home that was accompanied with varying levels of emotional pain. The students' ecological systems changed substantially. Students were unable to attend school, family members and friends were killed or separated, and communities were destroyed.

The trans-migration phase might have included living in a refugee camp for years waiting to be relocated or it could have been a relatively short period of a few weeks that included leaving home and relocating to Canada. The majority of the students encountered years of displacement from camp to camp with broken promises for relocation. The four boys from Sudan had lived in various refugee camps for approximately 10 years. Life in the refugee camps was reported as "difficult," unpleasant," "violent," and "unsafe." Camps were overcrowded, food was rationed, and neighbours could not be trusted. The students indicated that they waited and hoped that they would be chosen by the United Nations for relocation. The process of applying for relocation was complicated, and students reported that they "felt like they won a lottery" when they were finally chosen to come to Canada.

The trans-migration phase was characterized as tending to basic survival needs and working toward relocation. Some students experienced several phases of relocation and they had to go through the process of resettlement numerous times. The experiences of the latter phase of trans-migration included leaving the country of origin and travelling to Canada, which was typically accompanied by hope and happiness about starting a new life.

As the following chapter illustrates, long-term post-migration challenges and obstacles are ubiquitous to the students' experiences; however, their capacity to adjust and overcome their challenges are recognized, which supports a trajectory that is hopeful and positive. It is absolutely imperative that, as a society, it is not assumed that because students have been relocated to Canada, they will be better off. For many of them, the challenges are enormous, their life is not as it was imagined, and they no longer have the social, cultural, or familial networks that would typically carry them through the difficult times of their lives.

What emerged from much of the data related to post-migration is that the students are generally happy to be in Canada and to be free from persecution, poverty, and conflict. Although many of the students miss people, places, and their former culture, most look forward to the future. Students seem to carry on as best as they can, despite numerous barriers, with their hopes and aspirations for a new life in Canada. Various comments also emerged from the students about how appreciative they were for Canada to accept them. They proceeded to discuss their problems and challenges with a disclaimer stating that they were so thankful they were here, but they still faced so many challenges. It was almost as if they were thanking a host for receiving a bad dinner.

Several key individuals were identified by the students as being people they could trust in their school. It was through these participants that the students opened up and shared their personal stories in numerous ways, both verbally and in written or electronic forms. It is from talking with these people that I was able to see the connection that still exists between the pre-migration, trans-migration, and post-migration phases and how the students' past experiences continue to affect their current lives. The subtle hints from the students became more obvious and led me to uncover new information.

Despite the experiences many of the students have had, their resolve to get an education, to work to support themselves and their families, is what drives many of them forward despite their past. Whether the memories are suppressed or forgotten, consciously remembered or problematic, all of the students exhibited perseverance to achieve their goals and aspirations. A positive focus on the future was evident in all of the interviews.

The theory of segmented assimilation purported by Portes and Zhou (1993) did not necessarily encapsulate what was discovered in the exploration of the students' experiences. Segmented assimilation suggests that there are three paths to assimilation. The students' post-migration experiences most closely resembled an oscillating pattern of adjustment. This fluctuating model incorporates progressive movement of the individual, who encounters challenges and obstacles, as well as successes and accomplishments, throughout all phases of migration.

Most people who work in the education system will be able to name students who have dropped out of school, become involved in criminal activity, and then turned their lives around to be more productive members of society. Even the justice system has developed programs to turn the most hardened criminals around. A downward spiral denotes no movement upward and no exit points on the way down. That said, perhaps the individuals who might have been considered part of the downward spiral were not part of the study, as they likely would not be attending school. Having said that, with the right resources and the best people working with the individuals who are having difficulties, one cannot guarantee that these people will not change for the better.

As most people who work with young offenders, or students who choose a path leading to deviant behaviour or criminal activity, can attest, there is almost always a point of departure from this path. As was revealed in an interview with both a government representative and Tim MacKay, who coordinates a family reception centre in the city of Winnipeg, approximately 17 years ago a program was put in place with 13 Vietnamese youth who were engaged in criminal activity and who also had dropped out of school. With immediate attention to the problem and an intensive program of support, all of these students were put on another path. As Tim MacKay explained,

> The issue with the Vietnamese kids and the gangs is almost identical to the problem that arose last summer. The Vietnamese children arrived on their own and they were 17 or 18 years of age. These kids were in a refugee camp in excess of 10 years and they had limited literacy in their own language. They had very limited school experiences and they were dropped into high schools. Within six months they were out and they were a problem. So the youth re-entry programs said, "we need to fix this." They got an anonymous donor from the Vietnamese community to grant a block of money. These kids were already involved in petty crime and other sort of criminal activity. In order to get back into the classroom, they were paid four dollars an hour to go to class for the year. It was the only way they could get them to stay, with an incentive. And the focus was

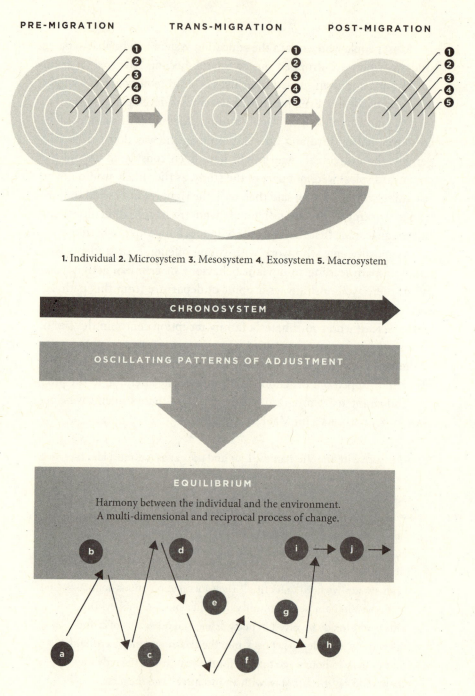

1. Individual 2. Microsystem 3. Mesosystem 4. Exosystem 5. Macrosystem

FIGURE 2.1 *Reconstituted Conceptual Framework*

specifically on literacy and numeracy and some group counselling around some of the behaviours that were happening. After five-year follow-up, all of those kids finished high school. Three went on to university. The remaining ten are employed. There's no question that works, and if we had a program in place like that at the beginning, it wouldn't cost a quarter of a million dollars (personal communication, March 3, 2007).

Although this was not a large-scale longitudinal study, there was evidence to suggest that these 13 students were turned around with an intensive educational and support program that essentially paid the students to attend school. School is one of the most influential ecological systems for students. If the students are not successful in this system, there is little opportunity for them to adjust to Canadian life and to become successful members of society. Although the challenges are numerous and there are many facets of the system that need improvement, the best chance that these students have is to get an education.

Figure 2.1 represents what was revealed in the stories from the students and teachers. The reconstituted conceptual framework reflects two major changes. First, the connection from the pre-migration to post-migration demonstrates the potential for the individual to continue to be affected by many of the same factors that influenced his or her life during pre-migration. This is particularly influential because wars continue to rage in many of their former homelands and many of the individuals continue to worry about the safety of loved ones. Many of the students continue to financially support family members, who depend on this support to survive. In sum, many of the same factors that affected these individuals during pre-migration continue to affect their development and adjustment. Despite being physically removed from war and violence, students continue to be emotionally connected to these experiences.

The second change to the conceptual framework more accurately reflects the oscillating patterns of adjustment that were found in the students at this point. Refugees encounter a plethora of challenges that appear to bring them down or set them back. That said, they also experience remarkable achievements and successes that push them forward.

This process was referred to by Len as "soaring and crashing," and it more accurately denotes the patterns of adjustment observed in this study. As Figure 2.1 (see p. 56) illustrates, the example identifies various upward and downward points, labelled *a* through *j*. There are times when the individual has attained harmony with his or her needs and has achieved a level of satisfaction. There are also times that the individual's needs are not being met and they are unsatisfied. Consider the following (letters *a* through *j* on the figure), which correspond to some of the experiences that Sokut discussed in his interview.

Sokut's experiences included the following: (a) arriving in Canada and not knowing any English, (b) acquiring basic conversational English, (c) being put in an age-appropriate classroom and not understanding how to do the work, (d) connecting with a teacher and a group of friends who are in a similar circumstance, (e) being mistaken for a gang member and getting beaten up, (f) someone breaking in to his home and threatening to kill him with a gun, (g) connecting with a politician who advocates for a change in housing, (h) failing three courses, (i) getting a mentor and a tutor to help after school, and (j) being hired at a local restaurant. Each experience in this example shows the varying levels of adjustment. While some experiences propelled the student forward and closer to adjustment, other experiences pulled the student down and farther away from attaining harmony with his or her needs and wants. The purpose of this example is to show the varying levels of adjustment and how experiences, luck, good timing, or hard work can dramatically change the outcome for the individual. While there are some individuals who experience less success and far more challenges, there is always a point of departure for someone who is headed in a downward spiral.

CHAPTER THREE

Educational Issues and Challenges

THE FOLLOWING TWO CHAPTERS present some of the challenges and obstacles that confront war-affected children who are now living in Canada. The information has been subdivided into four main sections: (1) racism and discrimination, (2) educational challenges, (3) psycho-social challenges, and (4) environmental challenges. Although there are numerous points of intersections between these categories, I have grouped the themes into general clusters to organize the discussion. Educational issues and challenges will be discussed in Chapter 4, as this cluster has specific implications for teachers and school leaders.

RACISM AND DISCRIMINATION

Whether racism or discrimination is perceived or real, it has been noted as a prominent and recurring challenge within all of the ecological systems and from a variety of participants. Sandra's quote outlines just how pervasive the problem is:

> I definitely see kids that feel that they have no avenues. I've had students that have told me that they lived in a racist country before and now they have come to Canada, and they thought that Canada was going to be this total ideal place and then they realized that this place is just as bad to them. They thought that they would feel safe on the street and they wouldn't be persecuted for the colour of their skin. And now they know that they are profiled by the police, they are profiled by the administration, by teachers and by other students who just see them as a nasty black man or a gang member. So they feel that the promised land that they worked so hard to get into is not what they wanted it to be.

Sandra's words not only illustrate how widespread the discrimination is from an ecological perspective, but also the disappointment that she thinks the students feel about being in Canada. Scott informed me that, in his class, there is an obvious division in where the students sit. He said you can physically see the division; there is a white section, an Aboriginal section, and a section where the immigrants sit. When I asked Scott whether there was racism because of this division, his response was, "Oh yeah, by other students and by teachers and by administration."

The perceived school culture highlights the division between the main groups of students as well as the opinions that some of the teachers have regarding the attitudes and behaviours of their colleagues toward the refugee students. The division recognized in the microsystem mirrors what is also observed in the exosystem or the larger community. While some of the conflict is played out in the school, a considerable amount of violence occurs in the community, which ultimately affects what happens in the school. Most of the teachers and the community members believe that the school has not done enough to encourage cultural understanding.

Participants, on numerous occasions, identified the administration as needing to play a key role in creating a fair and accepting culture in the school. Some of the participants indicated that the perceived unfairness by the administrators toward certain ethnic groups contributed to the racial division in the school. The importance of leadership and the notion of fairness were deemed to be prominent in much of the discussion on racism and discrimination. The perception of inequality heightens the likelihood of situations being considered racially motivated or discriminatory. As long as the perception is there, the students believe that they are being treated unfairly because of their race or culture. Whether it is true, the students' perceptions need to be addressed. Scott indicates that accusing people of racism is sometimes the only power that some of the students will have because they have learned that white people are scared of the word. He notes, "And they think that that's the only power that they have, that 'I can make you feel feel guilty for having power'. It's scary because you can see them internalizing this." This statement provides valuable insight into what schools need to do in terms of liberating the students and attempting to combat racism and discrimination.

Ingrid, a divisional consultant, believes that racism is "highly existing" in many schools in the school division. She is concerned because once she sees progress in one school, she recognizes another problem in another school. She also indicated that she has received phone calls from parents who said that they do not want their child sitting beside a black student. The parents do not want their child to sit with another student who has come from another country.

Many students indicate that they have had encounters with the police that they perceived to be related to racism or discrimination. Afem indicated that he had trouble with the police on numerous occasions. He attributed most of the dealings with the police as being racially motivated. I have left the following quote in its entirety to illustrate the consecutive episodes that were discussed when I asked him if there were any racism or discrimination.

> It's good, not like last year. It wasn't safe. The police, they stop people like us. When I was new to Canada, like two months, the police stopped us on our way home from reception centre. They asked us who we are and they asked to see our identification.

We give them the ID. And they say, "Where you guys from?" and we say, "We're from Sudan." And they say, "Where are you guys going?" And we say, "We are going to 7-11 to buy a phone card to call to Africa." And they say to us, "Are you guys mad cow?" (gang) and we say, "No." And they said, "We're looking for some people and you look like the people we're looking for." We thought we were in trouble.

And another time, they said I was driving without a licence, but I wasn't driving. They said, "Why would you be driving tonight without a licence?" And I said, "I wasn't driving." This makes us wonder why these things happen. The police are telling you that you have no rights. They can do whatever they want to do, but they shouldn't do this to a person. Pull them over and then they were telling me I was driving tonight without a licence.

They stopped us again with a gun and they said, "Put your hands up." Then we stopped and they checked me, and after I asked him, "What's the reason that you guys stopping us for no reason?" And they said, "Because you're a black asshole." And I said, "Why you say that?" He said, "Whatever, go back to Africa, where you guys come from." What they did—that's racist. And you know, we have no power. This is a different country, they can do whatever they want us. And they're going to do it. So you just let them do whatever. After what they did, I was thinking, "He was right, I should go back to my country." They just want me to go back to Africa. So I don't think that's very good and I was thinking maybe I should just go back to Sudan and die there.

Scott also discussed an incident that he heard from one of the refugee students.

I talked to one student who talked about being jumped on the street and his friend was hit with the bottle. And they were being called gang members so they called the police. The police were horrible to them. They immediately assumed that these guys were, in fact, gang members. They handcuffed them, brought them to some room somewhere, and interrogated them. And meanwhile they are bleeding and beaten. And they were the ones who called police. So they experienced being presumed guilty, and being assaulted. And I said, "Why didn't you tell anybody at the school?" and they said, "It was the police, what did the school have to do with that?" And most kids know that the school is just part of the community. And if you talk to another adult, they will help you. But these African boys don't have that experience, and they don't want to bother me with their issues. And furthermore, when I really pushed them he says, "I don't think the school would really do anything anyway." They have this feeling that this is their problem, and "just leave us to be."

The aforementioned examples illustrate some of the dealings the students have had with the police and the resulting opinions they have about racism and discrimination. As Scott identified, many of the students have not talked to people in the school community who could potentially offer some support. Many of the students consider these issues to be their own responsibility and it is not something they would discuss with the school staff. There was an obvious lack of trust between the majority of the students and the police that seemed to be the result of encounters they have had with police in the community.

In many of the interviews, students identified a clear distinction between the roles of the school staff in their home countries and the roles of their Canadian teachers. Most identified their former school-teachers as being the ultimate authority figure and someone who should not be questioned. Many of their former teachers used corporal punishment as a common form of discipline. Many students commented how little authority Canadian teachers have and how little respect Canadian children afford to their teachers. Most found it completely unbelievable that students could yell and swear at teachers and suffer no major consequence. Considering many of the pre-migration experiences that refugee children have had with school, it seems entirely plausible that these students would not even consider discussing their personal matters or problems with their current teachers. It appeared that, once

again, there were only three or four teachers who knew about many of
the details of the aforementioned situations.

Some of the racism and discrimination that students reported was
related to how teachers responded to them in the classroom and how
students interacted with them in the school. I asked Afem if he had ever
experienced racism or discrimination in school and his response went
as follows:

> Yes. Like, they are racist sometimes. Because if you ask them
> questions they don't answer sometimes. That's what I think.
> They answer questions for other kids. So if I go up to this
> teacher and ask him a question he just says to me, "Shut up and
> sit down and shut your mouth." And they just say, "Sit down,"
> and that is all they do. I think this school is not racist. Just some
> teachers are the racists. That's what I think. And like sometimes
> kids call me that N-word and I don't even want to say it. The
> N-word I'm not even going to say it and sometimes I just ignore
> them.

Levia recounts an altercation with some of the Aboriginal girls in
school.

> At school, there are some kids that tried to get me on the way
> home. And they say, "You black kid." And they'd be racey. And if
> they call somebody black in colour they are racist. And like they
> call me, this girl, she met me on the road and you know they are
> cheering and they want a fight and I told her that I didn't come
> to Canada for fighting. I didn't leave my country to fight here.
> I said, "If you want to fight you go to my country and join the
> war." They call me the "N word." They call me a nigger. All the
> time, they say that to black people in here. And it's racey. That's
> hurtful. These girls are Aboriginal and they are racist to me. Not
> the white people. The white people are nice to me, but not the
> Aboriginal, they are very racey. And they always like to fight
> people like with black people.

An Aboriginal Student's Perspective: Toward a Solution

As more students reported that there was conflict with the Aboriginal population, I decided that it would be beneficial to interview an Aboriginal student to get her perspective on the issue of discrimination. I asked Sandra to suggest the name of a student who might be willing to participate in the study. I was introduced to Teresa, who volunteered to participate in the study. I asked her the same question I posed to the refugee students: Is racism or discrimination a problem in the school? Her response was as follows.

> To me it seems like the Aboriginal students and the black students are trying to find out who is better, then they get mad at each other. Aboriginal people stick up for what they believe in, and same with those people. I kind of think Aboriginals are kind of racist and because they think that all black people are in gangs, because that's what it used to be at the school.... Well, you know we have a different program for people who come from another country. I don't think they should do that. I don't think they should put them in a separate group. I think they should put them in a classroom with regular students and have like a teacher there, that understands them to show them whatever. I think that's so we can get a better understanding of them. So that we know who they are and stuff. Then he gets to know them because you have all different kinds of school programs here.

> *Do you have refugee students in your classrooms?*
> No.

> *Where are they?*
> They like to have their own program so that the teachers can help them understand better because they don't speak English that good. In one class I was in advanced keyboarding and they had to take me out so other students could get in there because they had lots of refugees and they couldn't

understand typing so they didn't want us to be in there
because we already knew how to type. So they transferred us
to a different class.

Teresa's insights into the issue of racism and discrimination were helpful for three reasons: she clearly articulated what she saw in the school in terms of racism from both an Aboriginal and a refugee perspective; secondly, she outlined a clear distinction between the roles of both the males and females; and thirdly, she discussed the importance of integrating refugee students into the regular classrooms. Teresa continued to discuss what should happen in the school to encourage more integration. She suggested that at the beginning of the year there should be two days devoted to getting students together to get to know each other better. She also suggested that there be a club for refugees to come to meet people from the school so they could be introduced to other students. Although this may appear to be an overly simplistic solution, she has clearly presented her perspective on the issue, as well as offered a suggestion for addressing the problem.

It appears that much of the racism and discrimination was a result of two marginalized groups clearly not understanding each other. The divisive lines between the cultures were quite clear in both the school and in the community. Having said this, I did not observe much opportunity for students to integrate with one another in either the school or the community. The after-school program was all African students, there was a "Black Student" Internship program, and there were several programs for Aboriginal students that were a part of the school or part of a satellite program linked to the school. Based on my visits to the EAL classes, many of the immigrant and refugee children were brought together into the same classrooms, but their out-of-class relationships were with students of a similar culture and there was little integration with the white students or the Aboriginal students.

It was interesting to note that only three of the student participants indicated that there was no racism and two of these participants were boys who were heavily involved in sports. The other, Ugot, said that he did not insult others, and they did not insult him. He mentioned that he stayed to himself. Ugot is currently in the pre-beginner EAL class and does not attend classes with other students who are not EAL learners. Two of the girls, Banya and Anna, indicated that racism occurs but not to them because they stick to themselves and they have respect for others. Both Banya and Anna are strong students who work part-time and intend to pursue secondary education. Although it would be premature to make a generalization based on such a small sample, it did appear that the students who were more self-assured, articulate, and connected with sports or after-school work were less likely to report that they were directly affected by racism.

EDUCATIONAL CHALLENGES

School emerged as one of the most important systems for the students. Unfortunately, for many of these students, their insatiable appetite for education was impeded by numerous personal, organizational, and systemic challenges. Although there was evidence to support the fact that there were a considerable number of students who dropped out or were pushed out of the school system, there were also many students who progressed quite well, both socially and academically.

Participants discussed several challenges and obstacles that the students faced when they attended school. To begin the discussion, I will first provide evidence to support the importance placed on education by the students. Secondly, I will discuss some of the more prominent educational challenges that emanated from the various discussions. Lastly, I will provide evidence to support the importance of providing a systemic response to address the challenges for the benefit of both the individual and the collective society.

Education as the First Priority

Without exception, every student that I interviewed indicated that being educated was his or her first priority in life. They all referred to getting an education as their only hope for a better future. Many of them saw education as an agent of change. Sokut indicated that after he finished his education he would go back to Sudan to help people live peacefully. The importance of getting an education was clearly articulated in the following quote from Sokut:

> Although there are difficulties, it cannot stop me from going to school. Although I don't have anything to eat today, I cannot stop going to school. I have to go to school. I have to drink some water, and then go to school. I have to get my education. Unless I died, nothing will get in my way. I go to school even though I have no money. Now I live with a cousin who helps me get money for food.

Not only was education a priority for the students, but it was also indicated as being one of the best things about being in Canada. Access to what the students referred to as "free education" was frequently referred to during the interviews with the students.

Len, a counsellor at a refugee centre, confirmed the importance of education in the lives of the students.

> I agree with you the social component is so important. School is the area of socialization. It is everything for these children. It is their first encounter and so much that they identify with the culture and the environment is what they see in the school community. I am of the opinion that we need to invest some more into what happens in school and to support the school system and help the schools get more equipped and have more proactive programs to deal with the social issues because once they leave the school, it is the first stage of deterioration. They drop out of school. It's really hard to get them back. There'll be a very short period of time from the time they drop out of school until they end up in the justice system. So what happens in schools is extremely important for society in general.

Considering the importance of education in the lives of the students, it seems reasonable to delineate what the challenges are for students and to provide focused programs, structures, and systems to help them overcome the challenges. As the following section reveals, there are times when the challenges appear to be too numerous and they pave the path out of school.

The Pathway Out of School

A pattern emerged when discussing school-based challenges. If students were not successful in school, many left the system and it was not long before they were involved in the justice system. Paul, the vice-principal, noted,

> We have a difficult problem with retention. When students do not find success in our school, they are quickly drawn to the life on the street. For many of these kids, the challenges are numerous and life on the street is much easier. Unfortunately, it does not take long to be lured into the street life of selling drugs, committing crimes, and joining street gangs just as a means of survival.

There was also a direct link that was revealed between the need for money, illegal activity, and joining gangs. Tim MacKay argues,

> The truth of the matter is that newcomers do not arrive, get off an airplane, and go downtown and join a gang. That's not how it works. Typically, the pathway is: newcomers arrive, we put them in school, and they leave in six months to a year and then they look for success elsewhere. Kids would rather be bad than stupid. So we set them up in a situation where they cannot succeed and they will find iden-tity, success, and welcoming elsewhere. (Personal communication, March 3, 2007)

Heather, who is a representative from Justice and Youth Court, pro-vides evidence not only to support the pathway from school to criminal behaviour, but she also suggests that there is little to help students who are not successful in school.

> At noon today, I am picking up a woman whose son is now in Brinkston [maximum security prison] and she tells a very

compelling story. She dragged her kids through ... she is from Somalia. She dragged several kids around from camp to camp. And talking about not knowing where these kids come from, her son, who is now 20, was actually in a pit, in a huge pit, full of dead bodies that were going to be burned. And her son was in there and she was watching them going to set them on fire. Because she thought her son was dead. And then she just saw his body twitch, and she pulled him out of this mass grave of about a thousand people. She pulled him out and he lived. And she said to me, I went through hell. My husband was murdered and my other children were murdered, and I dragged my kids all around and finally I got here to Canada with the hope of having a wonderful life.

And if you thought my life was hell in Somalia, my life has been more hell since I've gotten here. My son has never been in school.... He didn't know his ABCs in his own language. He didn't know his ABCs when he came to Canada, and he was 12 years old and he was dumped into a grade 6 class. He learned English very quickly; probably within three months he could speak pretty good English. But he couldn't read or write. He had no literacy whatsoever, he still doesn't. He immediately felt out of place. He didn't feel part of that group. They lived here in the Central area. And somehow he just couldn't cope. And within six months, he was out of school. He has never been back to school. I don't know from the school, whether they reached out to the mother or not. And he has been in the justice system ever since he was 12 years old.

Heather continued to recount her frustration in finding school placements for the children she works with. She has had to send some children back to Africa to keep them safe. She states,

I could tell you right now, I was looking at the gang list for the two African street gangs. There are probably 150 names. I didn't count them, but there's about 150 and I am sure that none of them have gone through school; they have all fallen through the cracks. Our system has not worked well with them.

It is difficult to ascertain what it is that ultimately leads students away from school. For the most part, the school just does not seem to be a place where the student finds success. In both of the above quotations there was a similar reason for the student leaving the school system—academic difficulty. A common challenge brought forth by teachers, parents, and students is the fact that students have had disrupted schooling or the absence of schooling. Two of the parents also suggested that students drop out of school because they do not get support from their parents. They also suggested that the school needs to engage with the parents to connect them to the school. Manley declared, "Some students drop out because of the failure of their parents. In order to make sure all of these things are addressed with the parents. The school has to talk with the parents."

Disrupted Schooling

Consider the following statement made by Ugot: "I have never been to school until I came to Walter Duncan." Ugot is 18 years old and his goal is to become either a teacher or a medical doctor. He has no previous educational experience and no language, literacy, or computational skills. The school system is presented with a unique problem. How best should children at the age of 16, 17, or 18 be schooled when they have never been to school before? Furthermore, does the school have the adequate resources to deal with this issue?

Some of the students have had some schooling, although much of it has been disrupted by war, relocation, and the lack of financial resources needed to pay school fees. The disruption or absence of schooling is further complicated by the age of the student. What is the appropriate placement for the student who has little or no education? As Mike from the welcoming centre states, "We see it as a problem to just drop these kids because of their age to a lower level of school. It creates enormous problems." Although Mike admits that there are pre-beginner programs offered in the school division, his staff has told him that there is too much bureaucracy for getting into the program and it needs to be a lot more flexible. The coordinator in charge of the newly designed centres also suggests that numbers of students in the pre-beginner classes are very low and she had anticipated that more students would have been enrolled in these centres. Students who have basic conversational English skills also struggle because they do not generally have the academic skills to engage in the coursework.

Working and Going to School

Marleen, an educational coordinator of a refugee counselling centre, states, "We tend to put every obstacle we can in front of these kids who are working and going to school every day. We put every obstacle in front of these children who are just trying to get an education." Most of the refugee students work; however, many of them work full-time jobs while attending school. More than half of the students that I interviewed left school at 3:30 and then worked until 11:30 or 12:00. Bill comments about how many students have to work and the difficulties this poses for them when they try to attend school.

> Some of the students who are now 17 and 18, they have to go to work because they have to support themselves and their family. And this is a challenge, really. I've been through some refugee life, but not like the ones that these young people are going through.... I see that most of them actually work after school and in this case they don't really have time to do their homework. They may be tired the following day, and it would be hard for them to wake up and go to school. But I don't think there is any free money to provide to them. I don't know how that can be solved really. I really don't know. Maybe the government knows better. Sometimes it's hard really for you to bring other people to a new place. It is really appreciated to bring them, but what difference does it mean when there is no adequate support to help them resettle in a new country? It's like taking people from a plane and then just dumping them down there and just letting them fend for themselves. It's just really frustrating.

Paul also notes a similar pattern in one of the students he teaches:

> I know he works up to eight hours a day doing maintenance and security. He starts at 4:00 and finishes at 12:00 and by the time he

gets home, it might be 1:00 or 2:00, and he has four, five, six hours of sleep and then he gets up and goes to school. And he does this five or six days a week.

Rassan was so concerned about one of his students that he went to the student's place of work to complain about the shift the student was given. The student's shift started at 7:00 PM and went until 4:00 in the morning. Rassan went to the place of work and asked if they were aware what the student did during the day. The employer acknowledged that he knew the student attended school. Rassan explained, "They gave the schedule and it was impossible for the kid to come to class. And he has a family to support, an older mother to support, and a younger sister to support. The kid felt he had no choice. That is a shame." Rassan argues that it is imperative for the community to understand the student's circumstance. He indicates that if the student and the employer do not understand each other, then it is the student who gets fired.

Afem clearly articulates the difficulties that he and some of the others have in terms of going to work, attending school, and completing homework.

> The government gave us some money to go to school for about a year. And after that, we went to social assistance, and that wasn't good and because you need to go to school. And you have to have attendance, and they said you have to go to work. And they know in Canada, when you go to school, you don't need to be disturbed. There was a lady ... you had to bring your résumé and your attendance with you to prove if you go to school or not. And she said you have to look for a job. So now I go to school and go to work, both of them. And I don't even get time to do my own work because I go to start at 3:30 and I will go late because the school just finishes at 3:20. And so I go late, like 4:00. And then I finish at 12:00. When I come home, I do my homework and it takes time. Sometimes you have a lot of homework especially like reading, and we try to learn the language, but we take a lot of time. And once you get home at midnight it takes sometimes until 3:00 in the

morning to finish your work. And we get up at 7:30 and I don't
think it's good for us.

To understand more about the students' circumstances and how
they support each other, I have included the following exchange that I
had with Afem.

We live with ourselves. If you don't go to work, nobody will pay
your rent. So you need to survive for yourself. Right now I am
living with my friends. We go to work and go home at the same
time. When you come home, one person will cook, and then the
next day the other one will cook. That's how we do it.

Do you ever do any fun stuff?
No.

What other things do you do?
On the weekends, we do our homework, and we don't get time
to go nowhere. And we have friends over, and they asked us
to this place that we say we don't have time because we work
five days a week to get money. Monday to Friday. On Saturday
and Sunday we go to church. Sunday and Saturday we do our
homework. We don't have free time, we do everything, we
cook everything.

Very similar conversations occurred with additional students.
Although there were exceptions to the amount of support that the student had from family members, most of the students worked to pay for
basic necessities or to support the family, either in Canada or in their
countries of origin. As the teachers indicated, in some instances, students have dropped out of school because they need to work full-time
to help send younger family members to school. James dropped out of
school because he was getting home at 3:00 in the morning and he said
that he could not cope with all the work. He subsequently came back to
school and he is hoping to graduate this year.

Akot works and lives with Afem, and the two of them take turns cooking and cleaning. Both of them have indicated that the challenge of working full-time and going to school full-time has taken a toll on their schoolwork and their social life. At the end of the interview with Akot, I posed a question, "How could we make this situation better for you?" His response was, "Maybe the government could help. That way I could concentrate on my school. Maybe if I only worked two or three days ..." The answer to this particular challenge has already been advanced by the students—it does not have to be an overly complicated solution. For years, the educational community has struggled trying to motivate learners who had no desire to be in school. We have expended time, resources, money, and talent trying to devise creative ways at keeping kids in school. This is clearly a group of students who have the drive and the will to attend school; we need to remove the financial burden and allow them to stay in school.

Perceived Attitudes of Teachers

Some of the teachers openly discussed their dissatisfaction with how other teachers and the administrators treat the refugee students. Examples were provided by various participants to substantiate their claims that some teachers do not want refugee students in their classes. For example, a teacher in the focus group states, "And that's the issue that teachers are—instead of compassionate and empathetic—are asking, why are they even here? Why do they bother coming to this country if they don't know how to behave?" Some of the participants explained that teachers assume that refugee children are like every other immigrant and they should not be given preferential treatment. One of the more difficult comments to hear and one that has resonated with me throughout this study was a comment from one of the teachers at Walter Duncan School. At the end of our interview, he emotionally and with a defeatist tone states, "And the only thing we have going for us is that they don't know that they're being treated like crap because they're not physically under threat as much as they were. But they will figure it out." On the more positive side of this comment, it was clearly coming from a teacher who struggled with some of the attitudes and behaviours that he witnessed; that in itself shows that there are people who are concerned for the children in the school.

Laurie discussed an incident that occurred in one of the technical classes. She concludes that there are some teachers who refuse to have immigrant students in their classes.

> I'll give you an example. There is one girl, I can't remember where she was from in Africa, but she was a new immigrant at the time. And so she walked into the classroom and she was visibly one of those students who are new to the school. She said that she kept trying to get the teacher's attention, asking him how to work a machine. Apparently, the teacher kept putting her off and putting her off and she waited almost half the class doing nothing. So she decided to try it by herself and she broke the darn thing. A piece of glass in it got broken and it was $200 to fix it. He went completely nuts on her. Anyway, the poor girl came down to my office crying, saying, "I will pay for it, I will pay for it. I don't know how, but I will pay for it and I don't want to go back into that class." And now the teacher uses that as an excuse not to bring any more ESL students into his class because they don't understand and they are a safety issue for themselves and other students. A big challenge for kids is feeling unwelcome ... I think it's just feeling unwelcome in a school that's just unable to program for these kids, so I think that's tough for them.

Some of the participants in the microsystem also commented on what might best be referred to as an indifference to the refugee students. For example, the participants indicated that there were teachers who taught the way they taught despite who was in their classroom. The teachers did what they felt they could do and unfortunately it was too bad for those who could not keep up with the expectations.

Sandra emphatically states her discontent with how some teachers treat the refugee students and she comments on how she believes this affects the students.

Every time I hear them bragging about how many immigrants we have in this province, I just think how many of them are just going to fall through the cracks, just to fill some quota or some number. There's a huge divide between those who see it and those who get it. Like there are people who just don't get it. Unfortunately, these are the ones who are teaching these kids that make them feel like they're absolute crap.

And you hear them saying to kids, "What, are you stupid?" All of those little things that we do as human beings that we don't necessarily mean. But I see some of those teachers doing the same thing over and over again to the same students. And these kids know very little English, but they certainly know what stupid means.

Sandra's comments are particularly unsettling because she was the teacher who has the most contact, on an informal basis, with many of the refugee students. She was named most frequently by the student participants as someone whom they felt safe talking to should a problem arise. Each time I visited the school, students were always informally talking and joking with her. When I needed to find a student to talk to, I went to her room and she knew exactly where he or she would be. She was with the students before and after school and she ate lunch in her room all the days I was there. Although I was cautious not to assume that Sandra's comments represented the majority, I did hear other comments, from school staff, students, and members of the exosystem, that reinforced much of what she said. The fortunate part of this challenge concerning teachers' attitudes was that there were only a few people named as being particularly problematic and difficult for the students. Moreover, it was clearly stated that the cause of these attitudes and behaviours is usually the result of ignorance and a lack of knowledge about the students and their circumstances, rather than the result of malice or contempt.

One of the teachers also discusses her anger about a situation that she was brought into by an administrator concerning an African student who wanted to change classes so that he could be in her class. The teacher feels that the treatment from the administrator would not have occurred if the student were not an immigrant. She clearly indicates that she thinks the administrator could "get away" with her behaviour because the student did not have a parent or guardian who would come back to the school to hold the administrator accountable for her words.

> I distinctly remember sitting in the cafeteria and I remember an administrator coming into the cafeteria toward me, red-faced and I thought, Oh my god, what have I done? She was with one of the African students and she says to the student [yelling], "You sit down there, you tell Mrs. R. what is going on, you tell her what happened in the office. And she will tell you what the difference is between those classes." And I'm thinking, What is she talking about? Then I realized it was because the boy did not want to be in the other class. He wanted to be in my class. So I had to say they are exactly the same because I'm right in front of my administrator. And he is trying to explain how all he wanted was to be in this class where he felt comfortable, where the teacher understood him, and he was afraid to go to another class because he had friends who were uncomfortable in a class. They felt that they weren't good enough to be in the other class. So he's trying to explain to her that was all he wanted and "I went to you because you are the boss of the school. You're the only person that I thought I could talk to, to change this on my timetable." And she stood up and she said, "I am not your servant." And I was thinking, "Please Lord, don't let her say I'm not your slave." And she walked out. And I was thinking, there is no way on this earth that she would ever have said that to a student who was not an immigrant. There's no way she would have said that to a well-off white person—*I am not your servant*—because that family would be down here saying, "Don't talk to my child like that." And I see that time and time again, families with power and privilege and support get to decide what classes their kids will get into, and the ones who have nothing—they have nobody to defend them, they are stuck in classes where they don't belong and no one does anything about it…. And then who suffers because of that? We watch students suffer semester after semester, feeling totally helpless. To watch them

walk out of a classroom crying because they're told that it is a waste of their time to be there, based on what? Their second day in class? What do you know about what they can and cannot do?... This student I am referring to, he wrote in his essay, "I am just so disappointed about all the things that I hoped for are not going to happen. And I'll never be able to change anything." And you know what? He's right.

It was obvious that the teacher was quite distressed about how some of the students were treated by the administrator and by some of the teachers who might not be as sensitive as they should be in terms of the social and emotional needs of some students. The students that I interviewed knew very well who the teachers were that they could go to if they had a problem or who would be more sympathetic to their needs. As with any high school setting, teachers will have a reputation, whether it is true, that precedes them and often influences how they are perceived by the students. That said, once there are actions or words to reinforce this opinion, it becomes quite difficult to reverse.

It was noted that teachers must be willing to adapt and modify their curriculum to meet the changing demographics of the Canadian classroom. Rassan clearly articulates the need for teachers to respond to the changing needs of the children.

Our classroom right now is not the classroom of the 1980s or the '70s or '60s, where you had a majority of white kids in your classroom. There were very few immigrants. You would have a curriculum and you could say this is what we're going to accomplish by the end. We have to do a lot of modifications, and that doesn't mean to bring the level down or to water the curriculum down. Modification means find a different way to teach the material to different people. And that is the challenge for a lot of people. Very simple. I have a colleague who has a test that was done in the 1990s and he puts it in front of these kids, assuming that the language is okay and the comprehension will be okay. And kids fail. Why? Because they don't understand the language that was used. So you have to make modifications, you have to know what your demographics are and make modifications if you want success for students. But if the point for me was to get the curriculum covered no matter what consequence, it will happen, but what will be the price? Kids will pay for it. That's the bottom line. I worked with teachers and different departments and this worked 10 years ago, but look at class now, 50 per cent of your kids are EAL students. Make the adjustment. I had to go through this. I am not just speaking because I have read an article. I went through it. I have the experience, and that's what kids want.

Additional knowledge and resources were identified as key challenges that would be needed to meet the needs of the refugee students. The teachers' willingness to change their teaching style for the betterment of the students also figured prominently in the data. The frustration that I sensed from many of the statements made by school staff was that some teachers were not willing to take the time to make adjustments to better fit the needs of their students, and this seriously hampered the students' academic success.

Language and Literacy

A major obstacle for non-English-speaking refugees is to learn the language so that they can function in society. There was a clear distinction made between oral English and academic literacy. It seemed that once the students learned enough English to carry on a conversation, they thought they had mastered the language and they would be able to succeed in advanced-level courses. There appears to be two levels of challenges that the students encountered related to communication. First, they needed to acquire basic communication skills to navigate their way through the various systems. Second, they needed academic language and literacy skills to advance their level of education.

As many of the EAL teachers explained, many of the students did not have adequate written English or English comprehension skills to be successful in some of the academic classes. The problem many of the teachers encountered was convincing the students that they needed the academic literacy skills to understand and complete the work in the courses. Many of the students took the high-level courses only to be disappointed that they were not successful and they needed to take the courses again. Many of the students had to repeat courses until their language skills improved enough to complete the coursework. Bev states,

> I explain to them that they need to take four basic English courses in EAL before they are ready to take regular courses. But not all of them listen. I tell them that they need to have at least 80 per cent or higher in these classes to be able to handle the regular courses just to get a decent mark around 60 per cent. They don't listen and then they fail the courses, over and over. I cannot insist that they not go into the regular classes. If they don't listen, they go in and learn the hard way. What makes it worse is when teachers feel sorry for them and just give them a pass. This doesn't help anyone.

Scott also notes,

> I have kids in my grade 10 Geography class taking it for the third time, this is just ridiculous. How can they stand doing the same thing over and over? What tends to happen is they just end up getting bored or frustrated and then just give up.

Banya indicated that she knew three languages. She struggled the first couple of years after coming to Canada, and now she says it is better. "I only know a bit of English so is very hard for me at the beginning. It was a big challenge. I know how to write everything but not really. For some people it is very hard, they don't even know how to write ABC." Afem also stated that he should have graduated but because of the language it has been very difficult.

Bill discusses the importance of the EAL programs, as well as the need to support the teachers who provide these programs.

> I think the schools are really trying to do their best to support the EAL problem. Because imagine if you bring these newcomers without any English, just put them in the mainstream class. They will never perform better. But they are helping them with the EAL

program, and it gives them the foundation and the entry into the system. They don't just come here and, bang, there they go. And teachers are not made aware of the students in the classrooms and they might think the students are dumb. They don't know anything and they don't treat them right. I think this is some of the things that teachers need to be made aware of. And I think the government needs to provide more support to teachers or volunteers who are willing to come to the schools to support these newcomers with their language.

Learning English is also a major challenge for the parents, and many of the parents also attend EAL classes. As Rumbaut and Portes (2001) state, "… immigrant adolescents experience much faster linguistic adaptation than their parents …" (p. 219). Because the child develops language skills at a much faster pace than the parent, it complicates the parent-child power relationship, especially when the child is used as a translator for the parent. As Parsa outlined in the following excerpt, her limited English meant that she could not attend parent-teacher conferences to find out how her children were doing in school.

Hard for me was the language. It is very hard to learn a new language, and I didn't understand the culture in Canada. My counsellor had to teach me and another person got a house for me, downtown. And another counsellor talked to the Walter Duncan School and my children go to Walter Duncan School. This was a hard job for me because I didn't understand English. I know a little bit now. And sometimes I can go to my children's school and I can talk with my children's teachers. I like it because I didn't understand before. It is hard for me. I didn't know the English so I didn't know how my children were doing in school and I just had to look at my children's report cards and they explained it to me. I've only been to school for my children twice. The school could give translation.

Learning either English or French and having the academic literacy skills is paramount to being able to work and be educated in Canada. Having said this, the data in this study revealed that there was so much more beyond just reading and writing that needed to be done to support these students. Although programs and services have been noted as being beneficial, many blank spots clearly need to be addressed. Sandra states that it is all of the things beyond reading that students need more help with. She believes that the challenge is both to help students adjust to Canadian customs and to provide more knowledge on basic life skills.

> The education system—absolutely something needs to be done. We can put all the supports in place to make them learn how to read but to read is not going to be their problem. It is everything else around the reading. They don't have sex ed, they don't know about personal hygiene.... There has to be more supports in place, we just have to. There is tons of money going into literacy, but how much is going into teaching them about, you know, how to respect women or how to get along with people who are culturally different. Those are the big issues that I see.

Language and literacy issues were a challenge for both the students and their parents. The language was a barrier for parents to become more involved with their child's education. Acquiring the basic communication skills needed to function in society was one challenge and acquiring the academic literacy skills needed to be educated in Canada was another challenge. While these two challenges were mentioned, other challenges related to education and living in Manitoba were mentioned more frequently by both the students and the participants representing the microsystem and the exosystem.

Academic Literacy, Aspirations, and Ability

Several participants suggest that the career aspirations and the future goals that the students have are unrealistic given their current academic level. As one of the counsellors indicates, many of the students want to be doctors, engineers, or lawyers, but their reading skills and math skills are at a grade 1–3 level and they are 17 or 18 years of age and in grade 11. Even after being in school for a year or two, they struggle with basic skills, yet many of the students want to take the highest level of math or English so they could pursue university entrance requirements. One of the other counsellors said that she has an ethical issue putting students in high-level courses and then seeing them fail in excess of three times.

The EAL teacher indicates that once students learn enough English to carry on a conversation, they think that they are able to jump into the regular stream of specialized university preparation courses. It appears that there are two different issues related to language and literacy challenges. First, there is the need to develop basic conversational skills that the students need to navigate their way through the systems to satisfy their basic needs. Second, there is the academic literacy necessary to take courses in school and to pursue a more advanced academic program. For example, students would have to learn basic English to shop at a grocery store, take a bus, or to go to a meeting with their reception counsellor. Once the students reached a certain level of basic conversational English, the teachers indicate that they thought they had mastered the language and they could take any course they wanted in school. The business teacher states, "They just want to get that Canadian dream, you know, they come here and they think they can be all of these things, but...." Essentially, many of the teachers suggest that the students have an unrealistic outlook for their future, given their current academic level.

The challenge for educators is that the academic level of the students is, in most cases, a long way away from where they need to be in order to fulfill their dreams. The students' understanding of the level of academic literacy necessary to complete the courses is incongruent with what the staff members think students need to realistically pass the course. In addition, some of the teachers clearly indicated that the cognitive ability of the student was compromised, particularly when they had years of disrupted schooling. This left what one teacher referred to as "serious gaps in their learning and functioning and this complicated their ability to transfer learning skills to a new environment."

The purpose of suggesting that students take alternative courses better suited to their ability is not to limit their choices by encouraging them to choose a different career path. Moreover, most of the teachers suggested that they would like students to achieve some success at one level before progressing to a more difficult level. That said, the students need to have a much better idea of what it will take to achieve their goals. A second observation about this issue is the fact that the school staff has indicated that most of the students aspire to the same grouping of occupations: a doctor, a lawyer, a dentist, or an engineer. That in itself suggests that these students are in dire need of learning more about high- and low-prestige jobs, expected earnings, and the future job outlook for Canada. Many students were motivated to become employed and financially secure within the next four to five years so that they could support themselves and their family members. The latter was mentioned when the students discussed their future plans, in addition to their wish to sponsor more family members to come to Canada.

Much empirical evidence in the domain of career counselling supports the influential role that parents have on the career choices that their children make (Bregman & Killen, 1999; Middleton & Loughead, 1993; Sebald, 1989; Trusty, Watts, & Crawford, 1996). Considering the fact that students in the west make most of their career choices based on what their parents do, or what friends of their parents do, it is not surprising that these students would choose the occupations they did. The people that refugee children would come in contact with, who would represent the west and the wealth that accompanies this perception of the west, would likely be those from the list of careers that the students aspired toward. Many of the student participants did not live with parents and, in many cases, if they did have parents, they were unable to work because of the conflict. The interactions that the students had with foreign workers may have influenced their career choices. It is quite possible that if students received a more comprehensive career development program, they might have different aspirations that were better suited to their interests. Although this is only speculation, there could potentially be some work that is needed in the area of career awareness and realistic goal setting.

Preparation of Teachers

The school system is in a unique position because virtually every refugee child who comes to Canada will be enrolled in school. For many families, outside of the initial contact with the welcoming centre, the school will be their first point of contact with any form of support agency. As the discussion in the following chapter illustrates, school has been identified as the most important ecological system for the refugee family; all of the children and their families will have some form of contact with the school, albeit for varying lengths of time. The challenge that has been identified is that the school does not have adequate resources and the personnel does not have the training to identify or respond to all of the issues. This will become particularly concerning if anticipated numbers of newcomers immigrate to the province. Although some of these issues are happening at a micro level, with numbers of immigrants to Canada expected to increase over the next five years, the issues are likely to be exacerbated at the macro level. Most of the participants indicated that the school was not ready for the onslaught of newcomers.

Donna, the principal of Walter Duncan School, notes that there is very limited time for professional development (PD). Although the school was granted additional time to train the staff to deal with a substantial increase of refugees in a short time, Donna believes that this was a one-time occurrence that she would likely not receive again in the future.

> I think we need more PD time and then that is restricted. I know in one week we got 19 kids and that is almost a whole classroom in one week. These kids showed up from Iraq. And then the other superintendent, I phoned him and I was almost hysterical because these girls after a few weeks were showing anger and fighting and pulling hair, all kinds of strange things, and it turned out that one of the families had arrived and the father had been killed after they got here. He [the superintendent] gave us permission to use two half-days to talk about what was going on and we talked to an Iraqi psychiatrist. And this person came and talked to our staff. But that's because the superintendent granted us that day, but usually we're not allowed. And actually, I don't think I would've gotten that from my own superintendent.

Rassan adamantly argues the dire need for classroom-level support because of the multiple roles that are expected of a teacher.

> Put yourself in the students' shoes and you travel back in time. You put yourself in a refugee camp and go into their country and live and learn their language and their life. You do that. In a perfect world I would say you've got to find the right person to deal with these people. You just can't put them in a classroom and assume that this poor teacher is going to do the job of a teacher, the job of a disciplinarian, the job of a parent and a counsellor and a community leader. Provide them support. I don't expect you to go into a classroom and be successful with all these kids without any support. Without support, we are nothing. Find the support.

Scott informed me that the only preparation in the school for the influx of African and Middle Eastern students was to know that they were coming. He states, "That was it. We didn't receive any in-servicing, we didn't receive any background apart from a few words at a staff meeting." While there was clearly a need to better prepare the school staff for teaching refugee children, time was not allocated at either staff meetings or professional development days for this purpose. One of the teachers indicated that improving literacy skills for all learners was the focus of their professional development activities over the past few years. Although the school principal indicated that the topic was of immediate concern, additional days were not provided by the school division administration for additional training of the staff.

As the executive director of a reception centre, Mike states that he had a workbook of resources available for teachers to use, but it was sitting on the shelf gathering dust. He indicates that his staff has also developed an Ambassador program to assist refugee students when they arrive in a new school and this was also not being utilized. He then concludes,

> We are not out there to market ourselves. Hey, if the school division doesn't recognize the resources that they have, it's not my job. It's

their problem. If they are not using us, the same way they're not using the Ambassador program that we spent a whole lot of time developing and it just sits there. If they're not using this stuff that is available, there's a brick wall between the regular kids and the irregular kids. You know, we deal with the irregular kids. And if they're not interested, what are we supposed to do about it? If they have the resources and they do want to take advantage of it, Okay.

There was quite clearly a lack of communication between the school division and the personnel who had developed the programs. Mike banged his hand repeatedly on the table throughout this portion of the interview. A few members of the focus group collected Mike's contact information after the meeting so that they could inquire further about the resources. It was clear that the program and the workbook were of interest, but it was also evident that there was a previous lack of communication about what resources were available and how they could be distributed to schools.

Parental Assistance

One of the teachers pointed out that if the children do not know the English language, then it is likely that the parents do not either. Many references were made as to the importance of the school connecting with the parents or caregivers and the need for parents to be more responsible for their child's schooling. One of the parents that I interviewed suggests,

A successful child in education needs supervision between the school and the home. And if they are just left to go to school, that child is not going to because a child is a child. And they don't know what is wrong. Those parents, they have to monitor from time to time and check the kids and check what they did today. And most of the times, I don't think, especially immigrant parents, they don't even look into their kids' work because they think education is the responsibility of the school. The school is alone because they don't have, may I say, knowledge.

It was suggested that more work was needed to improve the communication between the school and the home. This communication is particularly difficult when the parents do not speak the language and the school uses the student as a translator. This creates an unequal power structure that complicates the roles between the child and the parents.

Bill, a Sudanese community liaison representative, suggests that more resources need to be provided to the parents on the weekend because many of them work during the week. He adds that if the school had programs on the weekend that were designed for parents, for example, on the topic of discipline, it would be easier for parents to attend. Bill also indicates that there are some parents who are working two jobs and it is not feasible for them to miss work time.

Educational Organizational and Policy Issues

The overall organization of the system and the policies, or lack of policies, pertaining to the education of refugee children were noted as challenges at the government, the divisional, and the school levels. A thorough investigation of the organizational and policy issues concerning this topic would extend far beyond the scope of this study. For the purpose of this discussion, I will highlight some of the challenges that were noted as these related to providing an appropriate education for refugee children. I will discuss the perspectives of the government representatives as well as that of the school and divisional staff.

Debbie, a government consultant in the area of EAL, states, "There are a lot of times when they [the teachers] are held back just by policies that have not kept up with the changes." Will, also a government consultant in the area of EAL, informed me that up until quite recently there had been no real planning mechanism or divisional direction for refugee youth in the school divisions, including those divisions with the greatest number of refugee students. He indicated that most of the schools were locally responsible for developing policy, which was usually dependent on the "whims of the principals to give it any support." In some cases, there were no additional resources for EAL learners. Will suggests that the province is moving toward a more consistent approach that he hopes is based on research and good practice.

Will noted that he knows of a school division that has received an additional $400,000 because of the number of EAL learners. He questioned what was done with the resources because there was no additional support staff and no additional EAL consultants put in place.

In some cases the schools have established programming and progressive approaches that were said to be appropriate, but once there was a change in the administrator the programs were not sustainable. Will notes, "And then there's the change in the school administrator. The person doesn't come in with that knowledge, or believes there's a different set of priorities. So everything that was built up over time can be totally destroyed." If the priorities have not been articulated and included in the principal's mandate or the school plan, then it is left up to the individual principal to determine whether it is important and worthy of attention. Historically, the EAL programs have been informal, inconsistent, and unsustainable after a major change in leadership.

In many school divisions, EAL programming was not a priority and schools had a "sink or swim" situation where the students showed up, were placed in an age-appropriate classroom, and teachers were encouraged to support them as much as possible. Some school divisions who had a larger number of EAL students might put in an EAL support teacher to help in the classroom. An interesting comparison was brought forth in the focus group by Karen, who stated that, "We don't just put kids in a French immersion program, we actually have a program designed for them where teachers are knowledgeable about second-language methodology." She elaborated, saying, "We don't just dump them into the regular classroom and say, 'You learn that way,' this is how they learn." Karen refers to this as a double standard.

Will and Debbie both indicate that a big challenge is to come up with "standard practice and formal policies and protocols that draw on good research and practice and to get schools to implement that." As was revealed in the focus group and by the interviews with the school administrators and divisional consultants, there was also a disparity between the written policy and its implementation.

Ingrid, an EAL support teacher for the school division, states, "It seems that some of the policy of the school divisions that I'm representing ... it's not getting to the individual schools. It seems that different things are being done in different schools, and they're not following the policy." She indicated that schools are either "ignoring the number of students that are EAL learners" or they are "deferring to other kids who are just regular learners and they've grown up in an English-speaking home." It appeared that whether there was an EAL program was dependent on whether the individual principal thought it was a priority for the school. Ingrid states, "It's really catch-as-you-can as to whether one administrator thinks it is important to have an EAL program and to support it properly or whether they'll just be immersed." Ingrid provided the following example,

> Last year, when I began the job and was visiting, one principal told
> me, "They are just in the regular classroom. They don't have any
> supports. They will learn English...." And even if we are talking just
> about immigrant children, and not just refugees, I already knew
> that there was a brick wall to my ever coming back there, until the
> administration changed.

In one leader's defence, Paul states, "Policies are more paper-based than they are action-based. And so that action bogs us down even more." Considering the demographics of the school and the issues that Paul raised in his interview, policies might need to be more aligned with the realities of the school environment. That said, articulating clear and realistic policies that have been developed cooperatively might lead to more successful implementation.

At the provincial level, Will indicates that the government has started work on an EAL program framework and he notes that they are moving to a more provincial approach in terms of expectations for programming. Will also states that they are trying to "build capacity for programming," as well as trying to "implement more accountability measures, particularly for EAL."

Despite some of the forward movement from the education department in terms of a framework, course development, and more accountability, it does not necessarily mean that this change will occur quickly or in the way that it was intended. As Will illustrates, there are also schools that set policy on something that is not pedagogically sound. He talked about an example in one school division where there are two high schools with EAL programs. In one school, the beginning learners are not allowed to be in Physical Education or in Home Economics because of safety concerns. That school argues that the students do not understand enough English to follow directions and this could be a safety concern. The students in this school are not permitted to attend these option courses until they move into the intermediate-level classroom. This could take in excess of a year. To link to an earlier argument, this is another example where students are not given the opportunity to interact with other children in the school, thus exacerbating the already difficult process of socializing to a new ecological system. This situation is completely different from another high school in that same division that says beginning learners will be in the beginner class but they will also be in Art, Physical Education, Home Economics, Sports, and Music because even if the students do not speak or understand higher level English, they may be good at one of these other subjects.

These are examples of two schools in the same school division. Because there is no standard or coordination between the schools, there is no consistency across the division. In addition, when the staffing changes, there is also no retention of knowledge and, in many cases, teachers need to reinvent the programs. Will notes, "There needs to be a retention of knowledge so that when a school's teachers change, someone can come in and continue on with the program without struggling and relearning things that should be available within that school." Will also suggests that school divisions need to document best practice, decide what support materials they need, and then determine what programming should look like. Because there has not been consistency and coordination in terms of policy, it often means that schools are going to be more reactive than proactive. Essentially, what participants noted was the overwhelming desire for a more formal approach that was proactive in nature, collaboratively developed, consistent and sustainable.

Although this discussion has focused primarily on the policy issue at the provincial level, I questioned why none of the participants suggested that it must also be examined federally. Immigration is under the federal jurisdiction, and education is a provincial issue. It appears that if we are truly going to collaborate on solving many of the organi-zational and policy issues, it might be more useful to look at the issues from a broader perspective. What responsibility does Citizenship and Immigration Canada have for ensuring that the refugee children who are brought to Canada are given an appropriate education? Using an ecological framework and a multitiered federal, provincial, and local approach for investigating and solving many of these challenges might be more advantageous.

Several educational challenges have been discussed in the pre-ceding section. Although evidence suggested some students become overwhelmed by the challenges and subsequently leave the school system, most forge ahead despite the adversity. Challenges related to difficulties with the coursework, perceived teacher attitudes, and limited support from home made it more difficult for students to be successful. In addition, the lack of policies related to refugee education limited the availability and consistency of programs and services provided to these students.

CHAPTER FOUR

Psychosocial and Environmental Challenges

PSYCHOSOCIAL ISSUES

A DICHOTOMY EXISTED between those who thought refugee students needed help to work through psychological issues, in particular trauma, and those who thought refugee students seemed to be doing quite well without any intervention. It became important to not only examine what was said by various participants but to also consider the context in which this was said. The information that was divulged, the role that each of them played in the microsystem, and the personal relationship that the person had with the student seemed to influence where they each stood on the issue.

When I first began talking to the refugee students, there were times where I assumed that they were so resilient because they had lived through war, witnessed conflict, lost their parents, and yet still carried on with seemingly little effect. Although the students hinted

95

at how difficult their lives were, it seemed that they had put the war behind them and then moved on with life in Canada. After I spoke with more students and with teachers who had a closer relationship with the students, I altered my thinking about what many of these students continue to experience.

I asked Anna, who is from Liberia, only one question throughout the entire one-and-a-half-hour interview. I asked her to tell me a little about herself. She talked about her trans-migration experience and the issues she had with the adult who accompanied her to Canada. Divulging serious issues of both physical and emotional abuse, she had just recently attempted to kill herself. At the time, fleeing the abuse, she lived alone with her young child. After the attempt, the child was subsequently removed from her home by Child Welfare.

I had no idea before commencing the interview what Anna was going to discuss with me. Following the interview, I followed ethical protocol and ensured that she was safe and that she had appropriate support. The following is a short excerpt of the interview, which is only intended to provide evidence for the extent to which a student is struggling with mental health issues and to question our beliefs about how best to provide assistance to these students.

> I was having seizures from back home and from memories of being with my aunt. And I said I've never heard about anything like this kind of thing. And these weird things are happening to me. I'm seeing visions. Like the same people are in them. Bad people and witches; they are in my mind. And it was bothering me. And on Tuesday morning. I was just in the house ... I don't know ... I was so confused and people were just talking to me in my mind. And they said, "Who do you think you are, what is going on here?" And I went into the kitchen and I just took a knife. I opened the drawer. I took a knife and another person said, "Take that knife and put that into yourself." I was on the floor. I was so lucky that my cousin came in. And all I was trying to do is to cut something and my eyes were just going on like this [rolling]. And I cannot see, and I didn't even see my cousin come in. And my cousin took my knife from me. I was laying on

the floor with the knife to my stomach…. I told her, "I'm listen-
ing to voices," and I try to hurt myself. One voice tells me to kill
myself and the other voice says not to. And I can't hear with
both of them talking to me in both ears. And every time I go
home, I can be so worried. It is so scary, to go home by myself,
living by myself, with nobody around me to talk to. And I told
her that every night, every night, I listen to the voices and I can
be so scared to go to bed. Sometimes I just leave the lights on
all night. Or I leave the music or the TV on really loud all night.
And then I go to bed.

Anna's words certainly raise serious questions about her current
mental status. It is also quite obvious that she is frightened to be alone.
Later in the interview, Anna divulged that the two people talking to her
are deceased family members. Considering this information within a
western medical model, one might question whether Anna was schizo-
phrenic or delusional. Using a non-western model based on spirituality
and cultural teachings, the reason that Anna hears the voices might
possibly be a result of not providing the deceased a proper burial. In
some cultures the souls of the dead haunt the living until they are properly laid to rest. Considering these two orientations, treatment might
look completely different depending on who worked with Anna.

Anna was not willing to seek medical attention; in fact, she signed
herself out of the hospital and refused care. She states, "And I told them,
taking pills is not going to make this thing go away, and no one wants to
believe me." She later indicates that prayer is the only thing she thought
would help her. She explains,

And I called the pastor and asked him to come and see if he
could save me from the people. And he explained everything to
me and I went to church, and he prayed for me. And he said he
prayed for me and the thing is going to go away and he went
and prayed for me. And he anointed me, and he came to my
house and he prayed for me and the whole house. And the next
day I went to bed very, very good, and I woke up. I called him
and I said, "Oh pastor, thank you," and I said, "You really saved

my life." And he said, "That's okay, no problem." And everything
is okay, I can go to bed good; I am not scared anymore.... Now
I'm okay as free as you. I'm fine.

The overarching question that emerges from this conversation is,
Are we willing to work with Anna within the latter paradigm or are
we going to insist that she seeks medical treatment? The argument put
forth in this book suggests that we must provide assistance that is both
culturally and linguistically appropriate. In Anna's case, she was told
that if she did not attend the treatment program, she would not get her
baby back. This is a considerable stretch from being culturally sensitive.
If we are not willing, as a society, to open ourselves to alternative, non-
westernized models of support and care, we will continue to oppress
and further marginalize this group of people.

The issues of self-harm and suicide were discussed by other participants, and it was apparent how potentially serious many of the mental
health issues could be for some students. Laurie, one of the school counsellors, commented on the severity of the mental health issues.

> The suicide attempts that I've seen have not been the kids that are
> from the African countries, they are the kids from the Middle East.
> And very much the kids from Iraq and Syria. I have a lot of experi-
> ence with those students. When I was at a different school, there
> was a lot. I worked with a student there that ended up coming here.
> Her older sister was killed and left under rocks north of the city. I'm
> not sure if you remember that situation ... they were accusing the
> father and the older brother of murdering the girl. The girl had dis-
> honoured the family so she was killed. The younger sister was living
> with this and she made numerous suicide attempts. When she came
> here we had her put into psychiatric care for several weeks.

There were also several references to students whose symptoms
manifested in less overt behaviour. James indicates that he woke up several times a night with memories of murders that he witnessed when he
was ten. James does not live with parents, so the nights were a particularly lonely time.

> I just think people are crazy because we are all the same
> blood, and you go and you kill your own sister and your own
> brother and that is strange. And I saw that thing when I was
> young. I was 10 years old, and it's still coming back in my mind.
> Sometimes it comes in my dreaming. But I have to get up three
> or four times in the night.

Helen comments that her source of help and support is a lady from her church. When I asked her about some of the challenges that students had in school, she replies, "I think those kids should have their own counsellor. The problems they have, just tell them, tell them things to comfort them, to feel this way, don't be scared of this. If you feel this way, you need someone to talk to. A counsellor helps."

Laurie also discussed her position as a counsellor and the ability she has to develop a relationship with students and to learn more about their lives. She explained that a male student came in to see her with his girlfriend, who was pregnant. Before the student could tell her about the pregnancy, it was important to him to talk about his life in Sudan. Laurie explains,

> His dad was shot in front of him. And forever he wakes up. He still
> wakes up thinking he has the blood of his father on him. He still
> wakes up dreaming about that. What that was like, with his father's
> blood splashed all over him. He wakes up still to this day. They don't
> just forget, he could not. I mean, it is a trust issue too; they need
> time to develop a relationship with you. So I am often getting things
> because I am in a very trusting place for them. So before they could
> tell me that she was pregnant, he had to tell me about his past so that
> I could understand what this means to him today. He is genuinely
> afraid that her brothers are going to kill him. Genuinely afraid.

Laurie also discusses the difficulty she has working with some of the teachers who seem to have "blinders on when it comes to this kind of thing." She suggests that these kinds of stories create blinders because of the time it takes to deal with issues and because of the teachers' workload. She indicates that she could excuse it for many reasons, but she believes that there were some teachers that did not understand, or they chose not to try to understand, what some of the students were experiencing—which made her work exceptionally difficult. She used the following example of an experience she had with a teacher the previous week.

> I had a teacher in here who was upset with me, extremely upset with me because I had called out a student who was doing a practice exam because her brother had just tried to hang himself in the school. And the teacher was upset with me because I called the student out, knowing full well why. Because she was just so focused on that exam, and that's all she could see.

Although Laurie's position in the school is a support role to both students and teachers, she notes that it is particularly difficult to share information and to educate the adults about all of the issues related to teaching war-affected children. She states that for some people the issues are just too emotionally difficult to cope with, so it is easier just to "put the blinders on and focus on teaching." Having said this, as was previously noted, there are trained professionals who have the best intentions but for numerous reasons never come to know what a student might be living through each day as they sit in their class or walk beside them in the halls.

Debbie, a government consultant for EAL and a former EAL teacher for more than 20 years, identifies how difficult it is to know just how fragile a student is and, secondly, how important the role of the teacher is to the students.

> I can't tell you how many students have come back to my colleague and I years later and said, "I would have committed suicide if I hadn't known that you two would be really mad at me." And you don't realize it at the time, what you're doing for them. And you don't think that that makes a difference, and sometimes you don't know how fragile a student is any given day. And then they come back and tell you that. I think most kids will identify a certain person, I know I've been in other schools, and they will identify another teacher as being their lifeline.

Considering all of the barriers to acquiring information that were stated in the previous discussion, it is somewhat assuring to know that there are students who managed to find someone in their school or community who was their "lifeline." Whether it was a teacher, a counsellor, a clergy member, or an administrator, someone was indicated from most students' microsystems as a person to whom they could talk to and find some level of support.

Seeking Services

One of the first issues to advance is the legitimate concern for the students' well-being and how difficult it is to provide assistance or support. As with many confidential and personal issues, it is not always obvious who is struggling with psychological issues. Many of these issues cannot be empirically measured, such as a test of English or computational skills. Although westernized checklists are often used to measure mental health issues, many cultural and linguistic factors could potentially skew the results found using these instruments. This is further complicated by the fact that many students do not readily seek assistance for mental health issues. It could be a source of embarrassment for the students, who may have been told to keep personal issues to themselves, or that seeking help may be perceived as a weakness. Also, they might not understand the school-based systems of support. Many of these factors are included in the following excerpt from the focus group. Sara, an EAL teacher, states,

> I think also with the mental health thing, [there are] the cultural norms around secrecy and privacy and what to talk about and what not to talk about. I have had a range, from a mother being open to many things [to] the opposite, where parents are saying there's nothing happening and the kid's sitting right next to me saying, "No, that's not true. I saw this and this and this." So there is a lot of, I guess, there is a lot of stigma attached to mental health issues.

When referring to mental health issues, one of the teachers explains, "You suspect that there are mental health issues, but it's almost as though they are very private about revealing any of their needs."

From a student's perspective, Imran indicates that kids do not have a chance to express what is inside, and he further suggests that there are cultural or personal issues that explain why students may not ask for help.

> And some kids, they have something and they don't have a chance
> to express it out. Some kids, they keep these things inside of them.
> You know what I am saying, in the culture too? In some cultures you
> don't have anything and there is nobody to help you, and sometimes
> you feel like maybe you will be embarrassed to have to ask some-
> body for something. So some people, they keep these things inside.
> They don't ask for help. They need help, but they don't ask. So just
> ask people how they are doing and stuff like that.

The aforementioned examples suggest that it would not be sufficient to assume that just because students do not seek assistance, they are not struggling with issues. Although there could be many reasons for not accessing services, the examples provided in the excerpts are a reminder to consider other factors that might influence how and when students seek help and from whom.

When I discussed the issue of students not seeking assistance with Laurie and Taylor, two of the other counsellors, they suggested a slightly different angle to the psychosocial needs of students. Laurie states, "Well, the first thing that comes to my mind is gender issues for the girls. The girls really struggle fitting in socially, and conflicting with parental and family values or cultural values. That's a big piece of a lot of the work that I do." Taylor notes that although students do not currently discuss issues of trauma with him personally, he explains that "the major challenges are to throw off the trauma that they have just been through, especially if they are older and when they have very little support, very little counselling support, if any."

Sandra, who was identified by the majority of the students as being a person to whom many of them could go to for help, asserts,

> We have just developed a course for teachers to address the EAL
> problem of war-affected families. And they have these reception

centres, and we are one of the schools that house them, but they hire people who have no background in counselling kids through this and what that might mean. And you're the first person that those kids see when they walk through the door. How should you present yourself in that situation? We don't provide training for that; we don't hire for that; we don't think about that. So they are thrown to the wolves. Absolutely. I really think it's common sense. That common sense is not always so common, is it?

Later in the interview Sandra expresses her concern for the fact that many of the students come to her and she does not feel like she can professionally deal with many of their issues.

Christine [a former counsellor] is the same way, and when she left [maternity leave], I took on double the load. All the things that they would've gone to her about, they all come to me. And I'm not a guidance counsellor; I don't know what I'm supposed to say. When I go home I tell my husband that a student asked me the difference between what sex and rape is and he looks appalled and says, "How dare they ask you that question? That's inappropriate." How many other people would say that same thing?

There are two major issues that are advanced by Sandra. First, she suggests that people are not trained to know what to look for in children, and secondly, when students do disclose personal information it is often to people who feel that they do not have the knowledge or the skills needed to respond appropriately.

A similar statement was made by Paul, the vice-principal.

You need a month of administrator boot camp where you go through stuff like counselling and interviewing skills. When it comes to dangerous issues, we haven't really been taught how to deal with these circumstances. I am more and more convinced that you need a boot camp where you are taught the actual survival skills, in order to do the job well.

A recurring theme in many of the interviews, both with people in the microsystem and the exosystem, was the need for more training and knowledge on how to better assist the students. This issue will be more thoroughly discussed in the following section on the preparation of teachers.

Larry, who is the superintendent in the school division and who formerly coordinated EAL services for the school division for numerous years, notes a puzzling absence in students accessing services.

> So they aren't presenting in the school, so there doesn't seem to be a large number of referrals for therapy or whatever the case may be, which is kind of puzzling to me because I would expect that there would be lots, particularly in light of the fact that the initial reception centre for most of the government-sponsored refugees is located within the boundaries of this school division.... So where are these children with this trauma and needs for therapy and all those kinds of things? I still haven't seen it. So it's presenting a very interesting situation.... None of that trauma that we were anticipating has really presented itself.

Larry's statement is certainly puzzling because of what the principal and the vice-principal and several teachers from Walter Duncan School had previously stated. It also contradicts what another consultant indicated during the focus group interview. Ingrid states,

> The biggest challenge that I've seen within the school systems, and I am in every classroom in every school, is the after-effect, the psychological effects. After about two years, once the children are settled in a stable and more consistent environment, what we are really finding, based on teacher feedback and a lot of interviews, is that the parents are really seeing changes in their child's behaviour.... It is really now that it's starting to surface, what they have been through or what they have experienced.

Paul refers to the intensity and frequency of the numbers of students who bring these kinds of issues to the school. He says that he feels like he is doing "triage." He also says that if you talk to triage people, they wear out after a while. Ultimately, he suggests that the school should be doing integrated emotional and spiritual health care for the students. He also indicates that "we feel very much that we are alone" and "we work with what we have."

I began to question why there would be such disparity between the teachers and administrators of the school versus the divisional representatives, who quite clearly worked with the same demographic group of people. I wondered whether this information had not been channelled up to the divisional level. It was evident that the literacy and language needs of the refugee learners were a priority, given that the division had piloted four pre-beginner classrooms, so obviously some information was channelled up to the divisional office. Another statement that Larry made later in the interview hinted that there may be other factors influencing the exchange of information. He states, "Maybe we are not recognizing it, maybe we don't, maybe the counsellors and psychologists or clinicians or whatever, do not have the tools to really identify that and then respond to it." Combining this information with the fact that some of the students do not seek or request services adds another dimension to the situation. Larry also suggests that it could be quite similar to other cases where there have been traumatic experiences and children do not actually disclose the information until years later.

Another key point that was discussed regarding a lack of information was that, in most cases, the information received from students was confidential; as such, we might never really know what students are discussing with a school staff member. Larry also asserts that much of school counselling is reactive and that there really was not a formal means to assess what personal issues the students may be experiencing. What became quite obvious was that consistent information was either not tracked or not passed on to the appropriate people. It was evident that this was a significant policy issue that needed to be addressed.

Mental Health Issues with Parents

In several of the interviews, participants indicated that the mental health status of the parent had a large influence on the child. In some cases, the students were placed in the role of the caregiver to help look after their parent or to look after other children when the parent was not capable. Bev, the EAL teacher, comments that many of the students tell her that their mothers are sick. She notes, "A lot of the students come and say they are taking their mother to the doctor. Mothers seem to have all sorts of difficulties and I think it's the stress and the responsibility and very few of those mothers work." She believes that there is a lot of illness and stress and she notes that this often comes out after a time when the family is a little more settled.

During the interview with Banya, she indicated that her mother was sick. During only one interview that was just over an hour, Banya made reference to her mom 30 times and she talked about how sick her mom was at six different points of time. Banya and her siblings fled from Afghanistan to Pakistan and later immigrated to Canada, leaving two sisters [ages 14 and 16] who lived with their husbands.

Banya mentions on one occasion that her mom cries all the time worrying about her daughters that she had to leave in Pakistan. Another time she states,

> My mom has a problem with blood pressure because of the war. My father died. She lost her brain. So when she heard some noise and problems, we applied for housing and we had to wait for two years.

Prior to the interview with Banya, I had already arranged to interview her mother as one of the parent participants. Banya insisted that her mother wanted to take part in the study. Her mother invited me to her home and she confirmed that she has medical and mental health issues because of her past experiences in Pakistan and Afghanistan. She states,

> My husband died, my children are still there. My house is finished and after I buy everything, it is finished. No heat, no house, everything was wrong with me. My heart and my brain were damaged. And there is no fighting in this country. Sixty-two people in my family died in the fighting and all of them were young. My heart is no good working and my head is no good working. And sometimes,

I am sick in my chest. Everything comes back to my mind. I remember.

Banya made numerous endearing references to her mother during her interview. It seemed reasonable to assume that Banya and her mother were very close. Banya opted to take part in the optional photography activity, and all 10 of the pictures she took were of her mother or of her baby cousin. Banya wants nothing more than to make her mother proud. Toward the end of the interview she says, "My mom's wish is that me and my brothers—we just do our best and we have a good life. And so if my mom's dreams come true, then I am happy too." In reference to her mom she states, "So she is doing her best because she spent her whole life for us. She is trying to give us a better life.... When I get my paycheque, I go, 'Mom, this is yours. Do anything you want.'" Considering how close Banya is with her mother, it could be assumed that her mother's sickness has a great effect on Banya's life. She does not have a father, and she is the oldest child of the three who are living in Canada.

During the interview with Banya's mother, all of the children were present in the living room where we were talking. Ahearn (2000) refers to this as a cultural style based on collectivity that is particularly seen in Afghani families. "Afghans do not see themselves as individuals, but as part of a family. It would be rare for them to invite someone into their home and exclude others in the family from joining in" (p. 52). When Parsa was talking, Banya's tears welled up on two occasions and she states, "It is very hard." Integrating the literature with what occurred during the interview with Parsa clearly substantiated my hunch that the welfare of her mother certainly had an effect on Banya's mental health.

Some of the other participants who had parents also made reference to their sadness, sickness, or their personal stress. Mahad comments about his mother's sickness; Helen discusses how difficult life was for her father, who was a single-parent looking after five children; and Anna discusses the shouting, yelling, and physically abusive behaviour she received from her aunt.

The mental and physical health of the parent or caregiver seemed to have an effect on the student, either socially, mentally, or physically.

Debbie, a government consultant in EAL, also suggests that many of the adults are trying to work through their own problems around learning English, finding where to live and to get settled, as well as their own grief and loss. She states that "many of the parents may not have the emotional energy to really be there for the kids."

To summarize, the psychosocial needs and challenges for war-affected children living in Canada appear to be difficult to identify, complicated to understand, and even more troubling to address. Evidence suggests that there are teachers and other school staff members who do not have the necessary skills to identify a student who is in need of help. Evidence also suggests that there are some people who choose not to acknowledge signs of distress visible in the students, nor do they respond in the most culturally sensitive or appropriate ways to students who have mental health issues.

The debate surrounding the trauma discourse is prevalent but of little support to the student who wakes up in the middle of the night with disturbing thoughts and images. Providing a medical term to this experience is also of little help to the individual experiencing these events. What appears to be helpful is providing these students with a venue and a medium to express themselves, if and when it is needed. In addition, providing a safe place where the student is accepted without having to relive their past experiences may also be of assistance. The limitations of the school staff must be recognized and the capacity of these individuals should be substantially increased so that they more appropriately recognize and respond to the psychosocial issues of the students who are war-affected.

ENVIRONMENTAL CHALLENGES

The three far-reaching categories of challenges—namely, racism and discrimination, psychosocial issues, and educational challenges—illustrate the numerous and often insurmountable barriers and obstacles for many of the students who have come from countries of conflict. Moreover, there are numerous other challenges that were also mentioned that did not necessarily originate in the school system but did complicate other interactions with the ecological systems. Although I have categorized the various challenges, and put them into a format to ease the discussion, I do not suggest that these challenges occur in isolation. As the discussion continues, it should become increasingly more obvious how interrelated the issues are, and how complicated many of the problems can be. The seven most frequently mentioned challenges will be discussed as they were revealed in the data.

Gang-Related Issues

There is a commonly held perception among the students: African students think all the Aboriginal students are in an Aboriginal gang, and the Aboriginal students think all of the African students are in an African gang. While these assumptions are not factual, it does not lessen the fear and resentment and the accompanying violence that occurs as a result of these beliefs.

Although there are some youth in the community who have formed gangs, there was no evidence to support that actual gang members attended Walter Duncan School. The youth who were in the gangs were said to have left the school when their criminal behaviour became more serious. In fact, it appeared that the result of a failed school experience is what led many students to gang activity. Heather, from Youth Justice, states,

> I am hearing this story a lot from our gang members' families. The
> school system is where somehow it all falls apart. At that front end
> is: I'm not blaming the school system; I am just saying that that is
> what the parents perceive is happening is that the school piece is
> falling apart.

There appeared to be three main reasons why the participants believed students became involved in gang activity: (1) easy money, (2) lack of success in school, and (3) no family support. There was no mention of females being involved in gangs; rather, the problem appeared to be only with males.

As was outlined in the previous section, most of the students must work and most of them work full-time and go to school full-time. The draw to gang activity was said to offer students "easy and quick access to money" that would take months to accrue in a traditional work setting. Aran told me that the reason kids join gangs is because "they have nobody. So they end up in gangs because they can see the easy money and everything. It's easy money, but there are a lot of problems." Aran also mentioned that he had a friend who had joined a gang and he commented on what he thinks lured his friend to the gang life.

> Because there's no chance of them getting out. I told him so many times, but they didn't listen. Because they're alone in everything. They just join a gang and they don't have any support for the government helping them. They got culture differences when they come here and they have to work. And the way we see it on TV in Sudan they think being in a gang is a cool thing. They're carrying guns and when we see them in movies; it affects a lot of people there. So when they come here, they think it's that easy. If you're in a gang you get a lot of money and they think they can just tell them they don't want to be in the gang anymore, but it's not that easy. It's not.

Mike explains that some of the kids innocently become involved in entry-level gang activity. Someone might approach them in the Central Park area and ask the youth to take a bag from one place to another and they will give them $20. As he points out, $20 is a lot of money to some of these kids, so they are easily drawn into activity that quickly escalates to being more serious. Manley, a parent, suggests that "they don't go to school anymore because they know they will make money quickly being in a gang."

As was discussed in the previous section, there are numerous challenges for refugee students who are trying to pursue an education. Bill, who is a community liaison worker, reinforced how these challenges might overwhelm the student to such a degree that gang activity looks like an easier way to achieve his or her means.

> Some of them drop out of high school, and they become involved in counterproductive activities. And I think this is because of the

challenges they face in school and sometimes their friends or the people in society. They tell them there are easy ways of getting money that they don't need to go to school, to sit in a classroom. And that brings us back to the original point that when students finish their classes they have to go to work, is like you're going from one difficult time to another time. I can't say that as a reason for sure about why they go to counterproductive activities, but probably it is the difficulties that lead them to these activities.

Whether it was a lack of success in school that led to gang activity or whether the lure of money was what made the student leave school, it was obvious that these two themes were closely aligned. Bill also suggests that people misunderstand the issue and they think that the government has let in these criminal people to Canada. An argument he made was that we need to remember that before these people could come to Canada, they had to have a very clean criminal record and medical checkup. Although he states that he is not blaming Canada, he suggests that it is a community problem that is not just affecting the immigrant population. In his opinion, we should focus on making one or two schools better for all students and then extend this to the whole community.

The third reason that led students toward gang activity was a lack of support. Donna states that she has seen a few cases when you think that students are "shining stars, and they just turn around because of the lack of support that they have." In some cases the families and parents have very little understanding of the youth justice system. Heather mentioned that she needs to help parents understand the concept of court orders and the role of Child Welfare, and her office was in the process of hiring two additional staff members to perform this role.

Laurie, a counsellor from Walter Duncan School, blamed the school system for not providing a young student and his family the support he needed. Her statement also illustrates the severity of the violence that is linked to gang activity.

I worked with a boy from Eritrea, who was killed, who was 14 years old, and he was killed for running drugs. He was shot in the stomach and died on the street. He was my student and he was a really great kid. He was charming, but he had no sense of belonging. We didn't give it to him…. We've failed him. We failed him by not understanding his needs, by not providing support for him and his family.

Whether the impetus for gang involvement is financially motivated, the result of a failed school experience, or because of a lack of support, there was a clearly identified problem in the community that has led to fear, insecurity, and violence. Culturally based groups of students have organized themselves into gangs and now there are youth who think the only chance they have to protect themselves is to be in a gang.

Imran was attacked at school by someone he identified as a gang member. The youth threatened him with a knife following a basketball game. As this boy came in front of Imran, another boy hit him over the head with a glass bottle. When he turned around, he was struck in the face and three of his teeth were knocked out. Imran was taken to the hospital and he subsequently enrolled himself at a different school. Imran indicated that there were associates of this person who still attended Walter Duncan School and he felt that he was no longer safe.

Two other student participants also indicated that they had been "attacked by gang members" with a weapon or bear spray, just for being in the wrong place at the wrong time. The reason they gave me for the attack was because the members of the Aboriginal gang accused them of being in an African gang; they indicated that they had no prior dealings with these youth. Larry indicates that, from his perspective as a superintendent, the youth are involved in a different kind of violence. He noted that it was different from other kinds of violent gang activities and was a "whole different level or intensity of violence that we haven't had experience with."

The participants representing the microsystem also discussed several "gang-related" violent attacks that they heard about through the students. One of the teachers indicates that it is so hard for some of the African boys not to be noticed because they are so "dark and tall" and they really "stick out on the street." She also mentions that these students are often coming home late from work and it is difficult for them to pass certain areas because of the "gang turf" issues.

Numerous members of the microsystem commented about housing issues and how this ties into the gang problem. Because most of the refugees are forced to settle in areas of inexpensive and subsidized housing, they are right in the middle of gang territory. In summary, the level of violence that has been noted by the participants in this study is undeniable. Students have been killed, threatened, and physically hurt because of gang-related violence. Although some people question if it is truly a "gang-related incident" or if it is merely indiscriminate violence from a group of disgruntled youth, from the perspective of the students, it is gang related and they are frightened. One student has left the province and one student has left the school because they were scared they would be killed. It is quite clear that the students are fearful of their safety and it is obvious that they are not receiving a great deal of support. If the ecological systems do not provide the support that is necessary both to keep students in school and to deal with the threat of gang behaviour, there is not likely to be an end to the violence. As Paul notes,

> [I]f you don't provide them with the hope that they need and the access to the kind of opportunities and training and education that allows them to be productive members of society and to live a life of dignity, then that critical mass will turn on you. So, the city has to be aware of that.

Although there is hope that some youth can ultimately leave the gang life, there is more evidence to suggest that it is easier to keep them out of it in the first place.

Economic Challenges

The former discussion links the issue of having financial difficulty to the need to access money in whatever way possible. The federal government provides a subsidy for one year, and after this time, the family or student is expected to cover all of their expenses. A dire need for a longer term commitment from the government was noted by numerous participants. After one year of support, students are expected to work.

The students who were without a family indicated that they needed to prove that they were looking for a job and they had to prove that they were in a full-time regular high school program so that they could continue to receive subsidized housing. Mike insists that the government needs to stop "harassing kids to go and get a job." He argues, "You are condemning these kids to beginning-level jobs for the rest of their lives and also the potential for a life of crime."

The biggest financial challenge for both the unaccompanied youths and the families was paying back the government debt that they owed for their transportation to Canada. About a month after arriving in Canada, all refugees receive a bill in the mail, accompanied by a letter, indicating that they must repay the Government of Canada for their airfare from their country of origin. The cost per person is roughly $2,500. Multiply this number by five children and it will be quite obvious that families will have a substantial debt to pay. Considering the wages that many of the income earners make, this does put many of the refugees at an unfair disadvantage. For youth, paying back this amount of money was inconceivable.

> Right now I have to pay $2,500, and where can I get that? Now I have to pay the government the interest, every month three dollars more. So it's going to be $3,000, $4,000, $5,000, until I find a job that can pay that. So these are the conditions I say that sometimes it's better to go back to Sudan.

Sokut later discusses how difficult it was for him to deal with financial issues, but he remained focused on going to school.

> I have to struggle now to look for a job to help him, my uncle, so that I can pay the rent because he also has a mortgage. In this country, he cannot feed me and pay my rent and my school supplies. I have to look for a job. I have to pay for rent, food, a bus pass. What I have to do is work on food so that I can go to school. I believe God will see all of my problems, and he will see it one day.

The students that I interviewed were not lavishly buying up brand-name sports attire or loading up their iPods with the latest hip-hop selections; they were visiting food banks, rationing supplies, and furnishing their homes with discarded items from the school staff. Vivienne mentioned that none of the students in her class had appropriate winter wear so she had family members knit scarves and hats to give to the students. Karen, one of the counsellors in the focus group, noted that when she visited one of the student's apartments all he had was a mattress and a few dishes. She had the school staff donate enough furniture so that he could have a comfortable living space.

The majority of the students I interviewed sent money home to family members. Len, a counsellor at the refugee counselling centre, indicated that some of his clients rationed food or went without eating so they could support their families. "They might eat one day, but not the next, because they need to send money back." Some of the students commented about the enormous sense of responsibility that they have because people back home depend on them to make money and send it to them so that they can survive. Bango states,

> I look at it like life is kind of harder here compared to back home. You know, because back home, no one will depend on me. No one will look up to me, and at night, no one is expecting anything from me. But now that I am here going to school, I'm going to live on the small things that I am earning from work. I have to pay bills, and then from that I send some back home. Just for giving them to survive. I send money to my mom. I have to work.

There are also some students who were sent by their families to be the supporter and to send home money. This situation is clearly articulated in the following statement by Akot. His responsibility to provide for other family members was evident.

> Sometimes, it's hard. Because I work like five days a week. I have to send money for my family, for my brothers and uncles. But that's okay.

I have responsibilities, because I have to send money to my brothers. There is nothing back home. So ever since I came here, I have to send the money. Every month, I send him $200, $250, $300. Because $200 in my country is like $800. I always call them about twice a month. I want them to come here, but I don't know how to do that. Because back home, it's too tough. It is hard to work. There is not enough food. There are not enough jobs.

Because they're my brothers, I have to help them. And I'm thankful that I'm in Canada. Someday I'll go back to visit them. Because my mom is dead. My dad is dead. So there's no point to go back to Sierra Leone. I'll just go and visit. Because my brothers and sisters are there. If I don't send money, they don't eat. And they don't work back home. I'm like [pause] their hope. Because every time I call them, they tell me I am their hope.

Despite many of these challenges, many of the students and their families have proven to be extremely resourceful. Similar to what Len notes, Marleen states that she has clients who will go without eating so that they can send money back home. Many of the families will ration and go to food banks. Following this comment she adds,

… they are extremely resourceful, but the stakes are higher for them because often I have had clients that tell me that people back home will either live or die based on their sending them this money. The cost there is life or death. And what impresses me is their resourcefulness. I think we tend to forget how resourceful these people are. In some ways we minimize these incredible skills and resources they bring, and let's see what we can do. You know, sometimes just modifying it, so they can be successful.

Helen's statement below illustrates her personal resourcefulness and hope for the future. Although it took a little longer to finish high school, she will graduate this year and she is pursuing post-secondary studies. Helen states that in her country it is horrible if you do not remember the people that you have left behind.

And another thing is when we finished government assistance, I was saying, "Oh my god, how am I going to deal with study-ing and working and going to school?" This was hard for me. In Africa, you don't do that. You go to school. And if you decide not to go to school then you go to work. And now I have to save money for my people in Africa. I have to pay the government, and how I didn't think I could do it, but I said yes, I am going to do it. I am going to put my heart in this and try this experience. I have to try it. And I did [smiling].

As the previous statements reveal, most of the students feel that they have a responsibility to help others in their country of origin. In some cases, the student was sent by the family as the person who would provide for the others. While some of the students have been resource-ful and have been able to fulfill this responsibility, others have been overburdened by the difficulties and challenges that they encounter while trying to stay in school and also to work. Most of the students envisioned that they would live affluent lives after coming to Canada. Many were not prepared for the realities of making a living in a con-sumer-driven society. Sokut indicated that it is hard for some kids to see the others who have the nice clothes and who can afford to eat at restaurants because if they cannot have this, "it makes them want to be a street kid and to sell drugs to get money to have these things."

Criminal Activity

The general theme of criminal activity included drug use, violence, drug trafficking, and theft. For the most part, references to criminal activity were usually provided within the context of discussing the community where most of the refugees live. Mike states,

This integration into the existing violent system ... in the school where drug dealing, prostitution, theft, and violence are prevalent. If you settle a single mother of six in and you give her a three-bedroom house on Blockside Avenue and the kids are going to Billings School, where everything is a problem, it's not necessarily a reflection of the kids. It is them incorporating and adding what they had to the existing problems of the school and the community.... What you see is the mixture of all of the toxic ingredients. Not to stigmatize or to label, but that is the reality. The reality is, a lot of these refugee kids are settled in areas of violence.

Because housing is less expensive, the reception centre settles most of the refugees within the inner city, where the perception is that there is substantial poverty, gang activity, and criminal activity. Mike also stated that there is a lack of short-term affordable housing and the Aboriginal communities are having the same problem as the low-income people because the city has not built any additional social housing for several years.

Again, similar to the gang-related challenges, there was a noted relationship between references to financial challenges, leaving school, and criminal activity. Participants suggested that illegal activities were a lure for the students who were financially at risk. As Paul states,

Pretty soon, you have to start making your own wages and paying your own way. And there is that inducement to try to take a shortcut the illegal way. Maybe it's to get involved in gangs or drugs or the temptation to go on welfare or working under the table and all those things.

Similar to the gang-related challenges, participants indicate that they feel insecure living in the area and they are fearful of the people in the community and where their property is damaged or their personal objects are stolen. The importance of keeping students in school and of drawing them back to school, if they have left, figured prominently in the discussion concerning challenges. Most of the participants indicated that criminal activity was something that might have started while the student was attending school but certainly intensified shortly after the student left the school system.

Heather states that one of her main concerns is that once students leave the school system, there is a two-year window until the students come to her attention in the youth justice system. She comments,

My question to begin with is, unfortunately, we don't see these kids until about two years down the road, so they may leave school at 12 or 13, and they float around and they get into a little bit of trouble. But they don't really come to us until about 14 or 15. So I'm wondering, why don't we really know them until typically they are two years out of the school system? What can we do in those two years to help those kids?

The first three general challenges emerged throughout the interviews as interrelated and connected issues. It appeared that the lack of financial resources served as a draw toward gang-related issues and other criminal activity. Coupled with the influences from the community, in particular the proximity to drugs and violence, participants indicated that these counterproductive activities were the most difficult challenges for refugee students to deal with in Canada.

No Support in Canada and the Need for an Advocate

Students indicated that they felt alone and they were unsure of how to access services in Canada. With the exception of the school, the only source of support that the students mentioned in the interviews was the reception centre. This agency was an initial support when they first arrived in Canada, but none of the students were currently involved with the centre. It was because of this perceived lack of support that students and adults noted that refugees who settle in Canada need to have an advocate. They need someone to help them understand how all of the agencies work, they need direction on who to go to for help and how they could access support if necessary.

Suggestions for support for parents included: legal rights concerning housing; how to purchase and finance a home; how the school system works; the parents' role in assisting their child and engaging with the school; how to discipline children; signs to look for when you think your child is in danger or involved in criminal activity; and how to access medical services.

Suggestions for support for students included: how to dress for the weather; how to access medical services and interpret the information;

how to budget; how to shop; how to prepare nutritional food; how to look after personal hygiene issues and protect yourself against diseases and infections; how to use public transportation and banking facilities; and information on who can help you in the community when you have a problem at school, home, or your workplace.

Participants indicated that they did not have support after coming to Canada. Many stated that they thought the government brought them here and then forgot about them. After discussing all of his problems in Canada and all of his attempts to contact government officials and local leaders who he thought might help him, Sokut concludes, "I feel like they let me down." Vivienne, who works with the newest refugees in the school, states, "Are they lost in the system? Probably." Vivienne suggests that because of this lack of support, many of the students now question whether Canada is really where they want to be. She argues,

> And then they think I would I have been better off living in my own country as a refugee. I do not know what is going to happen to those students who are on welfare now, when it ends. Do they realize it is ending soon? Will they quit school and try to find a job? Because it's going to be a low-paying job. They can't speak English very well. They don't know how to bank, they don't know how to shop, they don't know how to budget.

A relationship between the lack of support for the students and the lack of interaction with the school and the various ecological systems emerged throughout the data. The result was that the school provided most, if not all, of the support to the student. There were two students who also indicated that their church provided support, but for the most part the majority of support that the students received was from or directly arranged by certain members of the school staff. Scott states, "Right now, I feel like we're really on our own. The only thing that makes me feel better about that is that I know that the kids feel like they are on their own. So they appreciate any help that they get from us. But it's not fair to them or to us." Vivienne also outlines the difficulty that students have because the various systems do not interact with one another, which further isolates the students. She explains,

I think the systems work in isolation of each other. I think if there were more interactions among and between the different systems then the student would more readily pick up what needs to be done and how to survive. The student is isolated. They don't know how to make a doctor's appointment, they don't know how to shop. Until we work together, the kids are going to be on the outside looking in and feeling lost.

Because Walter Duncan School is a site of a pilot program for the students who are not literate in any language, additional support is provided by a program such as Vivienne's. The program is for grade 10–12 students and Vivienne states, "But the 7s and 8s, there is nothing for them. They just get put in the regular stream." There are individual schools and some school divisions who have locally developed programs and services to support some of these aforementioned issues, although there is no overarching program or mechanism of support for refugee students.

The need for students, particularly those who are unaccompanied minors, to have an advocate or a mentor was also prominent. Christine states,

I think that's really important and not every student is going to have the luxury of having somebody who is like their Canadian mom or Canadian dad. You need to have somebody who can help them manoeuvre in these various systems and right now they don't know where to go, and they're locked in a system that doesn't work for them. You need somebody who is an advocate for them, you need somebody who's going to help them with all of these things that are done outside of school so that they can be totally integrated.

It seemed like the school staff was extending well beyond their roles as advocates and it appeared that the school as an ecological system was stretched beyond its means. Using the bioecological model, it was the mesosystem, or the interactions between those people in the microsystem, that was defunct, which further exacerbated many of the challenges for the students. Moreover, it seemed that the direction for change needed to be set at a divisional or provincial level. Although people in the school outlined the importance of needing an advocate for these students, they also suggested that it should be a defined role and responsibility given to a staff member as opposed to an adjunct responsibility imposed on specific teachers.

Adjustment to, and Navigation through, the Systems

The overall adjustment to a new way of life was stated as a challenge for all refugees. This meant adjusting to the climate, a way of life, cultures, traditions, food, and language. For many refugees, it also meant adjusting to a new family structure. Bill also suggested that because of these adjustment issues, many families break down. He has seen many families separate because of high levels of stress, which often lead to disputes and conflict between family members.

Learning how all of the social systems work—the tax system, Child Welfare, work environments, and education—requires effort for the refugees, who must make adjustments to carry on with their daily lives. Along with these adjustments, the refugees must learn how to navigate through all of the systems. Many of the adults in the microsystem and the exosystem indicated that refugees are bombarded with so much information when they first arrive that it is virtually impossible to keep everything straight and to remember everything. Most of this information is also delivered in the first couple of months after arriving in Canada, when families are still trying to tend to their basic needs.

Sokut indicates that after he was attacked he went to numerous people he thought could help him find a new place to live, with very limited success. Sokut explains,

> We try hard to talk to the government and Manitoba Housing, and they said no. They will not help young people. When I talked to them on the phone they said, Come to our office to talk to them and then when they see we are youth, they say they can't help us.... But because everything has a system, you have to just do it the way they say.

Paul mentioned that many of the Lost Boys have had to use political means to get what they want or need. He notes,

I'm sure you've heard of the Lost Boys. I have friends who work at
Income Assistance, and based on what I know from the wider community as well, the other nickname for them as well is that they
are called the "Golden Boys." They were brought here by someone
higher up, by a group of people who sponsored them and sometimes, no ... a lot of times, if they don't get what they want, they use
political ways to get what they want. And I think that's part of the
survival process, just what they had to do in order to survive. So
in terms of educators, I think we need to be wise of our students
because if you continue to buy into it, you can become enablers, in
terms of giving them what they want and basically allowing them to
set the tone and the agenda. When in fact, they are young men and
young women, and they are just learning about life, and they are
exploring and pushing the boundaries.

Learning to adjust to a new system and figuring out how to get what
you need from the system appeared to be an immensely difficult task for
not only the students but also those people who were trying to assist the
students. The use of political means to get what was needed became an
additional strategy that the students used to satisfy their needs. What also
became obvious was that they were frequently used by political actors.
The students were asked to come to "tell their story" at conferences and to
be interviewed for news stories and there was very little or no remunera-
tion or follow up debriefing for them afterward. In a six-month period,
Sokut spoke at five different conferences or meetings across Canada, and
he was interviewed for two different news stories and he spoke once on
national radio. Although the youth tried to use political means to navigate
their way through the system, they were also used politically in return.

Housing

As was mentioned earlier, the location that most of the families settle in
is typically an impoverished area, in what people refer to as the inner
city. Although the location of housing was a major challenge, so were
the accommodations and the living conditions. There are also issues
surrounding the transient nature of being in subsidized housing and
how difficult it is to maintain continuity in the students' education
when they do move. Afem remembers his first house:

It was not good. It was too horrible, it was too dirty. And it was too far from school, and they said we need a place that's near to school so that we have time to come. And so we went to another one on Brookside. And we went to look at it and we liked it and we moved into there. We stayed there since we came to Canada, until we just started moving.

Parsa and her family relocated to a second home in a housing complex. She discusses the problems she had in her first apartment and the effort she made to try to get a different home:

My neighbour was from Somalia, and I didn't really talk with her. The people every day they go to work and when the evening time comes, they just make food to eat and sleep. The dishes were very dirty and there was stuff, stuff, stuff. They no clean. There were cockroaches.

The neighbour moved, to another place. And every day now that cockroaches came to my house. So many things I used to finish cockroaches and nothing worked. There was more and more and more it made me very sick. My children were sick. And after we had food, in one minute there was a cockroach. In my oil, my sugar, my flour, in everything. That was my bad life. We had to buy all new furniture when we came here because everywhere there was a cockroach.

I had to go to Manitoba Housing and I said, "Please, help me. My children and I are sick." And it was right next door to a firehall and every night toot-toot-toot-toot. Because of the fire and all the noise I have high blood pressure. For my heart like this, now it is good. Thank God. I applied for a house when I first came to Canada in 2003. It took three years to get a house. They told us when our number came, they would call us, but because of the cockroach problem and the alarms, they said okay.

Parsa and her family were delighted with their new home, and she indicated that her health had improved. The lack of cleanliness of the subsidized housing was mentioned in numerous interviews. Several students commented that they were disgusted when they initially saw their home placement.

Christine, the counsellor at Walter Duncan School, said that she was reluctant to refer students or their families back to the reception centre because she knows that they are overwhelmed and that no one would be able to assist them. She notes,

> And I have had to go out to find housing for these kids, or I have taken them to the food bank to find food. Or I sit down and help them move from one place to another or to get furniture for their apartments, or I have spoken to a landlord. And I'm unsure if these things are part of my job or not. I just do them because I know these kids need it, and otherwise they are not going to be at school the next day and they not will be able to concentrate or focus on what they're doing.

For the most part, housing challenges related to the location and to the living conditions of the home. Personal safety was compromised on numerous occasions, and most of the students stated that they did not feel safe where they lived. Other complications arose when students were unaccompanied minors and they were not able to advocate for themselves when their home placement was unsuitable.

SUMMARY AND CONCLUSION

Refugee children must cope with numerous challenges and obstacles when they come to Canada. For many, this adjustment is, at times, an overwhelming experience coupled with regret and uncertainty. At other times the challenges are mediated by a powerful source of personal agency and with a drive propelled by hope. The challenges are multidimensional, occurring at all levels of the ecological systems.

Within each ecological system there are layers of bureaucracy, proce-
dures, norms, and rules that are imposed by Canadian society, and
refugees must adjust so that they are able to function as members of this
society. Common themes and trends have been expressed by various
people in the school and community. These themes assisted in cluster-
ing and organizing the challenges (see Figure 4.1 on the following page)
to discuss each category and to reveal how all of these challenges collectively affect the individual. Without suggesting that one cluster is
more important than another, simply because it was discussed more
frequently, I have chosen to summarize the clusters of challenges into
four main conceptual categories.

In reviewing the challenges presented in this chapter, the following
four clusters of challenges were delineated: (1) educational challenges,
(2) economic challenges, (3) environmental challenges, and (4) psychosocial challenges. These four categories encapsulated the four categories
presented in the discussion with some slight modification. Because the
issue of racism and discrimination was largely a problem in all facets
of the ecological systems, it would be clustered accordingly in the environmental challenges category; however, it was presented independently
for the purposes of organizing the discussion. Economic challenges
include issues related to having to work while simultaneously attending
school and issues related to poverty. Each individual challenge need not
fit neatly into one category; rather, it is more important to understand
conceptually what the main challenges are for the students so as to more
closely examine how to address these issues as an interconnected set of
ecological systems.

Combining the information from Chapters 3 and 4, I have developed a model to represent the major adjustment challenges for refugee
children who come to Canada. In Figure 4.1, the centre of the model represents the individual. Human capacity, hope, and resilience represent the
core characteristics of the individual that mediate the effects of the various challenges. As will be revealed in the following chapters, individuals
possess certain protective factors that emerge as a means of coping with
and working through the various challenges. The dashed line surrounding the centre circle was chosen to suggest that the process of building
human capacity is not static; rather, it is a continual and progressive

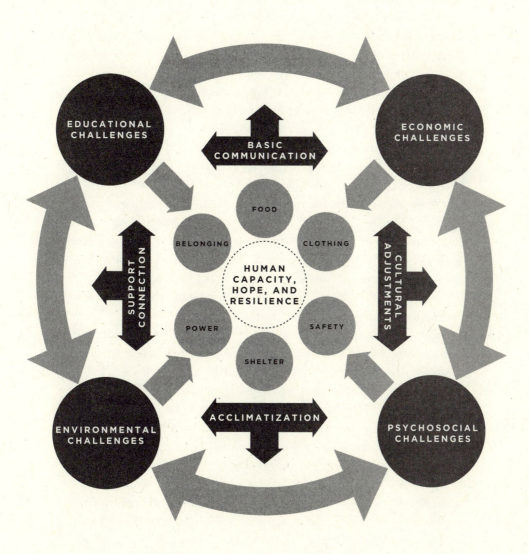

FIGURE 4.1 *Adjustment Challenges for Refugee Children*

developmental process. Six basic and essential needs have emerged from the data. Because the study included three phases of migration—namely, pre-migration, trans-migration, and post-migration—it was evident that first and foremost, the individuals' challenge was to struggle to satisfy their basic needs. This struggle was particularly evident upon arrival into Canada, although it was also a focus in post-migration, where students were continuing to look after their basic needs.

I have also delineated four intermediary categories that represent challenges that occur as a precursor to the four general topics. The four intermediary challenges are: (1) basic communication, (2) cultural adjustments, (3) acclimatization, and (4) support connection. These four will be briefly explained below.

There appeared to be two distinct phases of English-language learning. The first challenge was to learn basic conversational skills to navigate through the various systems and to attend to basic needs such as buying food, getting around the city, and talking to English-speaking teachers or students. The next phase was academic literacy, which relates to the level of oral and written English and comprehension skills to complete academic courses.

Cultural adjustments would refer to changes that the individual makes when coming into contact with another culture. Individuals will maintain varying levels of their former culture. The process is not static, and the process of acculturation varies depending on the development of the individual. Some students may elect to reject some of their traditional culture, only to later adopt these cultures back into their life. The individual may continue to wear traditional clothing or practise cultural rituals or may decline to wear typical Canadian dress representing a "kind of student" in a school. Scott informed me that some of the students elected to choose the "gangster look" while others chose the "jock look" or the "prep look." Some students will keep more of their former culture and some will choose to reject their former culture completely.

Acclimatization refers to the environmental challenges that the students must overcome. This is particularly prominent when children arrive from African climates to the Canadian climate in the middle of winter. The environmental shock is a physical challenge for the students, especially when they are ill equipped with clothing and strategies for keeping warm. Vivienne explained that she had to set up a clothing drive to get warm clothes, and she needed to instruct her students on how to function in a cold climate. For example, she had to explain that students must know when the bus will come so that they would not be standing out on the street in -45°C weather.

The final intermediary challenge was for the family or individual to find someone who would provide the essential link to the ecological systems. This support person might be a reception centre counsellor, a friend from the community, or a teacher who would help the newcomer find his or her way around the city and through the various systems. This personal support person was instrumental in assisting the individual or the family members upon first entering Manitoba.

The four main categories of challenges (educational challenges, economic challenges, environmental challenges, and psychosocial challenges) form the cornerstone of the model. Clearly, the students are not passive victims; they are active agents who negotiate, compromise, and forge ahead despite adversity. Although it was recognized that not all students will encounter the same level of success and all of them will face challenges in a different way, in most cases, the outlook was positive. A great deal of time is spent developing new and creative programs and services to help certain groups of students to be more successful. It might be more beneficial to look at what we are doing as a society and remove the barriers and challenges we impose on the students so that they have a chance at success. Combating racism, providing financial support to students so that we keep them in school, or developing culturally and linguistically sensitive programs might be a better use of intellectual energy and a good place to begin. From a societal point of view, the importance of schooling is paramount. The most compelling fact is that school is where these students most want to be. What remains frustrating is that there is a multitude of challenges that continue to complicate the chances of students being successful. That said, numerous suggestions and possibilities were discussed throughout many of the interviews that indicated viable solutions to many of the problems.

It is of utmost importance to understand and to be realistic about exactly what refugees need to make their transition to Canada successful. Evidence does support the fact that not all students are successful, and many have forfeited their hopes and dreams for a life of crime (Portes & Rumbaut, 2001; Rumbaut & Portes, 2001). That said, it is imperative that as a society we collectively, regardless of race, culture, religion, age, or gender, address these issues and strengthen all levels of the ecological systems if we hope to address the challenges facing this generation of refugee children.

The following chapter will examine the systems, structures, people, and programs that assist with the process of adjustment for refugee students.

CHAPTER FIVE

Systems, Structures, and Programs that Assist with Adjustment

THE FOLLOWING CHAPTER WILL DISCUSS the systems, structures, or programs that assist with the process of adjustment for war-affected children who now attend school in Canada. More specifically, (1) Who are the people who support the children from war-affected countries and what do they do to help? (2) What factors help students adjust to Canadian schools? I will examine the roles that were assumed by the people who support the children and what they did to assist the students. I will also discuss some of the suggestions that participants indicated would better help students adjust to life in Canada.

I will draw on the work from the previous chapters and use Figure 4.1 (see p. 127) as a foundation for organizing this discussion. The four main categories of challenges that were delineated in Chapter 4 will be used to provide examples of the systems, structures, and programs that could better assist children. To begin, I will discuss the issues related to the people who are currently assisting children in schools. Following this, I will outline some of the proposed ideas for addressing the challenges. I will then discuss some of the more recent initiatives implemented within the province to address the learning needs of refugee students.

ROLE OF THE SCHOOL SYSTEM IN THE LIVES OF STUDENTS

Based on what I observed from a systemic perspective, school was the most prominent ecological system in terms of providing support to the students. School was the point of contact with various other ecological systems, and apart from the family unit, the people within the school system had the most interaction with students. Within Walter Duncan School, the students and other staff members identified particular individuals who were the most influential in terms of providing support and helping children adjust to the school environment. Three key functions were typically performed by these influential members of the system. First, these people got to know the students personally and they formed a meaningful relationship with the students. Second, they helped the student connect with other ecological systems and support mechanisms, and last, they advocated on behalf of the student to ensure he or she was treated fairly both within the school and in the community. The three attributes will be discussed in more detail in the following section.

For the most part, these teachers had taken the time to get to know the students on a personal level and they understood their individual circumstances. The various students often identified the same teachers as being supportive. The students indicated that they liked to "hang" in the teacher's room at lunch or when they had a spare and the teacher did not have a class. Rassan is a practising Muslim, so he set up a space for Muslim students to come in to pray during the school day. Although the teachers had an informal relationship with the students, this relationship was still clearly defined as being "teacher and student" as opposed to "friend to friend." There were limits set to the relationships and both sides respected each other's role.

In 11 separate interviews, participants referred to acting as if they were being a parent to the students. The participants indicated that they helped the students access basic needs such as food, clothing, and housing. They helped them feel like they belonged in a system where they could feel safe. More importantly, they respected the students and treated them fairly. These teachers advocated for the students when they saw instances of inequality and injustice, and they went so far as to put their own selves at risk, physically or professionally, to protect a student. I witnessed and experienced events and interactions at Walter Duncan School that were evidence of the personal willingness and the professional commitment of staff members who were dedicated to improving the outcomes for all students, particularly those who they believed were marginalized. Although I have brought forth several concerns raised by staff members with regard to issues that contradict the values of these supportive teachers, it is imperative to realize that these are recognized as deficits, but that the focus of attention should be on mediating the challenges for students and creating a system that is more supportive.

These supportive teachers mentioned above also functioned as a link to the other ecological systems. They read and interpreted personal health care reports for the students or their parents, they called refugee counselling centres to access psychosocial assistance, they helped students apply for citizenship, they helped find housing or furnishings, and they contacted employers in the community to advocate on behalf of their students.

Teachers advocated for students both inside the school and in the community. Teachers called landlords to get students into new housing placements, they went to the students' workplaces to persuade the employers to schedule more appropriate shifts, or they spoke up about the unfair treatment by other staff members toward students. In a few cases, teachers put themselves in physical danger to stop students from fighting or to keep a dangerous student with a weapon away from other students.

These lists are by no means exhaustive. The roles that these various teachers assumed were extensive and far beyond merely "teaching students." Most of them said that they felt an obligation to help the students, because, they said, "If I don't do it, who will?" I asked Rassan, "In a perfect world, what could we do to better support the children who have been affected by war?" His response was, "In an ideal world, there would be harmony between myself and my students. There would be understanding between myself and my students about where they have come from. Education and academics is a secondary thing for them." In essence, these teachers purposely and intentionally endeavoured to get to know their students at a more intimate and personal level. In addition, they assumed roles and responsibilities beyond what was expected of a teacher.

Nanosystem

Within the microsystem there appeared to exist numerous other smaller and more intimate systems that provided support. For example, the African boys came to Sandra's room at lunch just to hang around and to get help with work, or to meet each other and decide what they would do that evening. Rassan set up a quiet and safe place to pray that the Muslim students could use at lunch or after school. He also helped these students with their science work and he coached many of the same students on his soccer team. Vivienne was in her classroom every morning by 7:00 AM to prepare for the day and to meet her students with a cup of hot chocolate. She brought her retired teacher friends in to her class to volunteer and help some of the weaker students. Her pre-beginner class formed another small hub of support within the microsystem. Bill, who was the Sudanese community liaison worker, organized an after-school program with a local university to run a tutoring, mentoring, and recreational program for other students. It seemed that different students gravitated to different people and different clusters of systems or networks within the school system were formed. I began to see that it was these small clusters of smaller and more intimate systems that provided the most support to the students.

I have elected to call these smaller systems "nanosystems," as they represent something smaller within the "microsystem" that provides this immediate circle of support to the student. This circle of support originated, or was created, by one of the people who connected with the students on a personal level. My assumption is that the circle of support naturally developed as trust was established and support was provided to the students. Extending Bronfenbrenner's model to include intimate "nanosystems" of support within the microsystem more clearly depicts what I witnessed in this closer examination of the ecological systems.

Some students did indicate that systems outside of the school were also a source of support and assistance. For example, Levia stated that her church was one of the most influential systems in her life. Fatya, who was her sponsor, is the person Levia goes to when she is sad or upset. Helen states, "I go to this lady, Tina, whenever I feel uncomfortable." Tina was also her sponsor from her church. The church is part of the microsystem for each of these women, but it is the active role of one person who is a part of this system that provides the immediate support to these two individuals.

DEFINING THE NANOSYSTEM

Reverting to the earlier definition of the microsystem provided in Chapter 1, we accept that a microsystem is the closest, most inner circle of relationships that the individual has with people, objects, or symbols in his or her immediate environment. It is the immediate environment in which the individual lives. How the nanosystem differs from the microsystem is the nature of the connection between the people. While the microsystem was observed to be more contextual, the nanosystem was more relational. Although the microsystem involves close relationships, the extent of this closeness is what differentiates the nanosystem from the microsystem. Everyone could be considered to exist within a microsystem, but only some connect to a nanosystem. A nanosystem may consist of the student and one other person or it may be comprised of several individuals.

The nanosystem is a close, interpersonal relationship or network that is integral to connecting the individual to the microsystem. The nanosystem is constructed by a significant person from the student's inner-most microsystem. It could be a parent, a teacher, a coach, or a best friend. The nanosystem is a network, a connection, and a close relationship. It may exist for only a short period of time in the person's development or it may be a lifelong connection.

Consider, for example, the student who is disengaged from school. There are teachers who interact with this student on a daily basis. He or she might work after school and then come home to a mother and four siblings. The people who interact with the student—his mother, siblings, co-workers, employer, teachers, and peers—would all be people with whom, to some degree, the student has formed a relationship. However, the student really does not have anyone that he or she could talk to if something has gone wrong at home or school. The mother might be busy with the other children, or she could possibly be having her own difficulties with adjusting to a new culture. Although the student knows of people, he or she really does not trust them or does not know them well enough to approach for help.

Conversely, there is another student who has the same demographic background, but every day at lunch this student meets with Rassan and two other students who share a similar passion for chemistry. Rassan is teaching these three students advanced chemistry work, and all three students hope to enter a science competition.

The latter student is part of a nanosystem, and the first student is not. The first student interacts and has relationships with people in the microsystem, but the nature of these relationships is not powerful enough to solidly connect the student with people in his or her microsystem. When adversity or problems arise for the student who is part of a nanosystem, the student is able to use the strength of this system and the skills of the people in the nanosystem to cope with or confront the problem.

Figure 5.1 reflects more clearly what I have observed in the microsystem: smaller, more intimate "nanosystems" existed and provided the support to the students. Integral to this concept is the importance of just one person who chooses to initiate and facilitate the growth of this nanosystem within the microsystem.

Referring to Figure 5.1, I have provided three different examples of what might constitute a nanosystem. While the students in this study only referred to one intimate nanosystem, it is possible to be a part of more than one. For each of the examples I have illustrated, I considered students from this study and I attempted to depict what their nanosystem might look like.

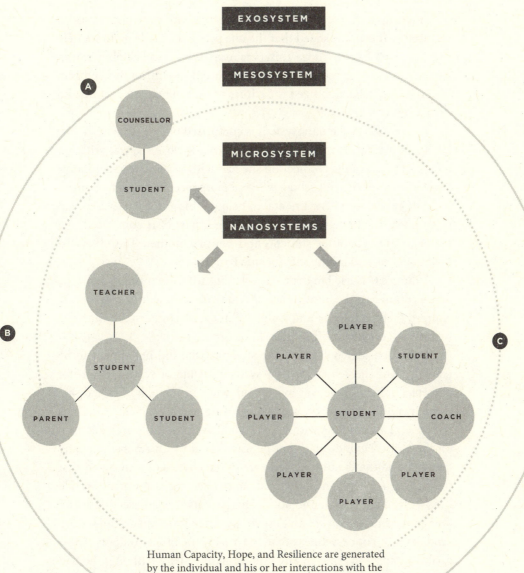

FIGURE 5.1 *The Microsystem, Mesosystem, and Nanosystems*

In example A, the student has connected with only one person, a counsellor. Imran indicated that the one person he could go to for help was his school counsellor. This person assisted with helping Imran relocate to another school, she has advocated for Imran to keep him in classes, and she mobilized the efforts of staff to help him set up and furnish his apartment.

In example B, the nanosystem is comprised of two students, a parent and a teacher. I considered Banya and how close she was with her mother, as well as the connection she had with her EAL teacher. Banya also has a close friend at school who is a more recent refugee to Canada, and Banya has been instrumental in helping this girl learn to read. For this reason, the nanosystem that Banya is a part of is comprised of a teacher, Banya, another student, and Banya's mother. The other student's nanosystem might only include Banya.

Example C is used to depict a larger but still very intimate nanosystem. I considered the importance of Aran's involvement in sports and I realized that his interest and skill level in sports connected him to the school and to people within the school.

I also considered some of the students who did not appear to be connected to the school or to a system outside of school. Akot, for example, stated that he was lonely and, when prompted, he stated that there was nobody that he could go to if he had a problem. Akot has had several altercations with people who have physically attacked him on the street. He indicated that he was shot at by an Aboriginal gang member and that he did not feel safe in the city. Akot also stated that the police, teachers, and other kids have been racist toward him. He lives with an older sister and both of his parents are deceased. Based on the limited time that Akot and I spent together, I was not able to see the same level of connectedness that I saw with the other students. I was unable to position Akot in any kind of nanosystem. Although he had relationships with people in the school and at work, these relationships appeared to be more contextual and superficial. When I asked Akot if there was anyone at the school who has helped him, his response was, "No." Akot also states that he has a hard time in school and that life is hard, he does not do anything for fun, sometimes the teachers are mean, and he often feels bad, especially when he thinks about home.

Based on the information provided by Akot, my opinion is that Akot is in dire need of connecting with one of the adults in the school. He has clearly delineated numerous challenges, and based on what I learned from the other students, these challenges can be mitigated by the power of a nanosystem. Out of the thirteen students, nine are considered to be part of a nanosystem (see Table 5.1).

TABLE 5.1 *Evidence of a Nanosystem*

STUDENT	EVIDENCE OF A NANOSYSTEM
Afem	Close peer group from Sudan and a teacher
Akot	Did not appear to be a part of a nanosystem
Anna	Did not appear to be a part of a nanosystem
Aran	Involvement in sports
Bango	Did not appear to be part of a nanosystem
Banya	Mother, a close friend, and the EAL teacher
Helen	A lady from church and friends from church
Imran	Close peer group from Sudan and a teacher
James	One close friend
Levia	Youth group at church
Mahad	Involvement in sports
Sokut	Was part of a close peer group before he moved
Ugot	Did not appear to be a part of a nanosystem

The students who were not part of a nanosystem reported that they did not have friends and all of them made reference to feeling alone. Ugot states, "I stay to myself, I go to school, I go back home, and I watch television. I can go shopping, and that is what I do.... The programs at school are too big for me, I feel lost." Anna made several references throughout the interview to feeling "alone" and "scared." Bango left school last year because he was having difficulty with his courses. This year, he has taken less courses and he indicated that he has not passed two of the courses. He states, "I really only have time to do my schoolwork, I don't really have time to talk to anyone. I don't like that much friends.... I don't like holding [having] friends. I don't like hanging out, that is just the way I am."

My hypothesis is that the nanosystem helps students adjust to school. It appeared that the nanosystem provided the student with a connection to the people in the school and these people helped to link the student to the other systems. Bronfenbrenner's notion of proximal processes suggests that human development takes place in progressively more complex interactions with the human being and his or her environment. Essentially, the nanosystem is the resulting network that is created by these complex interactions. That said, Bronfenbrenner's theory examines the broad context of human development in ever-changing, multilevel environments throughout time (Bronfenbrenner & Morris, 1999). This discussion was limited to the specific and dynamic interactions at a given point in time with individuals who had unique prior experiences. The pre-migration and trans-migration experiences of war-affected children and their numerous challenges post-migration might necessitate the development of a nanosystem more so than children who have encountered less turmoil and more stability in their ecological systems.

In a 1967 paper, Bronfenbrenner discussed the importance of engaging children and adults in common activities. This notion was later to be formally referred to as "proximal processes" (Bronfenbrenner, 2005). Bronfenbrenner (1977) referred to a 1966 study conducted by James Coleman, who studied the attitudes, behaviours, and school achievement of more than 600,000 children in grades 1 through 12 in 4,000 schools in the United States. Bronfenbrenner (1977) states,

> the expected finding was that home background was the most important element in determining how well the child did at school, more important than any aspect of the school that the child attended. This generalization, while especially true for northern whites, applied to a lesser degree to southern whites and northern African Americans, for whom the characteristics of the school were more important than those of the home. The child apparently drew sustenance from wherever it was most available. (p. 203)

Furthermore, in this same paper, Bronfenbrenner referred to a 1959 study conducted by John Kinch on the impact of the peer group on the child's attitude and behaviour. Bronfenbrenner noted that the study conducted by Kinch revealed that there was a turning point in grade 7. "Before that, the majority looked mainly to their parents as models, companions, and guides to behaviour; thereafter, the children's peers had equal or greater influence" (p. 203). These findings support the notion of the nanosystem and confirm the importance of other individuals, outside of the family, who also influence the development of the individual.

PROGRAMS AND STRUCTURES

Moving beyond the integral role of the people in the microsystem who create the nanosystem of immediate interpersonal support to the students, there were specific programs and structures that were discussed that assist, or could assist, with the adjustment of refugee children to the school system or the adjustment of the school system to better suit the needs of the refugee student.

Webb and Davies (2003) indicate that if we are unable to provide culturally sensitive assistance to refugee families, we are essentially replacing one form of adversity with another. Papageorgiou, Frangou-Garunovic, Iordanidou, Yule, Smith, and Vostanis (2000) state, "The cultural, religious, language and climate similarities or barriers with the receiving country or community are important factors to consider" (p. 88). Adjusting to the social system of a new country is very difficult, especially when children do not have the emotional support from home. Moreover, it must also be acknowledged that many refugees come to a host country as unaccompanied minors who may need specialized emotional support and information on legal assistance because they are children alone in a foreign country (Sadoway, 2001).

A coordinated program for transitioning students into Canadian schools would likely ameliorate many of the difficulties that refugee children experience. The first few months that refugees settle in a new country are considered to be critical to the post-migration experience. Putting a transition program in place could serve to centralize many of the services and link refugees to community programs.

Advice from the Students

I asked each student the same question, "If you could tell the principal or the teachers one thing that we need to do to better help the students who have come from war-affected countries, what would you say?" The following is a list of the seven major themes that emerged in the responses to this question.

DON'T LET STUDENTS BE RUDE

One of the most surprising and unexpected replies from two of the students was that they would tell the teachers to stop letting the Canadian kids talk to them so rudely. Anna commented, "Sometimes I say, 'Wow,' what makes the children so rude here?'" Mahad informed me that this was his first experience when he "got into a class and I saw kids swearing at the teachers." Mahad suggested that teachers might need to instill some fear into the students to let them know they are the bosses. Using Anna's word, she says "Don't put up with that." Anna and Mahad both came from schools in Africa where the teachers would hit the students if they misbehaved in class. They also indicated that if their parents found out, "they would get mad at you and smack you too." Mahad indicated that if you are too nice, the students will take advantage of it. Instead, he suggested that teachers should be "a strict person and a nice person at the same time."

BE LIKE A FAMILY

Aran indicated that many people that come to Canada do not have a family that provides support. His advice is to help these people join the community. "Like, be a family, be his family, because he has none, and then he will think the gang is his family." James's advice to the principal is to "take care of those kids and help them learn." He indicated that for kids like him, who do not have a mother or a father, it is hard for them to know what the right behaviour is for school. He states,

> They need to have the principal tell them what is the right thing to do and what you are not supposed to do. Some kids do not know what is the right thing to do. That is, most of the refugee

children. When they get here, everything looks different. So when they move here, and they just come to school, they don't know.... Talk to the kids not to do it again, but for the kids who don't have parents, you need to take care of those kids.

IMPROVE COMMUNICATION

Bango's advice is to help those people who have a different background. He notes, "So when you have a meeting or something, they have people who translate for you. Kids that don't understand what you're saying need help and I think that it is an important thing ... so communication." He elaborates further that if we improve communication, there would be less chance of misunderstanding each other and the students would be less likely to think that the teacher was saying something racist.

Banya also indicated that people must learn the language "as fast as they can for their education and for their life." She said the language is what they need to learn how to live in the community with people and to share things with them. She concluded by saying, "Just do as much as you can for the kids to help the new people, not for me, but for other people, because they need help for their families."

SUPPORT WITH SCHOOLWORK

Afem suggests that teachers give students more support to do their schoolwork. He indicates that students are not the same and that some kids need more time to complete work. He advised,

That's a good question, you know, because when you are new to the school, you need to be treated good. You don't know anybody, you're new to the school. You are like a blind person.... What makes it worse is when you give them too much work and they don't understand anything. You aren't going to have anybody when you get home and you are going to be think-ing how to do this assignment. Because in Africa, in the camp, we could ask an older student and they would help you and explain everything so that you understand. But here, we don't

know anybody and you give a lot of work and then more tomorrow. You know, teachers think that we are all the same level,
but we're not. We are different. We need to keep going to high
school.

LISTEN, RESPECT, AND SHOW THAT YOU CARE

Helen indicated that she would encourage teachers to talk to students
and to respect everybody and to listen to everyone's ideas. She indicated
that some people may not know how to express or say what they think
and they might be intimidated to say something because they will be
embarrassed in class. Her advice was to help students feel comfortable
speaking in class. After she spoke to me the following conversation took
place between us:

Do you get my accent when I am talking?

Yes.
Really?

Yes, I totally understand what you are saying.
Because when I talk, they say, "Come again, repeat it." And
I can't because what if I say the wrong stuff. And he comes
close to me and he says, "I don't get what you say at all." And
so I just say, "forget it."

Although it is difficult to explain the tone of Helen's statement, when
she was speaking for the teacher, she was appearing to be frustrated to
show that the teacher would be losing patience by not understanding
what she was saying. Overall, I sensed that she felt intimidated about
speaking in class, and although she had something to say, because
of her accent she hesitated because she worried about the teacher not
understanding her and embarrassing her in class.

Imran's advice was for teachers to show that they support students
because sometimes they do not have anyone else that supports them. He
indicated that some kids keep everything inside them and they do not
have a chance to express themselves because they do not have anyone to

help them. Imran stated that some people won't ask for help, so his advice to teachers is to go and talk to kids and find out how they are doing.

Levia's advice was, "I would tell them to make it easy, to be nice to the students. For the teacher to be nice to the students and the students to be nice to the teachers. There are some teachers that get on the students' nerves." Levia indicated that it is also helpful to be nice like Mrs. B (Bev), who gives her cans of milk, tins of food for her family, and bus tickets.

IMPROVE OPPORTUNITIES FOR SPORTS

Mahad is an accomplished athlete, and his link to school is his love for sports. Mahad suggests that the school give students the opportunities to get loans and bursaries to play more sports with the school. Mahad has a friend who is over 18, so he is not allowed to play on a school team. Mahad suggests, "I think we should open that up and it would be an excuse to keep people in school." Mahad, Aran, Imran, Sokut, and Akot all indicated that playing sports was personally important.

DON'T GIVE UP

Sokut explains that, if students do not have the desire to come to school, it is their choice and the result is that they will not improve themselves. He further notes that these students need to be told about the benefits of school and that they need to learn that they must improve themselves. He explains that there are some people who have problems and they need teachers to keep trying to teach them, despite their problems. He concludes by stating, "Sometimes teachers are not the same, like, not even in Canada. There are nice teachers and there are bad teachers. But sometimes, there are big problems with kids too. I would tell them not to give up and we need you."

The seven simple, yet powerful suggestions from the students provide useful advice for any new or experienced teacher, whether or not he or she teaches refugee children. For the most part, the seven segments of advice provide further evidence to support how essential the role of the teacher is to the students. Most of the advice is centred on how to be a more supportive and understanding person who accepts the fact that students are diverse people who need to feel like they belong to a system.

Essentially, this is what appeared to be what most of the students in this study wanted. Naturally, students would not typically discuss new and innovative curricula that would better help students, nor would they usually discuss multi-agency networking ideas to encourage partnerships across the systems. These suggestions would more likely come from adults who work in the various systems. Having said this, I did not find it surprising that the responses from the students were more personally based and the responses from the adults more systems-based.

SUGGESTIONS FROM THE ADULTS

Although I stated a similar question with different words to the adult participants, I essentially asked the adults the same question that I asked the students. I asked the members of the microsystem and exosystem the following: "In a perfect world, what could we do to better assist students who have come from war-affected countries?" The responses have been categorized according to the four categories of challenges that were delineated in the preceding chapter: educational challenges, economic challenges, ecological and systemic challenges, and psychosocial challenges. Most of the ideas will cut across multiple categories; however, to keep the suggestions organized, I have elected to cluster them to the most appropriate category and to separate the tables into two parts (see Table 5.2 and Table 5.3).

Additional recommendations and more specific suggestions will be provided in the closing chapter.

Many of the aforementioned suggestions offered by the adult participants centred on the development and implementation of programs and services and the refinement of communication between the systems. In contrast, most of the students indicated that they just wanted people to be more supportive, respectful, and understanding of one another. Reverting to the previously stated philosophical position and assumptions of the researcher, the active engagement of the oppressed in their own process of liberation is essential. Students in this study suggested that we begin with how we personally relate to and support them in the systems in which they belong. While the suggestions above contain an agenda for reform that may change the lives of participants

TABLE 5.2 *Initiatives to Address Educational and Environmental Challenges*

EDUCATIONAL CHALLENGES	ENVIRONMENTAL CHALLENGES
Provide opportunities for mentoring.	Implement more community and school partnerships.
Provide academic and vocational tutoring.	Provide more liaison workers.
Coordinate a re-entry program to help bring students back to school after they have dropped out.	Designate specific teachers as case managers who provide links to the ecological systems.
Teach pre-service courses in EAL strategies for all teachers and on refugee issues.	Designate a person who is able to advocate for the student.
Coordinate provincial and divisional policy development.	Implement multi-agency partnering on projects (justice and education, and non-government agencies, immigration).
Conduct leadership seminars on teaching in multi-ethnic cities and on utilizing community sources and resources.	Coordinate a sustained and intensive anti-racism and discrimination campaign in the school, community, private sector, and public services.
Acknowledge foreign-based professional programs.	Provide information for newcomers in video format in several languages.
Set up a school-based resource site that links to agencies.	Develop parent modules for helping children through school and for identifying signs of trouble.
Teach basic skills and social development.	Provide more student-to-student assistance.
Offer scholarships and bursaries to encourage involvement in sport.	Create and implement a culturally and linguistically appropriate assessment process.
Teach career development and awareness programs for all students.	
Train immigrant and refugee students to be mediators and peer counsellors.	
Provide training and education for refugee parents on issues related to discipline, personal safety, and adolescent development.	

TABLE 5.3 *Initiatives to Address Economic and Psychosocial Challenges*

EDUCATIONAL CHALLENGES	PSYCHOSOCIAL CHALLENGES
Build in an incentive program for staying in school, so students do not have to work full-time.	Provide more preventative programming.
Prepare students for independent living.	Provide group support programs to assist with the integration of the person with the community.
Provide more information on work skills and employee rights.	Implement initial screening and ongoing screening to identify psychosocial challenges.
Provide volunteer placement programs for refugee students who transition into job placements.	Provide arts-based activities (film, play, theatre, videography, dance) in school and the community.
Teach EAL programs for parents outside of school hours.	Train clinical staff on issues related to refugees.
Utilize technology-based communication and support.	Implement language and literacy programs that include trained professionals who know how to recognize and respond to psychosocial issues.
Remove the government loan for the cost of airfare from country of origin.	Implement language and literacy programs that include trained professionals who know how to recognize and respond to psychosocial issues.
	Train all students in conflict prevention.
	Provide integrated emotional, spiritual, and health care.

and the systems in which they belong, I suggest that the hope for change remains with the power and the drive of those who work and interact directly with the students. Nothing has become more obvious to me throughout all of my work with refugee children than that more needs to be done to assist and support the people who are doing the day-to-day work with the students. This is not to suggest that there is not a role for centralized planning, policy development, and improved programs and services; rather, we must extend the capacity of the systems by empowering those who work in it. It is essential that school leaders encourage and support the involvement of parents and community members in the school in an effort to create a more interconnected and sustainable network of support for refugee students. Moreover, school leaders must work collaboratively with all staff in order to articulate a clear plan for addressing the needs of refugee students. Manley, a parent, believes that some students "drop out because of the failure of their parents." He further suggests that it is imperative that the school talks to the parents to address the issues and challenges that students are encountering.

Although my intent is not to assess the strengths or inadequacies of the school leaders, there was evidence from several participants that supported the need for stronger and more supportive leaders. Participants indicated that they wanted a "clear vision" or a "strategic plan" for addressing the needs of refugee students. Several participants also suggested that the school leaders should "set a better example by being fair and equitable in their dealings with both staff and students." Although participants expressed numerous deficiencies in school leadership, others clearly indicated that the school leaders "had their hands tied" because of the lack of support from the provincial government, the limited divisional support, and the inadequate resources provided to the school. That said, although the participants indicated that the school leaders needed to make numerous improvements, the issues were far too complex to conclude that a "lack of leadership" was the primary problem.

Rassan also discusses the importance of the broader community and its role for supporting students. "Provide for them and they will succeed, whether in academics or sports." He suggests that if the community could support students by just providing them with a pair of runners to help them be on a team, that would help the students immensely. "That's how you build community, that's how you build a safer community. We have to be able to support these kids in their work, in their sports and in their lives."

SUMMARY AND CONCLUSION

Central to the process of adjustment was the role of one key person who formed a closer personal relationship with the student. This person provided an essential link from the student to the microsystem and to the other ecological systems. The bioecological model supports the assertion that, to adequately support and assist students with their adjustment to Canadian schools, the programs and services must be multidimensional and intersect the various ecological systems. The challenges that the children affected by war encounter extend over numerous systems, and so should the programs or services that are designed to assist them with adjusting to Canada. The school system is uniquely positioned to provide the necessary bridge to the other ecological systems; however, as the following chapter illustrates, it is the responsibility of all of the ecological systems and environments to ensure that this is possible and sustainable.

The following chapter will take a closer look at the ecological systems that interact with each other to influence the refugee student's personal, social, and academic development. Some of the individual characteristics of the individual child who is affected by war will be discussed and the child's interactions with the systems will be investigated. A closer and more revealing examination of the role reversal between the members of the ecological systems and the students will be discussed. In particular, the influence that the student has on certain members of the ecological systems will demonstrate an immediate need to improve the capacity of the system and the people in it.

CHAPTER SIX

Interaction of Ecological Systems to Influence Development

THIS CHAPTER WILL DISCUSS THE EXTENT to which the various ecological systems interact with one another to influence the refugee student's personal, social, and academic development. To begin, the ecological systems that influence and affect the student will be considered. This section will also explore how the individuals in the various ecological systems are affected by the student. The discussion of these interactions will be organized according to the various ecological systems: the microsystem, the mesosystem, the exosystem, and the macrosystem.

At different times, ecological systems will vary depending on the developmental stage of the student. For example, one of the students was directly involved with a child welfare service. At this particular time in her life, the people in this system and the agency as a whole played a key role in her daily life. Over time, this involvement may lessen, particularly if she is able to overcome some of her medical issues. As children develop and become more independent, the role of family members may also figure less prominently in their daily lives. The following discussion is intended to provide a summary of the various systems that interact with and influence the development of the student.

MICROSYSTEM

As discussed in the previous chapter, the school played a pivotal role in the students' lives. Sports and after-school programs that were closely aligned with the school were also influential systems that connected the students to a peer group and contributed to their personal well-being. Considering the time that students spend in school, and their motivation to acquire knowledge to improve their lives, it is not surprising that it was an essential aspect of their lives. Portes and Rumbaut (2001) also acknowledged the importance of the school to the lives of children and adolescents and stated that "schools play a critical role in their development, shaping what they learn as well as their motivation and aspirations to learn" (p. 203).

In addition to the school, other systems within the microsystem were also key determinants in the child's development. These systems included the family, the community, and the peer group. A photography activity with students illustrated the roles of these other systems. With the exception of Banya, whose 10 pictures were all of her family, the other seven participants took only pictures of their friends at school, their workplace, places within the school, and the outside of their apartment complex. None of the other participants took pictures of family members. Sandra was the only teacher whose picture was taken.

The family and the community will be discussed in more detail because of the numerous times they were both referenced in the interviews and because of the way in which they influenced the child. Furthermore, the overall way in which these systems interact reveals pertinent information to this study that is worthy of discussion.

Family

FAMILY SEPARATION

Although the nurturing and supporting roles of family members were brought forth, participants discussed the challenges concerning families to a much greater extent. Several recurring themes emerged when the topic of families was discussed: separation, role changes, stress and breakdown, and family violence and abuse. Separation of the family members and family breakdown were two of the most prevalent issues. Bill discusses the issues related to separation:

> There are a lot of cases where parents are separated from their children. Sometimes the children are in a separate country, in a different country than the parents are, so when the parents applied for resettlement, the child is somewhere else. The child's name may be in the file, but the child is not physically there. When it comes time for the parents to travel, they may need to leave that child there. Hopefully they will sponsor that child in the future, but in most cases it takes too long and the child has to be left with the relatives or friends in the hope that the child will join the parents later on. Sometimes the parents leave very young children. I know a family that has left behind two young children. It is very difficult.

Some students have come to Canada on their own, leaving their family behind. Some have lost all their family in the war. Some may have travelled to Canada with other children from the same refugee camp, and these children are now living as a family. Paul illustrates the support that he has observed through this reconstituted family:

> And there is a support factor that is built in to the community and many of the boys I know. There are not too many females and they tend to be groupings of people. You know, four of them in a two-bedroom apartment and when one gets a job he pulls another one in and then another one. They have learned to rely on each other if they have lost their parents and their family.

Ten out of the thirteen students whom I interviewed reported losing members of their immediate family (mom, dad, sister, or brother) from either death or displacement. Only two students had both a mother and a father. Many of the students reported coming over with a parent but leaving siblings behind. Some students indicated that they hope some-day to sponsor their family to come to Canada, although none of them knew how they would go about sponsoring someone.

Understanding the dynamics of the family was complicated, as it was often difficult to discern who made up the student's family. The familial ties and the bonds of friendship appeared to intersect and it was often difficult to differentiate between the two terms. Moreover, most families had undergone restructuring, and as was previously discussed, there were some individuals who formed a family for the purposes of immigrating to Canada.

ROLE CHANGES

As a result of the family separation, there was often a marked change in the roles of people in the family. Joanne reported that the separation, in particular the absence of the father, results in the older sibling taking on the role of the parent. With this change is a tremendous amount of pres-sure and responsibility to succeed and to provide for the family. Joanne states, "They go from being an infant to an adult, and there seems to be nothing in between." Bev also indicates that she worked with a boy who graduated last year who worked the night shift as a tow truck driver to support his siblings while he went to school. He now works at a local pizza shop. Bev states,

> This is the case of an Afghani mother who didn't work and she had an older son and four younger ones, and many other older ones are in Iran. So he has to give up his goals to support the family by working these long shift hours. Now his little brother who is in grade 7 has been suspended several times for acting up. And this guy has given up his life for these younger ones and the youngest one is just throwing it all away. The older one is doing really well and his sister is doing really well. The younger one is in a lot of trouble.

It was common for the eldest child to assume the role of the absent parent, as seen in the following example.

Helen states that her role was "like a mom." I asked her to explain what kinds of things she did and her response was: "I have to teach them how to behave themselves and I have to teach them about things about going outside and keeping safe. I have to give them advice on how to behave yourself."

It appeared that one child in the family emerged in more of a "parenting like" role when one parent was gone. I also witnessed an example of what Portes and Rumbaut (2001) described as a role reversal due to social and economic isolation of parents. Banya, for example, is teaching her mother to drive, she translates for her mother, and she helps her mother with her homework. The difference, however, is that Portes and Rumbaut suggest that this role reversal leads to "generational conflicts or Irvin Child's 'rebel' reaction of embarrassment and resentment of dissonant acculturation," which they suggest gives children a measure of psychological leverage over their parents (Portes & Rumbaut, 2001, pp. 192–93). Although Banya was deeply enmeshed with her mother's life, I saw more pity and guilt expressed by Banya as opposed to embarrassment and resentment. As Portes and Rumbaut (2001) indicate, second-generation children of immigrants believe that they are the sole reason for the immigration of the parents. This in turn results in guilt on behalf of the child, which then gives the parents a degree of psychological leverage. On numerous occasions, Banya commented on how difficult life was for her mother and how she had given up her whole life for her children. I sensed Banya felt a tremendous amount of guilt, but instead of this guilt causing dissonance, I observed more consonance. It seemed that the family unit was more cohesive and this guilt or pity that the children felt motivated them to work harder.

STRESS AND BREAKDOWN

In addition to the change in roles and the separation of family members, issues related to family stress and family conflict also emerged. In some cases, the conflicts resulted in family breakdown.

Christine indicates that she worked with a "made-up family" and there was a lot of conflict in the home. She believes that it was because the three people really did not have the same level of commitment to one another. She stated, "These three people were not really jelled as a family.... There wasn't that same level of respect or a response or support that you can get with family." Anna also comments that the lady who accompanied her to Canada also changed after their arrival into the country.

> On the day before we came she was very, very nice to me and she treated me like her own daughter. And I treated her just like my mom. And then she came here and she changed. And I said, What? And I said, What is going on in this house that she has changed? And every five minutes she had to be shouting, yelling, beating the children. You know, hitting the children with her hands. Not feeding us very well.

Bill, who works with numerous Sudanese families, describes what he called a "disconnect" between the teenaged children and the parents, and he indicates that he thinks many of the parents are losing control. He also states that other factors complicate the family relationships, such as parents having to work two jobs and not having time to spend with their children. Bill talks about a friend who works two jobs. He leaves the home at 2:30 PM to start a shift at 3:00. He works until 11:30 PM and then goes to another job until 5:00 AM. He sleeps for two hours and then his wife wakes him up at 7:00 AM to take his youngest child to daycare and then he comes back by 8:00 AM to sleep for two hours. He then wakes up and goes to work. He repeats this cycle five days a week.

Bill also indicated that some of these parents have a university education, but their credentials are not recognized in Canada. He indicated that it can be very frustrating because many of the parents must work more than one job to make enough money to support their large families. Bill offers the following solution:

> We need to just bridge that gap, and at least try to get them a good start, because I know these people, with any opportunity, would be able to do well. Let's remember that these new people are new Canadians, and they are going to live in Canada. If they don't succeed here then it will be a loss to all of us in Canada, not them alone, the parents, the children, and Canada as well.

Bill's statement outlines just how intertwined the systems are and how what occurs at the individual level of the family can have a ripple effect and consequences throughout all of the other systems. Ultimately, this issue affects everyone, even at the macro level. Combating some of these issues at the individual level could have dramatic effects on the family unit, the prosperity of the upcoming generation, and the overall macrosystem in which all other systems exist. As the following discussion reveals, if we do not deal with these issues, other social and personal problems are likely to worsen. Bill argues,

> Because of the limited income and personal earnings, there are
> family problems. There are family problems between husbands and
> wives. In most cases this results in divorce or separation, and at the
> end of the day it's the children who suffer.... There are family dis-
> putes, a lot of them.

Some of the stress results in medical complications. A couple of the teachers stated that they help students fill out forms and they often see confidential health information about students or their parents. In one instance, Sandra stated that she was given a parent's health file to help them figure out what specialist to see. Teachers indicated that they see a lot of stress-related illness, as well as anxiety and depression, reported in both the students' and the parents' health files.

FAMILY VIOLENCE AND ABUSE

In several interviews with students and teachers, issues related to physical and sexual abuse were discussed. These issues usually surfaced when discussing methods of discipline. Physical abuse was also discussed in relation to gender inequality, where the husband or older brother was the aggressor. Marleen, who works with some of the men, indicated that if men would get some "counselling or information, they would never be in the position that they are in now being prosecuted for domestic issues." She indicated that this dialogue is critical and that it is important to teach both responsibilities and rights together.

Sandra and Laurie both discussed their difficulties in talking to the males who believe that it is acceptable to hit your sister if she is doing something disrespectful, such as talking to a boy in the hallway. Sandra stated, "There are people who are coming to our country, to our schools, who believe that it is okay to kill your sister if she dishonours the family." Another participant stated, "I have a student who is 18 years old, and his mother beats him with an electrical cord because she has that right because the father is gone and she takes the place of the father and so she can do that." Participants indicated that in many of students' families, physical abuse is acceptable. Laurie states, "It's just the way they raise their family. Honour killings are an acceptable way to deal with girls who disrespect the family." She further suggests that gender issues are a priority and must be addressed in the school. Laurie states, "The girls really struggle fitting in socially, and conflicting with parental and family values or cultural values. That's a big piece of a lot of the counselling that I do." Laurie indicates that the boys do not treat women as equals, and she sees this both in their treatment of the other students and of the female staff members. It was also discussed that the girls are at risk of being sexually abused because they do not have a voice.

Rob indicates that many of the women go to church because it is the only place where their husbands will allow them to go. He states, "A lot of times, women are not allowed to go out, unless it's a religious gathering. So at our centre, we have a disproportionate number of women. This is about the only place where they can go for support."

Issues related to gender inequality and gender discrimination were discussed by numerous participants. Some of the teachers explained that it is difficult to know how to best assist the girls when they are being discriminated against. On the one hand, they want to respect the beliefs and values of another culture, but on the other hand, the teachers also want to empower these young girls to be assertive and not to be further marginalized by their family and their peers.

Community

The role of community was discussed as having both positive and negative influences. Manley and Bill discussed how the community members have formed a support network that responds to issues brought forth by the area residents. The group meets regularly to discuss issues related to education and parenting. Manley indicated that the group members formed an association and they are able to "give advice among ourselves and for society issues. If there is a problem in the community, we can call ourselves and we can discuss and give what we think." Manley and Bill both commented on the fact that parents need help identifying when something is going wrong with their children. "They don't know the signs of kids that are doing drugs." Furthermore, Manley commented that, when Canadian children are not doing well, most of the parents know about agencies that could help them, whereas immigrants need to "be reminded." Manley indicated that immigrant parents relied on the church in their country of origin, so many are not used to the kinds of services that are available in Canada. Both Bill and Manley indicated that the community parent groups were "ethnically based"; for example, their group was made up of Somalian parents.

CONCEPTUALIZATION OF A COMMUNITY

The conceptualization of a community changed for many newcomers to Canada. In many of their former countries, the community was a village with "tons of children running around" and where the adults took responsibility for children who were not necessarily their own. Marleen stated that she has had to educate parents not to leave their children unattended on the assumption that their neighbours will take care of them. Furthermore, she stated, "One loss that I hear a lot of them talk about is that sense of community. They miss that huge sense of community."

Despite the loss, there is evidence that the community is a source of support to varying degrees, depending on the individual. The Sudanese community, led by Bill, initiated a mentoring program funded by a community initiative and supported by students at a local university. Last year, the community members developed the program that currently runs out of Walter Duncan School. Although the program had a slow start during the year this study was undertaken, approximately 40 students were involved in the program the previous academic year. Some of the student participants in this study mentioned that the after-school program was important to them because the university students provided tutoring help and the recreational activities were fun. The parent group is hoping to extend the program to other schools in the area.

Beyond the programs and the continuing meetings, the community around Walter Duncan School is testament to the need for people to be with people from their own ethnic group. Small enclaves of Sudanese, Somalis, Afghanis, Iraqis, Cambodians, Ethiopians, and numerous other cultural groups and divisions between these cultural groups live in close proximity to one another and they have developed support systems throughout the city. Similarly, ethnically based peer groups have been established in the school. Some could argue it is because of the accessibility to inexpensive and government-subsidized housing that the people live in the same area; however, within the inner city, communities have clearly established robust ethnically based circles of support. While the scope of this study is limited and not intended to provide a sociological and anthropological investigation into the composition and interaction of the community systems, it would be fascinating to examine the numerous culturally based enclaves that have been erected throughout the city and in the surrounding rural areas.

COMMUNITY ISSUES

Community groups also have their own issues, and some are not always as supportive as one anticipates that they will be. Mike indicated that he has seen negative influences coming from the community. "They tell people from their own communities, 'Don't go to the Canadians for help because it's an embarrassment to the community.' And that may be the reason why people pull out, because of the social pressure from people in their own community." There are also people in the community who are prejudiced and they tell people to stay away from certain ethnic groups. For example, Mike indicated that he has picked up people from the airport and they have told him that they would not live in a particular area because there were Aboriginal people living in the community. Reflecting on Parsa's comments, as a parent she was frightened to live where she was provided housing because of all of the negative comments she heard from her community members. She also was told that Aboriginal people were a threat and this stopped her from talking to her Aboriginal neighbours for nearly a year. Now she comments on how ridiculous these people were to say such things.

Despite some of the difficulties related to community groups, for the most part, the participants indicated that the community was a support when they first moved to the city. Some of the more intimate, ethnically based community groups also provide ongoing support and assistance. As demonstrated by the initiation of a mentoring program, the Sudanese community has been instrumental in providing direct support to the students, as well as a link from the school to the community. This program is promising and has already had an impact on the students' academic and social skills.

FAITH CONNECTION

Faith emerged both as an overarching belief that guided the thinking and behaviours of students as well as a connection to a support network in the community. The students reported varying degrees of involvement with either a church or a mosque. Levia, for example, attends Bible study, a youth group, and a women's group at her church. She is involved with the church three days a week. Students who are Muslim have a place in the school where they meet to pray throughout the school day. Other students might attend a place of worship less frequently, but it was still a system that they chose to mention in the interviews as being a place where they spent time in their community and where they received some support. Helen, for example, was sponsored to come to Canada by a church and she will occasionally contact her sponsor when she is having trouble.

Throughout some of the interviews, students made mention to God looking after them and protecting them in Canada. It appeared that their belief in God gave them the faith that things would work out, despite their challenges. Afem states, "I think God brought me to Canada to protect my life so that nothing will happen to me. So that I can do my own thing." Similarly, Sokut also suggests that one day things will get better for him. "Four months now is over so I have to look for a job. I have to pay for rent, food, a bus pass. I have to do is work on food so that I can go to school. I believe God will see all of my problems, and he will see it one day." As was previously mentioned, Anna believed that prayer would help her get rid of the voices in her head.

Although the interview questions did not include a direct question regarding the students' involvement in organized worship or questions pertaining to their faith, 12 out of the 13 students made reference to attending church or to a belief in God or a belief in Allah.

Peers

The peer group has emerged throughout the previous chapters as an essential base of support for the students. The essential role of the peer group was also discussed in this section as it related to the family system. Some might question why the peer group figures so prominently in the following discussion. There are two main reasons that illustrate the importance of the peers. First, some of the students do not have family members and the peer group is their Canadian family. Second, it is widely accepted in the psychological community that the importance of belonging to a peer group is prominent during adolescence (Santrock, 2001).

While almost all of the students' relationships are with people who are culturally similar, some students did indicate that they had friends from another culture. This was often exhibited in the sports teams.

The family, the community, the peer group, and the school figured most prominently in the day-to-day lives of the students. These systems in the students' immediate environment were the source of relationships that supported the students' personal, social, and academic development. As was previously discussed using the concept of the nanosystem, the majority, but not all of the students, were connected to a close network of people. While there is some evidence that these systems are somewhat connected, there is more evidence to suggest that more problems are created because of the lack of connections. The following discussion will focus on the mesosystem and the various linkages or connections between the different contexts.

MESOSYSTEM

As was discussed previously, the experiences in one context can have an effect on the other microsystems. For example, the parent who must work excessively is therefore unable to help the child with schoolwork or does not have the time to interact with the school system and provide educational support at home. Additionally, the peer group can support the students and satisfy their basic need to belong to the school system. This can be the motivating factor that keeps the child in school.

One of the major barriers to the child's development appeared to be the lack of a well-functioning mesosystem. I argue that the school was the dominant force in the child's microsystem, having substantial influence on the students' daily life and their future goals and aspirations. That said, there is considerable evidence to support the assertion that the school is functioning alone and there is very little connection to the other systems. Whether the school needs to reach out to the community more or the community needs to help out the school remains unanswered. What was certain was that the systems are not as effective as they could be because people are not working together. Moreover, those who are closest to the students and working diligently to support them are depleting their personal resources and becoming less effective. The following excerpts, from various participants representing the microsystem and the exosystem, best describe this lack of connection.

"All of us here are the lone voice in the wilderness." (Ingrid)

"There is a gap out there because there are skills in different professions and somehow there doesn't seem to be somebody who is pulling these things together." (Sara)

"I think the reason why the other agencies are not helping is because there is no connection between these agencies. If they could cooperate and coordinate with their work, it would probably be more helpful to the students and to their parents." (Mike)

"Who is doing these things, because when you're doing these programs you don't have time to connect to get the people in. You just don't have the time to go for lunch and go to coffee and whatever." (Sara)

"I think for the most part we're just on our own. I think that there is
a willingness and I've been involved with some meetings with various agencies and government departments. But everyone just kind
of does their own thing. There's no collaboration." (Larry)

"And that's what we need for the local community to come together."
(Manley)

Representing the microsystem, the participants also indicated that
there is a lack of communication between the systems. Rassan articulates what he sees as an "unhealthy gap" between the systems.

There is no real connection with the community and the school. You
come and tell me what kind of demographics you work with. That
is not helping me to understand why people are the way they are.
You coming here once a week and handing out Band-Aids or whatever. It's not going to solve my problems. There is a big gap. A big
unhealthy gap.... The kids are alone. They feel alone, and they may
not be alone, but they feel alone and then they come to class, here's
a test next class. Here's a quiz next class. Here's a project. When are
you going to take the time to understand the kid?

Taylor suggests that the school could play an integral role in
connecting the students and their families to support places in the
community. The school was referred to as "the gatekeeper of all of
these systems," and on numerous occasions was the essential link to
the greater community. In addition, certain community members were
referred to as a connection to the community. In fact, Taylor noted that
when he talks to some parents, he feels that he is talking to a much larger
group of people in the community. He said that when parents come in
to the school to discuss an issue, they are actually the spokesperson for
an entire group from the community. That said, the deficiencies in the
mesosystem are clearly delineated by the words of the various people
representing the microsystem and the exosystem. From an ecological
perspective, it is important to develop the formal linkages between the
systems by improving communication and developing shared initiatives to address the challenges facing students.

EXOSYSTEM

As was previously mentioned, the members of the exosystem also played a role in supporting children and their families, but as the aforementioned statements indicate, there is clearly a lack of coordination between all of the systems. There was also a noticeable gap between what was happening at the school division level and the government level and what was implemented at the school level. This disconnect between the exosystem and the microsystem was more thoroughly discussed in the preceding section on policy and government direction.

From the teachers' perspective, they are not getting the support that they believe is needed. The teachers who are working directly with the students want practical strategies that they can immediately use to help the student. The people in the microsystem, in particular the people in the nanosystem, have genuinely connected with the students and now play a pivotal role in the students' lives. The connections with the students can best be developed with the support that is generated from the connections within the individual contexts and the connections between the various systems. This system, however, is weakened by the isolation of the various systems. Figure 6.1 refers to the kind of mesosystem that participants suggested would be the most advantageous; all of the systems are connected, with each microsystem assuming equal responsibility for assisting and supporting the child.

Although the school might facilitate the coordination of the four systems, it is essential that the four groups are equal players who are committed to the dialogical process and the act of transformation. While there are promising connections that have occurred, a concerted effort is needed to build up more systemic power to better help all students. As the following section reveals, a weakened structure has numerous consequences.

MACROSYSTEM

Participants representing both the microsystem and the exosystem made comments that suggested more education is necessary to deal with negative perceptions and to prevent divisions that have the potential to bitterly divide and aggravate social, religious, and racial tensions within a country.

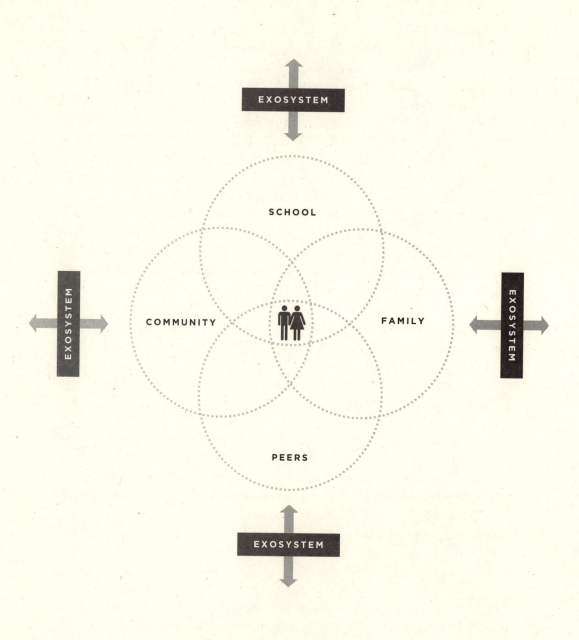

FIGURE 6.1. *A Well-Functioning Mesosystem*

Marleen states,

> Absolutely, there's almost a lack of education everywhere. And these
> people think that these refugees come here and the government
> gives them a lot of money and a wonderful life. If they actually knew
> the money that they got, they would think otherwise.

I argue that it is imperative that Canadians are educated on issues related to accepting immigrants, basic human rights, and the responsibilities of citizens who live in a multi-ethnic city. Newcomers must also have education on their rights in Canada as well as their responsibilities for living in a multi-ethnic city. There are non-negotiable issues, such as domestic violence and sexual abuse, that are not accepted in Canada, and it is the responsibility of all citizens to understand the laws governing the country. The Canadian Charter of Rights and Freedoms sets forth basic fundamental rights, democratic rights, mobility rights, legal rights, equality rights, and minority language and educational rights. Legislation and policy must adhere to these inherently basic but pre-eminent rights of all people who live in Canada. Without a preventative strategy for dealing with issues concerning culture, ideologies, and attitudes, we leave the door open to misunderstandings, misinterpretations, and potential conflict.

A Comparative Analysis

I interviewed several experts from the United Kingdom in Manchester, London, and Oxford. The purpose was to gather information from experts in England who had done extensive work with refugees, both within England and with people in various war zones throughout the world. I also collected documents, including newspaper articles, policy papers, publications from a refugee centre, educational materials, and academic papers. In those two weeks, I came to realize that, at the present time, compared to other countries, the majority of Canadians have a very different opinion about receiving refugees. While my fieldwork was relatively short in duration, it was long enough to accumulate data that led me to completely re-evaluate the role of the macrosystem.

There were also numerous similarities to the themes discussed by the Canadian participants and the English participants. The numerous challenges experienced by refugees often lead to a dropping out of the school system. Rivalry between other marginalized groups within the community was prominent. While the similarities were numerous, I also observed a distinct difference between the overarching reception or treatment of immigrants and refugees in England to that of Canada. Put simply, there was a clear and distinct "anti-refugee" sentiment that was referred to by the participants from England. This opinion was said to greatly influence many of the British and it has created an "anti-immigration" debate within the country. The participants in the study indicated that this opinion has been a source of constant struggle, as they encountered numerous obstacles and challenges while working with refugees and asylum-seekers.

The purpose I have for taking this approach to this discussion is two-fold. I want to outline the power of the macrosystem and the ability that a critical mass of people can have on the workings of the other systems. Secondly, I want to expose what I refer to as the fragility of a macrosystem and the potential for a shift in the ideologies or attitudes in a culture. My overall purpose in doing this is to illustrate the urgent need to develop preventative and proactive strategies to ensure that the foundation of public opinion and government policy in Canada is informed by accurate information and sound research. Moreover, our national and international obligations to the fundamental rights of human beings and to the protection of children must be at the centre of these policies and practices. Losing sight of this focus could have dramatic effects on the macrosystem and could potentially alter Canada's reputation as being a compassionate, democratic, and accepting nation. The scope of this discussion will focus primarily on what I observed to be four main themes that emerged in the interviews with participants and in the documents that I read from England: (1) anti-refugee sentiment, (2) detention centres and deportation, (3) the role of the media in shaping public opinion, and (4) economic and social cost to immigration.

ANTI-REFUGEE, ISLAMAPHOBIA, AND TERRORISM

The participants indicated that England was "very anti-refugee." Johnson, who works in a refugee assistance centre, stated, "The majority of the

British people do not like people on their doorstep." There is a negative image that they suggest has been built up due to numerous reasons and it is furthering the notion of terrorism. Johnson further comments that there are a lot of issues in schools and it can be a very isolating experience for children who are bullied and who feel alone.

> There is a very anti-refugee, there is an assumption that with the post–September 11, there is an assumption that refugees are ... they are actually terrorists, anyway, so there is more hostility now. The popular press treats it very badly. They make a big deal about the floods of refugees that are coming. It is horrendous. And I think in this country, we have such negative, negative stereotypes about asylum-seekers and refugees that when a lot of people come here, their identity straight away is asylum-seeker, refugee, and again that's a very, very negative identity, negative stereotype. A lot of people lie at school and don't tell their peers at school where they are from, which countries they are from, and they don't tell their peers that they are an asylum-seeker in order to conceal, basically to not say what has happened to them. To avoid the negative stuff that comes with that.

When I further questioned Johnson about the connotation of being an asylum-seeker, he elaborated, stating that there is an "extreme negative connotation." He indicated that there is conflict between the status of a child, who is typically perceived as being positive and innocent, and the status of an asylum-seeker. "And it is about what takes priority over the other. And I think in this country their status as asylum-seekers is taking priority. And as an organization, and personally, I very strongly believe that their identity as a child should take priority." In his role as an advocacy worker with young refugees, he indicates that this negative image affects the child and also influences his work with policy makers.

> I mean, we find it difficult to work with other agencies and to work with government in terms of advocacy and educational policy. That is really, really hard, but it is even harder if you are actually that young person living your everyday life. And you carry that negative image

around with you before you even speak to anybody, before you even see anybody. They have this perception of you and who you are.

Carson, who works in a Somali reception centre, referred to "a real Islamaphobia in this country." The anti-refugee opinions appeared to be fuelled by inaccurate reporting, sensationalization of facts, and a strong belief that "Britishness" is being jeopardized by immigrants who are "abusing the system," "taking away housing," and "depleting social services." Participants also indicated that these attitudes have furthered the notion of terrorism, particularly in London. Several participants from England made reference to the July 2005 bombings and how they have contributed to fear and panic about anyone who is Muslim.

There were numerous comments, both from the participants and in the press clippings, that provided evidence to suggest that there was a critical mass, though not necessarily the majority, of people who did not want refugees in England and whose perceptions of refugees or asylum-seekers was quite negative.

DETENTION CENTRES AND DEPORTATION

My fieldwork coincided with an 18-hour riot that occurred in England's largest detention centre for asylum-seekers. Harmondsworth Detention Centre housed 482 immigration detainees and foreign prisoners facing deportation. The riot began when a guard stood in front of a television when a critical report was being released about the centre by the chief inspector of prisons. Fires were set and property was damaged and detainees used bedsheets and toilet paper to write "sos" and "Help" in the courtyard.

Detention centres are places where individuals and families are detained while awaiting deportation. The new asylum model implemented by the Home Office processes asylum claims within a 14-day period, a "shockingly short" length of time, according to Johnson. As Crawley and Lester (2005) indicate in their report *No Place for a Child*, it is estimated that there are 2,000 children detained with their families every year for the purpose of immigration control. The length of detention ranged from 7 days to 268 days. Crawley and Lester document the impact of detention, which includes mental health deterioration, physical health concerns, and the disruption of education. As cited by Travis and Taylor in *The Guardian* on November 30, 2006, the chief inspector of prisons indicated that Harmondsworth was run with a regime as "strict as any high security prison." Johnson argues that "the government is sending out a very strong message by the way they treat asylum-seekers, by detaining them in prisons that are not fit for the UK prisoners to be in." He further indicated that "The only crimes they have committed is trying to claim asylum and trying to flee the country where they face persecution." Johnson stated that he must educate the young adults he works with about detention and what to do when they are detained. He commented about how difficult it was for him to talk to children and young adults about the possibility of being detained and he stated that the children will cry as they are being told about the process. He explains,

> They generally tend to pick people up in the morning. They are allowed to use restraints, people are handcuffed. Sometimes they pick the parents up at home and then travel to school to take the children out of classes. That is what we have to deal with in this country, that's what we are trying to fight.

Crawley (2006) states in a policy paper from the Immigration Law Practitioners' Association, "The view that immigration controls take precedence over welfare considerations is not new." Johnson indicated that his work on detention is about teaching children and adolescents how to advocate for themselves and what they should do if they are released to carry on with their lives. He further indicated that the "future is bleak" for young people, as only 2 per cent are ever granted refugee status and allowed to remain in the United Kingdom. Approximately 70 per cent are given discretionary leave, which means their claim has been refused but they can stay until they turn 18 and then a large proportion of these people are deported. Another issue in the country is whether the educational system should invest in these children if they have no future in the United Kingdom.

MEDIA INFLUENCE

The role of the media emerged as a major influence in shaping or fuel-ling public opinion that contributed to moral panic, anti-refugee sentiment, and incorrect assumptions about the impact that refugees have on the welfare state. Some participants suggested that the tabloids support bullying behaviour and the media is very keen on highlighting the bogus asylum-seekers who are just here to claim benefits and taking advantage of the British people.

I examined more than 200 separate newspaper articles or elec-tronic bulletins over a two-week period from both tabloids and national papers in England. From this collection, I pulled the first 45 articles that I found that related to immigrants and asylum-seekers. While there was some evidence of balanced reporting that was based on fact, there was also ample evidence to support the media spin on numerous issues related to immigrants. The following are only a brief sample of some of the attitudes or opinions that were expressed that I believe could easily contribute to the anti-refugee sentiment:

> Britain is the best of both worlds. It is easy to get a job and easy
> to live comfortably without one. No wonder so many have come.
> (Whitehead, November 22, 2006, p. 5)

> On arrival, the immigrants are instantly entitled to child benefit, tax
> credits and housing support. After 12 months they can also receive
> income-related benefits such as unemployment benefit, effectively
> the same level of support as a British citizen.... Britain is now the
> destination of choice for "feckless" migrants who are already claim-
> ing benefits back home. (Slack, November 22, 2006, p. 8)

> The bottom line is that we are a small island and are already over-
> crowded—especially in the South East.... But the biggest factor of
> all is how long our newcomers decide to stay. (Green, November 22,
> 2006, p. 9)

> Flats at the centre of a row over asylum seekers will no longer
> be used to house them.... The location of St. Albans Court was

completely unsuitable to house asylum seekers and the social makeup of the neighbourhood was put under severe stress ... which led
to a climate of fear and mistrust developing on both sides. (White,
November 23, 2006, p. 1)

Illegal immigrants to be freed after riot at detention centre.... At
least 150 illegal immigrants are to be let back on to the streets.... But
a large number, who should have been kicked out of the country,
could now slip under the radar and vanish again. (Whitehead &
Drake, November 30, 2006, p. 17)

The city council has set aside £400,000 of taxpayers' cash this
year to support asylum-seeking families living in Coventry. (Scott,
November 23, 2006, para. 1)

The purpose of providing these examples is to demonstrate that
there is some anti-refugee sentiment expressed by the various media
sources. That said, there would clearly be people who quickly dis-
counted the sources and would choose to believe other sources that
would represent more accurate and balanced reporting.

THE ECONOMIC COST OF IMMIGRATION

As some of the newspaper quotes imply, refugees and asylum-seekers
are seen as people who are taking resources from the British people
and taking advantage of the welfare state. Carson mentioned that, in
the area around where she works, there are many Somalians who live
in the community. She indicated that the community feels threatened
by this, and they are upset because they see people who they feel are
given housing that should be given to British people. Not knowing how
the housing works, some of the community members are openly hos-
tile toward the new immigrants. Gang-related violence, drug use, and
other criminal activity are continuing problems facing the community.
In addition, Carson states that the area where the housing is located
is characterized by "many social problems, and then they put a whole
other strain of people who have a lot of needs into that area." She further elaborates,

Because nobody wants to live in the Northside, the housing is empty, and they call it void housing. It is not fit for human habitation, but it's okay for asylum-seekers. This is how people perceive asylum-seekers in this country.... It is wet, it is full of mould and whatever, and so, you know, you house asylum-seekers there.... They have no choice. They have been told this is where you're going to live. The housing providers are happy. It is absolutely disgusting. There are rats. There are all sorts of really unpleasant things that I would not sleep in. And again, the implications for the family and their mental health and physical health and everything is dreadful.

Asylum-seekers are not permitted to work, so they have a separate system called the National Asylum Support Service that provides their basic needs and accommodation needs. Johnson indicated that this system is "a separate welfare state for asylum-seekers. Payments made to asylum-seekers are 30 per cent lower than those who are part of the welfare state.... So you are forcing people to live well below the poverty line." He further noted that this has encouraged many asylum-seekers to work illegally in restaurants, factories, and in homes where they are not protected by work legislation. In addition, Johnson noted that sexual exploitation, pornography, and trafficking young girls to work in brothels is also a major concern.

The four general themes briefly outline some of the issues that influence some peoples' perceptions about immigrants and asylum-seekers. Coupled with these perceptions are attitudes that influence how refugees and asylum-seekers are treated by the host county. The ideologies or attitudes reflected in the culture influence the functioning of other systems. Johnson and Carson indicated that asylum-seekers are not encouraged to engage with social services and newcomers do not trust the government or home office. Furthermore, Johnson argued, "It's all about inclusion. It's about including the people in an inclusive society. But asylum-seekers are about exclusion, and how much we can exclude them."

The participants from England added an entirely different dimension to my research. The macrosystem appeared to have a much larger impact on the other systems than I had originally presumed. What became even more prevalent was how imperative it is for a city, province, or a country to maintain a positive outlook on the benefits of immigration and the basic human entitlements that all people deserve. Although there were numerous references to racism and discrimination in this study, the overarching ideologies or attitudes reflected in the culture were dissimilar to what I heard from the participants in England. As previously mentioned, I did not sense the same level of "anti-refugee" sentiment in the Canadian participants. Many of the European countries, such as France and England, have immigration issues at the forefront of the various and often opposing political platforms (Rieff, April 15, 2007). Considering the role of the macrosystem, the overarching question is, What is Canada prepared to do to ensure that this does not happen? Immigration is projected to increase significantly over the next decade. As this study has revealed, there are numerous challenges for the newcomer in Canada, as well as barriers and obstacles in the various systems of support. As was outlined in the second chapter, Canada needs immigrants and the federal government has committed to increasing the number of immigrants admitted over the next five years. Without proper education, support programs, services, and resources, public opinion could easily change.

Looking no further than *The Globe and Mail*, a headline on February 24, 2007, read, "CANADA'S HOTTEST NEW IMPORT? EMPLOYEES." The article by Harding and Walton discusses a program by the federal and provincial government to bring in foreign workers to help Calgary address its labour shortage. The following quotes reveal the exploitation of refugees by Canadians. Furthermore, these statements illustrate the urgent need for education of both Canadians and newcomers on the topic of basic human rights and responsibilities.

A sign hanging outside Calgary-based JIR Solutions reads, "Get your foreign worker today!"

I think there's a lot of people trying to make money off this.

They don't have the workers' or the employer's interests at heart.

Newcomers are being abandoned.

> They claim the broker was breaking several labour laws, including
> illegally garnishing [*sic*] their weekly paycheques by 75 percent.

> It's naïve for the provincial governments to expect foreign workers
> to lodge complaints because they would likely be sent home. There is
> a dangerous power imbalance....

Recent media reports have also centred attention on the politicization of the wearing of the hijab (a head scarf), which is most recently
making front-page headlines in national papers. Muslim girls who have
come of age and wear the hijab are being excluded from sporting events,
with officials citing it as a safety hazard. Throughout Canada, debates
are ensuing and becoming more politicized regarding what is referred
to as "reasonable accommodation" of religious minorities.

PERCEPTIONS AND ATTITUDES REFLECTED IN CANADIAN CULTURE

Participants representing both the microsystem and the exosystem
made similar comments that further reinforced my assertion that more
education is necessary to deal with negative perceptions and to prevent
divisions that have the potential to bitterly divide and aggravate social,
religious, and racial tensions within a country. Marleen states,

> There is a lot of negative perceptions out there and these people are
> living on next to nothing. Where the education piece is lacking is
> telling people about the economic benefit of these people. This is a
> community issue. We need a lot of people with the right attitude to
> make a difference for these people. Everyone is needed to make a
> difference in a child's life.

Will states that people only focus on the bad stories that they see
in the newspapers and they extrapolate certain details and generalize
about all newcomers. He believes that it would not take much to get
public opinion to go against newcomers and refugees.

It is essential for learning to be reciprocal and it is imperative that
Canadians are educated on issues related to accepting immigrants,

basic human rights, and the responsibilities of citizens who live in a multi-ethnic country. Newcomers must also have educational programs to focus on their rights as citizens in Canada as well as their responsibilities for living in a multi-ethnic country.

THE IMPACT ON THE ADULTS WHO WORK WITH WAR-AFFECTED STUDENTS

As Bronfenbrenner (2001) indicated, much of the research thus far has focused on the development of children examined by the influences of the older generation. Little research has focused on the role reversal and the development of the adults as they are influenced by their children. Bronfenbrenner (2001) suggested that there was little empirical evidence to test this assertion. Although Bronfenbrenner was referring to the role reversal between parent and child, I extended this examination to include the reciprocal relationship between the student and the teacher or adult representative from the microsystem.

The basic premise of the bioecological model is that development occurs through the interactions between multiple settings and from the relations between these settings. I observed significant personal changes in the adults who worked with the children from war-affected countries. What was originally intended merely as an inquisitive exploration into the reciprocal development between the adult and the student became a major finding that led to a more critical examination of the deficits in the systems of support for these students. These deficits further strengthened the importance of using an ecological model for designing programs, processes, and systems to support refugee children in Canada.

Most of the teachers had their own personal reasons for choosing to work more intensively with refugee students. Some teachers naturally evolved into their roles and others had more personal reasons that motivated them to be in their current position. Rassan and Christine were both immigrants to Canada, and as Rassan states, "Myself being one, I can understand the kinds of experiences that they have had." Despite what brought these people to do the kind of work that they do, what was most meaningful is what the participants learned as a result of working with the students. For the most part, the outcomes of this reciprocal learning kept the adults motivated to continue working and it provided encouragement that what they were doing was meaningful.

I asked the adult participants the following question: "How have you changed, both personally and professionally, as a result of working with children who are from war-affected countries?" The answer to this question was often accompanied by a strong emotional response from the participants. Weaving through most of the participants' answers were bursts of frustration, underlying anger, humility, and a determination to effect change. Although it is difficult to convey this emotion with words, I have elected to include some of the non-verbal actions of the participants to suggest the tone of the speaker.

Participants indicated that their lives have changed dramatically since they started working with refugee students. Some indicated that their outlook on life has changed and their commitment to advocacy issues has been ignited. Some have come to realize the dramatic effect they can have on the life of a child. Renewed meanings, an overarching purpose to their work, and a focus on marginalized people in the world have been outcomes of the work that these people have undertaken. Sandra commented,

> My life has totally changed since I've met these kids. I am more interested in … [pause]. It makes me more socially involved. It makes me join things like Amnesty International, to go into politics, or to do something in social service agencies and do something that never would've crossed my mind before because I never knew about anything like this before. [crying] I had no idea, growing up as a high school student, about these kinds of things, what these kids are going through. It's like, pfff, when I was in high school, it was like, "So how did your perm turn out?" That's all that was. It has been a totally life-changing experience. Sorry, it just upsets me.

> My first experience was a child soldier from Liberia who had scars over his arms. And I remember one day he got stabbed because he got involved in a gang. Of course, he didn't have any supports, he joined a gang, and he got stabbed. And this was like blocks away on

the street. And he came to our classroom, you know, as a safe place. And that was my first indication that, holy crow, I can actually help people like him.

Bev also referred to the role she played in helping EAL students and how this kept her from leaving the school. This also further confirms the need for the support system to have a sustainable program in place, one that is not dependent on the work of only one person. In addition, Bev discussed the human connection she feels to what is happening in the world.

I'm glad that I have chosen this for the last 20 years. People ask me why I haven't left and I say, "I can't leave" because I would've left kids with nothing, because I was the only EAL person and you know what happens if the EAL person leaves, the whole program leaves. So you sort of have a commitment to them so you have to keep staying for them.

In an emotional statement, Vivienne explains how her students inspire her to come to work and how her relationships with the students have made her a better human being.

I have the reputation of being a very fair, but firm, person. And a very tough person, so my demeanour tends to be a little tough, because 30 years is a long time to work in a profession where the kids, some of them, don't really care if they're here or not. These kids melt your heart [voice cracks]. They really do because they want to be here. It makes me all emotional [tearing]. People just don't know the extent the teachers go to.... But these kids make you want to be here. They want me to get up every morning and be here by 7:00. They make you want to find them other things to do. They make me want to find all the resources I can. My sensitivity to their plight has really become way more empathetic. I'm a more empathetic human being. And a more humble human being. This is a rich country, and we have all of these privileges. So I am just try-ing to share what was given to me. I try to give back and that's what

I've taught these kids. Even though you may not have very much, it's always important to give back to your community.

Paul, an administrator at Walter Duncan School, responds to the question with the following quote and then he segues into a very emotional discussion about the effects that this work has had on him and on his staff.

It's a privilege to work with the students and I know that I am stronger because of it. The road to service is travelled with integrity and with compassion and understanding. So my compassion in those areas has certainly increased. And that's what I need to do for the sake of our students; to do as much as I am able. And see each child for what they are, despite what is coming out of their mouth and what they are doing. But you can't do that unless you have the commitment to serving them and to serve them with care. And to demonstrate this in tangible ways.

What did the adults in this study report that they learned from the refugee students? Empathy, humility, compassion, courage, faith in the human spirit, patience, commitment, and responsibility. I can best describe these aforementioned characteristics in one general statement: they learned how to be better human beings. The new meanings that these adults constructed about the world and their acknowledgment of the privileges that they took for granted refocused many of their priorities and some renewed their purpose in life and became even more committed and motivated to work with these students.

The people in the systems and the system as a whole are functioning independently, without the collective power of a fully functioning ecological system. This has weakened the ecological system and, as such, it has taken its toll on the people who are trying to help. While these people are still committed to what they are doing, it is very clear that if the system does not provide more support, or if the other systems do not work more closely with the school to provide support, the consequences could be potentially detrimental to both staff and students. Specific people have clearly emerged as being influential and supportive members of the microsystem who function as an essential link to the school system for numerous students. Keeping these people in this position and supporting them in their efforts seems to be the most logical solution at this time. Skills that have been exhibited by these individuals are not generally taught in a two-day professional development seminar. These skills and attitudes are inherent to the character and personality of an individual and they must be nurtured and supported so that they can continue to develop. Without this attention, these skills and attitudes can easily devolve to unsupportive, unhelpful, or even harmful actions, behaviours, and attitudes that will be much more difficult to change.

The present-day school system must now contend with issues related to poverty, health, parenting, cultural diversity, and changes to the structure of families. All layers of issues have complicated the role of the teacher and the ability the system has to respond to the various needs of the people in it. As the following excerpts reveal, issues related to teaching war-affected children have created another dimension of issues for the school. Those who elect to form a meaningful relationship with the students are trusted by these students and their role becomes increasingly more critical and personally more demanding.

As one of the administrators, Paul recognizes that there are some teachers who "go the extra mile" for students, and as he acknowledges, there is a cost to this.

> There is also a group of us who do have empathy for students, who are able and willing to see those glimpses of what is shown to us. They can see what the students have gone through and they are willing to go the extra mile for them to do what is needed. But then those of us who do that must understand that there is a price to pay.

> That person that I told you about earlier, the colleague who took the girl to the hospital because she was on suicide watch, the teacher went directly to her own doctor after that session with the student. One of the things that we identified is that administrators tend to do a lot of things in terms of counselling and all that stuff, but then what happens is we end up not taking care of ourselves. So then one day, all of a sudden, that last little straw pushes us over.

I think the key thing for me is increasing capacity. Across the board. Knowing that there's still so much to grow and capacity that needs to be built and maintained, because sometimes I feel like, this month actually, this year has been really bad. Vicarious trauma just keeps coming back. I cry. I'm crying more easily lately, and last week I cried at a city council meeting. I cried in front of my colleagues. And it's not because I'm weak, but your heart needs to be expressed in a safe place. But the hard task is for the heart to be married to the head. Totally. That's when the action comes in. Because otherwise you can become permissive and sentimental [looking down]. Yes, I think I need to take a retreat one of these days. I really need to get away for the weekend. It's too much.

Working with war-affected children brings individuals closer to the harrowing atrocities of violence and terrorism in the contemporary world. This knowledge is dealt with differently by each individual. Some will mentally barricade themselves within their classrooms or organizations and others will open their doors and invite students to join them in a reciprocal exchange of learning. Both of these responses could be from two people who both care deeply about the student but have chosen a different way to deal with the information. It might also be the result of an individual who has run out of energy to care and who now finds it necessary to put up a wall of protection.

The macrosystem mirrors what is evidenced in the microsystem. There are some individuals who will lead very insular lives—they are busy with their own issues and what happens across the ocean has very little effect on their day-to-day living. Some will choose not to listen to certain newscasts, or read certain articles, because they are too disturbing. They may care deeply about the nearly 30 wars currently occurring worldwide, but it is not enough to mobilize their efforts to do something about it.

Some of the participants in this study heard graphically disturbing stories that they will never forget. Students trusted these adults enough to share personal information about themselves and about their life experiences. In their roles as adults and helpers, these individuals were often at a loss to respond. Feeling the need to make the situation better, as is often the role between an adult and a hurt or sad child, many of these adults felt that they were unable to fulfill their role effectively. Some were surprised by their reactions and others were disappointed by their behaviours. The struggle to deal with the information and to help others understand the issues became a major factor that contributed to frustration, anger, and disappointment.

Sandra's words illustrate how emotionally difficult it is to deal with the information she hears. More importantly, she discusses the lack of power she feels in trying to help make a difference for her students.

> When my first group of grade 10s leave, because they are graduating this year, the ones I first started with, I don't even want to come back next year. I don't want to go through that. [crying] They are very ... I mean, they drive me crazy. It's emotionally draining. When I go home, I tell my husband. He's an accountant, he just doesn't get it. Who would? I would never give up, but I don't know how much longer I can do this. You can only ... I can only hear so many times ... and feel totally powerless, but I can't do anything but just sit there and listen and say, "I am sorry that your teacher makes you feel like you are stupid." And not being able to do anything about it. I can only take that for so much longer. And although I don't want to be teaching in some monocultural school, I don't really know how to do that, I don't know how much longer I can do this with someone in administration, or someone in a position of power acknowledging that these people have cultural capital. This kid can bring so much to everything and people just don't see it. They just say, "Oh my God, not another immigrant and a stupid kid that does not know how to read or write a sentence." It blows my mind. I sit here and I think, These are my colleagues, what am I supposed to do? What do I say? How do I react? Do I just smile and nod and walk out? Do I defend them? But when people in positions of power are saying these things to you, what do you do? I don't know. I can only see so many more kids getting involved in gangs and put into jail. Sometimes I think it would be just easier to work in a whitey school.

The frustration reported by the participants was often the result of being a part of a system that was not supportive. Energy was spent on defending their roles, convincing others in the system that they also needed to support the students, and politically positioning themselves within the system so that they had power to help liberate the students. As one participant mentioned, there are times when individuals lose their capacity to care and they surprise themselves with their responses.

> And the sad thing is, when we reach that point where our ability to care is tapped out, we do damage to kids. They come in and they get bad experiences. And it doesn't take many of those bad experiences before they're out of school. And they are saying bad things about teachers and they have reasons for it. And they know it because I've been that guy.

> My first year here, one of the guys did end up in the [name of African gang]. It was my first year of teaching. He pushed me right beyond my limit. And then he pushed again. And I was in a classroom that had an outside exit. And I called him over to the door, and I grabbed him by the back of the head and I said to him, "You better hope that I never see you outside of this school" and I pushed him out the door. I have never in my life ever said that to another human being or meant it, and I meant it completely. And this is a 14-year-old boy, who comes from the worst situation. He has no dad, he never had a father. He has no money at home and I know damn well what kind of a situation he's in. But my ability to care is tapped out. And I put the wall up.

The emotional expression from the participants throughout this portion of the interviews was intense. Their words were telling: "tired," "tapped out," "crying easily," "draining," "scary," "couldn't go to sleep," "burning out." Some of the participants made hints about leaving the school or choosing to become less involved with the refugee students because it was getting "too difficult without the support." Some indicated that support was needed to the system as a whole, and some indicated that it was the leadership within the school that needed to create an internal structure that would be more supportive and that focused on a vision that was collectively valued. The current challenge for all of the ecological systems is to collectively respond to the needs of the people in it. This requires the collaborative and creative efforts of everyone, starting from the individual and extending to the macrosystem. The need for direction in the area of policy and practice is evident.

HUMAN CAPACITY, HOPE, AND RESILIENCE

Woven though various chapters of this book are some qualities that have typified the descriptions of the students. First, the students are capable and they demonstrated that they had the remarkable ability to adjust to a completely different country, culture, environment, and set of ecological systems. Despite numerous challenges, they were attending school and many of them were also working full-time and living independently or with only some of their family members. Secondly, the students were hopeful that their current situation would improve and what they had worked so hard to achieve would be accomplished. Finally, they have exhibited resilience and demonstrated that despite the situations they have endured and the adversity that they have encountered, they have persevered to make a better life for themselves.

Banya describes the concept of resiliency.

> I don't think the other kids are ever going to forget the bad things and the bad memories. Especially if somebody has done something bad to you, they're never going to forget. It gives you experiences of life. They only have their own self. They just think, This is my life. That is why they make changes. It pushes them to make a better life. This is the life, there is happiness and sadness; it is like a relationship.

While the students' outlook is hopeful, the people in the school and the community who work with the students are frustrated with how they see the system functioning and how some of the people in the system are treating the students. The school is a fundamental system in the lives of the students, and if this system is not just, and there are students who are marginalized by the actions of the oppressors, it must be transformed. The inequities of what children have lived through and the unjust systems to which they have belonged provide the seeds for resentment, conflict, and violence. It is essential that people who recognize injustices collaborate together and work with the oppressed toward their own liberation.

Scott expresses his dissatisfaction with the school and what he perceives as an unjust system. Although he is proud of his students' accomplishments, he is frustrated and angered by what his students must endure to get an education. The following passage outlines the moral dilemma that Scott encounters. He knows that the students are marginalized and he wants to advocate for them and push them to stand for their rights. At the same time, he realizes that the students have risen above the adversity and they have focused on what they need, despite the treatment that they have received.

> Every year at grad, when I look at those students I can barely make
> it through because they are just so proud and it's this rite of passage
> that has been so much harder for them than for anybody else and
> it really means something to them that it can't mean to anybody
> else. You know, that's when I think there's just so much injustice
> and there's so much crap in here. And they never get a piece of rec-
> ognition, and they have learned not to ever seek justice because you
> usually won't get it, you get punishment. So they've learned not to
> do that and that should not be rewarded. I should be telling them,
> "No, you should stand on principle here because it matters. And we
> have this Constitution, and we have this protection of your rights.
> You shouldn't stand for it. Stand for your individuality." Schools are
> ostensibly democratic places and they should get experience with
> democracy here first. Not fight their way through this place and then
> get to the real world. But they have this wisdom that comes from
> experience that says, "I know what people like that are like. Just let
> them be like that, I'd be dead if I worried about those people who are
> like that. Every soldier that I ran from, every fight that I got through."
>
> So I see them graduate, and it's just such a good feeling. To see
> them face this world and to know that they're really going to kick
> ass. Like, honestly, if you can get through this, not speaking English

with teachers who think you're the biggest pain, with people calling you nigger when you're walking down the hallway, if you can get through this, hey, you are going to do just fine. But it shouldn't be that way. It's not the way it should be. That's why I'm really happy when people like you come around and you're looking at the big picture, it makes me think that there is some hope.

SUMMARY AND CONCLUSION

This chapter began with an examination of the three other environments that comprised the microsystem, namely, the family, the community, and the peer group. Although the school emerged as the dominant system in the microsystem, it became evident that a more balanced and collaborative interaction between the school, the community, the family, and the peer group are necessary to create a better functioning microsystem, exosystem, and mesosystem. The importance of the macrosystem was revealed, and particular attention was drawn to the importance of preventing negative attitudes toward refugees in the host culture.

The final section of this chapter discussed how the students have affected the people in the various ecological systems and what the participants have learned in this reciprocal developmental process of working with refugee students. A corollary to these relationships was the development of feelings associated with stress, fatigue, and exhaustion. Consequently, the people who provided the close interpersonal support to the students were the ones who reported these feelings most intensely. Despite feelings of frustration, anger, and disappointment, the participants were motivated by the hope and resilience that they observed in their students to continue trying to improve the lives of the refugee children.

It's a bit embarrassing to have been concerned with the human problem all one's life and find at the end that one has no more to offer by way of advice than: "Try to be a little kinder."
—Aldous Huxley

PART TWO

Praxis

CHAPTER SEVEN

Lessons Focused on Self-Expression and Personal Awareness

LESSONS AND ACTIVITIES TO SUPPORT REFUGEE CHILDREN

The following four chapters provide practical strategies and lessons to support refugee children. The lessons were piloted with groups of students in Canada and in Uganda (primarily northern Ugandan districts) in both non-government and government agencies and in secondary schools. The lessons are not a substitute for counselling or therapy; rather, they are suggestions from professionals who work with children and youth who come from some of the most war-affected areas of the world. The activities are designed for teachers or counsellors to use with groups or individual students to support their adjustment to life in Canada. I felt it was imperative that basic support materials be developed to assist teachers, counsellors, and school administrators with helping children cope with the key issues that were identified in the preceding research. The activities are introductory level and not designed to provide intensive psychotherapy or counselling. It is absolutely imperative that individuals using these strategies know how to recognize the signs of trauma, stress, anxiety, and other distressing emotions and they refer the individual to a professional who is qualified and capable of providing them with the support that they need. For additional resources and practical lessons related to anger, mental health issues, and personal and social management, see additional resources: *The Tough Stuff Series* (Stewart, 2000); *The Anger Workout Book for Teens* (Stewart, 2002); and *The STARS Program* (Stewart, 1998, 2004). Additional interventions and therapy resources are listed in the annotated bibliography.

LESSON DEVELOPMENT AND OVERVIEW

The following chapters are organized into four clusters. First, I have developed lessons that are focused on self-expression and personal understanding. The second cluster helps students work though difficult issues such as trauma, death, depression, anger, guilt, stress, and anxiety. The third cluster encourages students to focus on the support systems they have and the accomplishments they have made. This section also helps students to see how resilient they are and how far they have developed in the various stages of their journey. The final chapter offers strategies for promoting a culture of peace and planning for the future. It is also a compilation of activities that bring closure to groups or classes with a focus on group connections and cohesiveness.

The lessons included in the next four chapters include creative interventions and expressive arts techniques. For each lesson, I have attempted to rely less on text and more on other techniques (e.g., music, drama, art) to help students express themselves and learn positive coping strategies. After conducting a study in northern Uganda, I was able to observe how effective many of the creative and expressive strategies were for helping children heal after war. Drumming, art, poetry, drama, music, and dancing were found to be among the most useful and meaningful activities for supporting children.

The lessons have not been written using a typical formal lesson plan that includes activation suggestions, outcomes, or assessment strategies. Instead, I have provided a core activity or teaching strategy that teachers or counsellors can develop, modify, or adapt to suit his or her particular group of students. Processing, debriefing, and follow-up activities are necessary steps in creating a meaningful lesson. Moreover, it is essential that the following lessons are carefully selected to be consistent with the needs and developmental stage of the student. As with all basic steps to counselling or educating students, the first step is to form a meaningful and trusting relationship with the student. A meaningful, genuine, and trusting relationship between a teacher and a student is the very basic foundation that is needed to support students.

Expressive activities used in the following lessons include the use of art, music, drama, dance/movement, and poetry/creative writing within a context of counselling and teaching. For many refugees and survivors of trauma, creative arts therapies have a unique role in treatment, particularly when students have limited language skills (Malchiodi, 2008). Furthermore, creative interventions have been used for more than 50 years through such disciplines as art therapy, music therapy, dance/ movement therapy, drama therapy or psychodrama, poetry therapy, and play therapy, including sandtray therapy (Malchiodi, 2008). That said, many counselling and social work training programs focus on teaching individual and group "talk therapy" to prepare students for the helping profession. Interactive, creative, and expressive therapies have not typically received the same level of academic attention as basic counselling theories.

Many of the refugee students that I work with do not readily seek the assistance from a counsellor, psychologist, or social worker; in fact, many of the students confide in a teacher whom they trust. Some of the students reported that they didn't want people to think that there was something "wrong" with them so they were hesitant to see a counsellor. Other students felt that personal issues were to be kept private and not shared. Some feared that they could be deported if they raised any issue that would cause concern for themselves or their family. Once students learn more about school counsellors and the numerous roles these people play in the school and community, they might be more trusting and less hesitant to seek help. That said, it is necessary to provide activities and strategies that will assist teachers and counsellors who need practical and supportive lessons to assist refugee students.

Using creative interventions means that the counsellor or teacher must be prepared to use the lessons effectively. He or she must also keep in mind ethical and cultural considerations, particularly when working with students from a diverse culture. Artwork, poetry, and other creative forms of expression must be treated and handled in the same confidential manner as case notes or other documentation or recordings related to therapy or counselling. Therapists or counsellors who are not trained in these techniques should be careful not to interpret the product based on their own projections (Malchiodi, 2008). The role of the teacher or counsellor is to facilitate the process of self-expression and personal understanding with children, not to interpret what they have created. These activities are designed to facilitate communication and healing. I hope that children who take part in these lessons find relief from the challenges they encounter and that they discover more about themselves and gain new insights that enhance their personal well-being.

I encourage students to keep their work products in a portfolio so that after they complete the course or group they have a record of their journey of healing and personal understanding. I take digital pictures or digital video recordings of their work so they can put their work into a binder, box portfolio, or onto an electronic source. Students are encouraged to discuss how their work has had an impact on their feelings, thoughts, behaviours, relationships, goals, and hopes and dreams. The path or journey for a refugee child is complicated and long, and the challenges for these students occur in every aspect of their life. Being a patient, flexible, and understanding facilitator will help students feel safe and more willing to take part in the activities and share their experiences. I encourage students to share their work projects with other students; however, I always offer students the chance to pass. Art is very personal and students may not wish to share what they have done, and it is essential that students be given this opportunity to keep their work private.

I keep art supplies and material in a big suitcase on wheels. It is helpful to have some basic supplies on hand and to have these transportable.

The following list contains some suggestions for some basic art supplies.

- [ ] Poster paper
- [ ] Craft paper (comes in large roll, good for murals)
- [ ] Sketch paper
- [ ] Coloured construction paper
- [ ] Pencils
- [ ] Erasers
- [ ] Pencil crayons
- [ ] Crayons
- [ ] Charcoal sticks
- [ ] Feathers
- [ ] Felt markers
- [ ] Sponges
- [ ] Chalk pastels
- [ ] Scissors (basic and a set of craft scissors—they come in a kit of about 20 kinds of scissors in a variety of cutting styles)
- [ ] Glue sticks
- [ ] Rocks
- [ ] Cardboard
- [ ] Glue gun (good for gluing rocks and other heavy objects)
- [ ] Masking tape (good to display work)
- [ ] Clear tape
- [ ] Collage materials (newspapers, magazines, cloth, ribbon, yarn, glitter, beads, stickers, sequins, objects from nature such as sand, pebbles, sticks)
- [ ] Acrylic paint
- [ ] Washable paint
- [ ] Paintbrushes in a variety of sizes
- [ ] Paint dabbers
- [ ] A brick of clay
- [ ] Colour modelling clay or Plasticene
- [ ] Index cards (for writing down responses to art)
- [ ] Button maker kit
- [ ] Sticky notes
- [ ] Recycled materials (bags, string, foil, plastic wrap)
- [ ] Mask forms
- [ ] Culturally appropriate materials (e.g., pictures that represent people from a variety of cultures, artifacts or objects from other cultures, such as paper beads from Uganda)

In addition to a binder, box, or electronic portfolio, I also suggest that students keep a learning log or journal to record their thoughts, interpretations, or feelings associated with their work or the work of their classmates.

The following activities have been written to both a student audience and to the teacher facilitator. Where possible, I have attempted to write directly to the student audience to assist with presenting the activity to a class or individual student.

LESSON 1 BETWEEN TWO WORLDS

One of the newcomers in my university course said to me that he felt like he no longer belonged anywhere. He literally felt that he was in-between two worlds: one being his home country, which he fled from during the civil war, and the other being Canada, his host country and place where he was relocated to three years previous. Despite being in Canada and attending university, he felt that he remained largely disconnected from his peers in Canada, his family in his home country, and from the community in which he lived. Although peers and community members engaged in conversation and made him feel welcome, nobody invited him over for dinner, helped him register for courses, or simply asked him out to an activity or party. The challenge to really belong to Canada left him feeling sad, depressed, and even angry at times.

To begin, take a moment to consider how your two worlds are similar and different. How close do you think your two worlds are? Perhaps the two environments are very similar, or maybe they are completely different. On a blank piece of paper draw one circle to represent your Country, Village, or Community of Origin and draw another circle to represent where you live now in Canada. Write on each circle how they are similar or different. If you need to do this activity on two separate sheets of paper (one for each world), go ahead and do this.

Next, draw a picture of yourself and put yourself where you think you are in relation to the two worlds. Are you closer to one or the other? Are you in the middle, off to the side, or directly on one of the worlds? Talk about your world and share with others.

ILLUSTRATION 7.1 *Two Worlds*

LESSON 2 MY WORLD

One of the data collection strategies discussed in this book involved students taking pictures of the systems, objects, and people they interacted with. The pictures were developed and the students discussed why they took the picture and what it meant to them.

The purpose of this activity was to gain insight into the students' world without relying entirely on words. This helped to understand more about the activities the students were involved in, who they spent time with, and how they perceived their world.

The following lesson is an activity that can take place over a set period of time (1–2 weeks). Provide students with either a digital camera (best) or a disposable camera. Ask them to create a photo essay about who they are and the current world in which they live.

Encourage students to write captions for each picture. Mount the developed pictures on a piece of cardboard or a piece of poster paper. This could be in the shape of a circle to represent the students' world or in the shape of another object that symbolizes something about their world. Digital pictures can be displayed using a simple slide-show program. Music or sounds could also be added for effect.

Sample pictures might include:

- Where they live
- A place of work
- Where they hang around at school
- Places they visit in the community
- People they interact with in the community
- Family members
- Clubs or sports that they take part in
- Friends

Have students present their collection to peers or privately to the teacher/counsellor.

LESSON 3 THREE PHASES OF CULTURE SHOCK

The shock (of moving to a foreign country) is said to consist of specific stages or phases. Two phases were identified in the previous chapters: initial excitement followed by numerous challenges. The third phase that was referred to was the process of adjustment. For the purpose of this lesson, the following three phases will be referred to: (1) excitement, (2) challenges, and (3) adjustments.

Listing and defining some of the challenges and feelings that you are experiencing or have experienced before, during, and after coming to Canada is an initial step to working through some of the phases of culture shock. It can also be helpful in determining where you might need additional support and what steps you need to take to help yourself feel better and more in control of what is happening around you.

Consider the following questions:

- When you found out that you were moving to Canada, how did you feel? What did you think Canada would be like? When you first landed, what did you think? What were some of the thoughts that you had? What did you look forward to?

ILLUSTRATION 7.2 *Three Phases of Culture Shock*

- Think about some of the challenges you first had. Did it take a while to adjust to the culture? What did you struggle to figure out at first?

- You have likely made some adjustments to your life after coming to Canada. What have you changed? What are some of the behaviours that have changed? Has your thinking adjusted?

Take a moment to consider the three phases mentioned above. Make three circles and, using words or pictures, label them Excitement, Challenges, and Adjustments (see Illustration 7.2, on previous page). Fill in the circles with your own thoughts about these three phases.

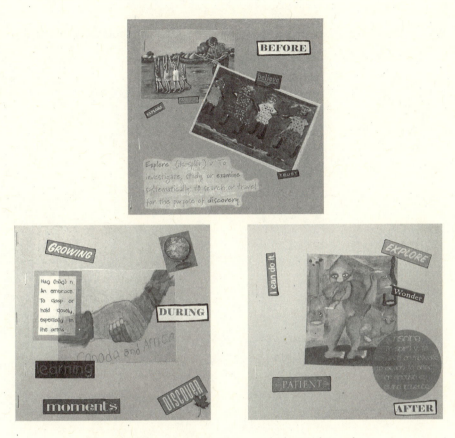

ILLUSTRATION 7.3 *Before, During, and After Work Samples*

LESSON 4 THREE DOORS

This lesson has been adapted from an activity in *A Kind of Friendship: Working for and with War Affected Children and Youth*, published by the Children as Peacebuilders (CAP) Project.

This activity can be done numerous ways. A large paper can be divided into three equal sections, or each student can be given three file folders. I prefer to use file folders so that they look more like doors and the student can keep the inside private. Label the three folders or sections of paper "Before," "During," and "After." There is no need to specify what the before, during, or after represent. Extra paper (coloured is best) should also be provided so that students can create an inside door in the middle of the folder.

The three outsides of the doors can be decorated. When the door is opened (folder opened) the student is to draw a situation and how it has changed over time: before the situation/experience, during the situation/experience, and after the situation/experience.

LESSON 5 INSIDE OUT

Some students who have come from countries where there has been conflict have difficulty adjusting because they have memories of violence or trauma. Many people assume that students are coping with their feelings because they look fine on the outside. What is problematic is that many people do not feel good on the inside because they have memories of unpleasant events that have happened to themselves or to people they cared about. These feelings or emotions tend to affect people in different ways. Some people experience headaches, stomachaches, or they have difficulty sleeping or concentrating. Some people talk about how they feel and others keep their feelings inside. There is no right or wrong way to deal with hurtful memories. If you do not feel like talking, there are other things that you can do to help yourself work through a difficult time.

Imagine yourself as a line drawing. Write some words or draw some pictures that represent how you feel inside. On the outside of the figure, write words or draw pictures that represent what you show others. How are these words/pictures similar or different?

LESSON 6 THE COLOURS OF ME AND MY WORLD

This lesson has been adapted from an activity in *A Kind of Friendship: Working for and with War Affected Children and Youth* published by the Children as Peacebuilders (CAP) Project.

If it is possible, read the book *My Many Coloured Days* by Dr. Seuss. Colour can be a useful medium to express yourself when words are more difficult.

Using a piece of chart paper, work with a partner and trace the outline of your profile (side portrait). Instead of using words, use colour as a code to describe how you feel inside as well as how the world feels to you.

Consider what colours mean to you. There are no wrong answers.

On the outside of the outline, the colours should reflect your feelings about the world around you. Crayons will work the best for this activity. Paint is also good.

In creating your colour portrait, think about how to represent your feelings. Do you feel the same way all of the time? Should there be more than one colour? What kinds of lines will you use? Will you use symbols?

If you are willing, this is usually an interesting activity to share with someone else.

LESSON 7 ABSTRACT SHAPES, MULTICOLOURS, AND VARIOUS SIZES

A microsystem represents your closest and most inner circle of relationships that you have with people, objects, or symbols in your environment. The microsystem is the immediate environment in which you live and it includes the close interpersonal relationships that you have with your family, relatives, peers, teachers, or others who are a part of your life.

Describe your microsystem using a series of shapes in different sizes and colours. Using different colours of construction paper, use your hands to tear up paper to make shapes that will represent your environment. You might include a school, a community club, and a refugee assistance centre as part of your microsystem. It can include places, people, or objects.

Once you have done this, think about the closest relationship you have at this very moment. If something was seriously wrong or troubling you, who would be the first person you would go to for help? Is it a group of friends? Is it a teacher or a counsellor? Is it a parent or a best friend? This is called your nanosystem.

Tear out a shape to represent yourself and put this on the large chart paper, but don't glue it down. Next, tear up shapes to represent the people in your nanosystem. Arrange your nanosystem (your closest relationship) to be the closest to you on the chart paper. After you have done this, tear up and then arrange your entire microsystem on the chart paper. Once you are satisfied with the arrangement, glue down the shapes.

NOTE: *I prefer tearing the shapes rather than using scissors. Using your hands to create the shapes and allowing imperfections that occur when you tear up construction paper seems to make this activity work better. Scissors tend to make very definite and hard lines, whereas tearing paper allows the creator to create frayed lines, jagged shapes, and fuzzy curves. If students want to create a hard line, they can create a fold and tear the paper. When I have used scissors, I tend to see students choose uniform shapes such as circles, triangles, and squares. When students tear out the shapes, there is much more diversity and less uniformity to the shapes.*

LESSON 8 DUAL-LANGUAGE STORYBOOKS

Folk literature is a form of expressive culture and can exist in many forms, including, but not limited to, myths, legends, fairy tales, fables, animal tales, short stories, and proverbs.

Have the students read a folktale such as *Qayb Libaax / The Lion's Share* by Said Salah Ahmed. This dual-language storybook tells a Somalian fable about the misuse of power. There are many websites devoted to dual-language storybooks and numerous possible stories that could be told. A quick search for "folktales" will yield hundreds of ideas and possible topics for students to write about. That said, it is most meaningful if students retell a story from their own culture or recall a story that has been told to them by someone from their family or community.

Have students read several forms of folk literature and discuss common elements (e.g., a moral, a hero, a lesson, elements of nature, or traditions of everyday life). Examples of dual-language storybooks are excellent resources to show how illustrations connect to the language and how the two languages tell a similar but not identical story. Discuss situations where there might not be an English word for a phrase or expression from their first language. Create a word wall of phrases or expressions in a variety of languages. Discuss sayings that have been passed on through generations. Discuss similarities between the stories from different cultures.

Ask students to think about a story from their culture that they could tell in a storybook format. Have them tell the story in both their first or most dominant language and in English. This activity could also be done in culture-specific groups. If students have difficulty thinking up a folktale from their culture, they might use a folktale from another culture and then translate it into their first/dominant language.

When books are completed, students should be encouraged to read the stories publicly to other classes or to younger children. This is a great way to share information about culture and to use literature to explore language and art.

Additional references for children's books are included in the Annotated Bibliography at the back of the book.

LESSON 9 BUILD A STORY

Storytelling allows students the opportunity to explore situations, identify feelings, and learn consequences for behaviours, actions, and events.

Gather up numerous miscellaneous objects to act as props. Small items from a craft or a dollar store are quite useful. Costumes, samples of material and fabric, and wigs can also be used.

Some additional items might include:

- Buttons
- Small action figures
- Mirrors
- Children's play house furniture
- Building blocks
- String or yarn
- Artificial flowers
- Plastic animals
- Small wooden dolls
- Clay or Plasticene

Have students build a story using a predetermined number of props. Three might be sufficient to start with. The story could teach a lesson or explore a serious issue such as racism, conflict with parents, or problems with friends.

This form of storytelling is well suited to students who might struggle with language or have difficulty writing. Oral storytelling is another form of expression that might be more appropriate for some students.

This process can be done in groups or individually. More props can be added or the teacher can challenge the students to find 10 props on their own to build a story. In a group of four to five students, each student could bring three props and the group can build a story together.

Topics might be randomly selected from a hat, or students might brainstorm for topics as part of the group process.

LESSON 10 MUSICAL STORYTELLING

A variation on storytelling is to use music to create a story. Provide a variety of musical instruments or have students create their own instruments. There are multitudes of ways to make instruments that can easily be accessed online.

Tambourines, shakers, triangles, drums, bells, and wooden sticks are excellent percussion instruments that could be used in this exercise.

Students may wish to do this activity for their own story or they may wish to work as a group to create a collaborative story such as "The Life of a Refugee." This story could be performed, with or without words.

Provide students with a series of sticky notes. Using a storyboard outline, have students create the "audio track" with the instruments and the script (using words or pictures) for the story they will tell. The storyboard is a rough sketch of the story and a timeline from the start to the finish of the piece. This format will allow students to match sound to the event or picture they wish to describe.

Allow sufficient time for students to experiment with the variety of instruments to create a variety of sounds. Encourage students to develop an overall message they want the audience to understand.

Develop a rough draft using the sticky notes and then transfer the notes on to the handout sheets in order to organize the story. Sticky notes can be moved around and rearranged easily with the storyboard handout.

Provide time for students to practise and rehearse and then allow students to perform their story.

STORYBOARD

Title of Song or Story...

Length .... Date ....

Instruments Required ....

....

....

STORYBOARD FOR .... **PAGE** ....

Storyboard
title of song or story
instruments required

LESSON 11 CD RELEASE

Music is often a source of comfort and relaxation for students who have experienced difficult times. Moreover, many students dream of being a star or music idol. Creating a stage persona and a style of music can be a useful activity for self-expression, relaxation, and plain old fun.

Provide each student with a blank CD jewel case. Offer magazines, newspapers, and a variety of art supplies.

Design the front and back covers for the CD and create a list of song titles that would represent yourself or tell something about your life. A short write-up or biography of yourself, including your musical background, would also add to the cover.

CD covers might also be designed electronically and then printed off to be inserted in the case.

You might also want to burn a selection of poetry, pictures, or samples of their artwork onto their CD to have as an electronic scrapbook or keepsake.

CHAPTER 8

Lessons to Help Work through Difficult Issues

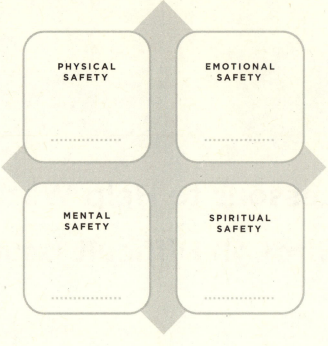

ILLUSTRATION 8.1. *Safety Squares*

LESSON 12 FEELING SAFE

There are four main types of safety: physical safety, mental safety, emotional safety, and spiritual safety. Physical safety relates to your body being free of danger. When you sense a dangerous situation, you are able to get yourself to safety. Mental safety refers to you making choices and thinking about what you need to do to get what you need. Emotional safety is using your emotions or feelings to alert you to a dangerous situation causing you to act in a way that is safe. Spiritual safety is believing in a higher being, a creator, or a God and using your beliefs to make good decisions. If you do not feel safe, it is difficult to progress with learning, making friends, or carrying on daily tasks.

On a scale of 1 to 10, how would you rate your level of safety? Put a number in the appropriate box in Illustration 8.1 above.

Considering your answers, think about yourself in relation to the various systems that you belong to.

Using the diagram in Illustration 8.2, shade in or colour an amount to represent how safe you feel in the following environments. The more colour, the safer you feel in that environment.

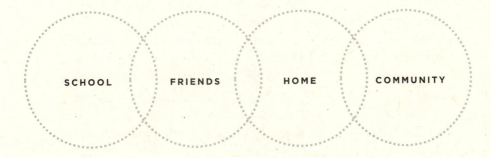

ILLUSTRATION 8.2 *Safety in Environments*

When do you feel the safest? ....

When do you feel the least safe? ....

How do you protect yourself? ....

Does this plan work? ....

What could you do to increase the level of safety you have in the four groupings above?

School: ....

Friends: ....

Home: ....

Community: ....

LESSON 13 WHAT YOUR BODY KNOWS

Whether you witnessed a traumatic event or you experienced trauma, you have a high chance of experiencing an intense emotional response. Witnessing violence is just as frightening and threatening as being the victim. Seeing someone get hurt is very stressful. Being hurt by someone is painful and can cause personal stress, anxiety, and fear. It is important to find a way to cope with these feelings so that you can heal and focus on getting better and achieving your dreams.

Your body will tell you to pay attention to it if you don't look after yourself. Some people get physically sick, some people get tired and grouchy, other people have difficulty concentrating or focusing on a task. Over time, these body signals can get worse and you could experience a more long-term medical issue. When your body signals to you that it needs attention, listen to it. Take some time for yourself and try to do something that brings you comfort.

Take a look at the list of symptoms or signs below. Circle the ones that you have experienced in the last couple of months. In the space beside the symptom, indicate how many times you would estimate that you had this feeling or symptom in the last month. If you experience side effects for a period of time, it is best to see a doctor, who will be able to determine how serious the situation is.

- headaches   [ ]
- frequently feeling sick   [ ]
- easily frustrated   [ ]
- excessively tired   [ ]
- restlessness   [ ]
- loss of appetite   [ ]
- irritable   [ ]
- being overly emotional
  or sensitive   [ ]
- tired   [ ]
- trouble sleeping   [ ]
- difficulty concentrating   [ ]

- trouble in school   [ ]
- nightmares   [ ]
- flashbacks   [ ]
- difficulty with
  relationships   [ ]
- fear   [ ]
- worrying   [ ]
- anxiety   [ ]
- withdrawn   [ ]
- constant sadness   [ ]
- low opinion of yourself   [ ]
- feeling overwhelmed   [ ]

LESSON 14 HOT SPOTS

Everyone shows and holds their emotions in different ways. For some people it is very easy to see if they are upset, angry, or happy. For others, it is difficult to see how they are feeling. Some people even have a hard time knowing how they personally feel. They have difficulty explaining what is making them happy or upset.

Different emotions or feelings affect our bodies in different ways. For example, if I am feeling stress, I have a stiff neck and my stomach feels like it is doing flips. When I am angry, my eyebrows slant and my chest feels heavy. When I am happy, I feel like my legs are floating and my face is warm.

Knowing how you hold your emotions is an important step in being aware of how your body is responding to various events or experiences. This awareness helps you cope with different situations more appropriately. In Illustration 8.3 (following page) eight emotions are listed. Assign a colour to each emotion. Pick a colour that you think best represents that feeling. Colour in the box next to the emotion. In the outline of the body shape, colour in with lines, objects, or shades where on your body you feel that emotion in your body. To the right of the outline, you can write a short explanation for what you have drawn.

What conclusions can you make based on this activity?

....

....

....

If your body could talk to you, what would it say?

....

....

....

....

....

FEELING	COLOUR	MY BODY	EXPLANATION
Anger			
Sadness			
Fear			
Comfort			
Happiness			
Anxiety			
Calmness			
Stress			

ILLUSTRATION 8.3 *Hot Spots*

LESSON 15 I REMEMBER

Many students find that sports, art activities, dramatic expression, or writing activities help them work through issues. It is not the product that matters in these activities; rather, it is the process of doing something positive to help yourself. When people do not find positive ways to work through issues, they often resort to harmful activities, such as smoking or drinking, or reckless behaviour as a way to cope.

Working through a traumatic experience does not mean that you need to relive the experience. For some people, it is not helpful to go back to the traumatic experience in their minds because it causes too much pain. For others, telling their story is cathartic; in other words, it makes them feel better. In some cases, telling their story releases it from their memories and they feel like they have gained more power or control over a circumstance or an event.

If you have times in your life that you are remembering an unpleasant memory and you want to take control of your thoughts, try to create a picture in your mind that is a safe place where you can mentally visit when you are feeling stress or anxiety.

ILLUSTRATION 8.4 *Visual Imagery Boxes*

Find yourself a cardboard box about the size that a piece of jewellery would be in. Something small that would fit in a jacket pocket would be best. Using modelling clay, design your real or imaginary place inside of that box. This place may be an actual place (e.g., a room in your house or a place in your community) or it may be a completely imaginary place (e.g., a place in space or underground). The purpose of this activity is to use your mind to create the place, to design it with your hands, and to later visualize this place when you have unpleasant feelings or thoughts. You might also keep this box in your pocket, or in a bag or knapsack, so that you can open the lid and be reminded of your calm and relaxing place.

LESSON 16 FEELING LOW, TAKE FIVE

At times, there might be events happening in your life that can bring your mood down. When you feel discouraged or sad, it is often difficult to think of things that can help you feel better again. You likely know what brings you happiness, but it might be difficult to think about these things when you are feeling low.

Trace your hand on a piece of paper. On each finger and your thumb, write down one activity that you might do that would help you feel better. Some students enjoy crafts, others enjoy sports. You might find enjoyment out of reading a book or going for a walk. Dancing or getting your hair done might also be activities that lift your spirits.

Think about what brings you a sense of happiness and write down these five suggestions so that you can go to this list when there is a time that you are feeling low. Even if you are not feeling low, you need to remember to do things that bring enjoyment to your life. Daily maintenance of your physical and mental health requires that you build in activities each day that you enjoy and that bring you comfort.

Find Out What Works for You
- Go for a Walk
- Play Football or Soccer
- Read a Magazine
- Cook
- Sit in the Sunshine
- Climb a Tree
- Play a Game on the Computer
- Make a Craft

and Next Time You are Feeling Blue, Take Five for a Quick Renew!

LESSON 17 TRIGGERS, FLASHBACKS, DAYDREAMS, AND NIGHTMARES

A trigger is something that reminds you of an unpleasant event. If you have experienced a traumatic event, a trigger (something presently happening) can bring back the same kind of response that you had when you experienced the traumatic event.

One refugee student discussed a time when the family member he was with was shot. The student was forced to run and hide in the bush. He was alone, scared, and feared for his life. The experience this student had during the war continues to come back to him at night through his dreams and sometimes during the day when he is at school. He says that he feels like he is right back in the bush, crying and thinking that he will be killed.

This student has several triggers. When he hears a loud noise, he thinks of gunshots. The day he ran from his home it was raining. When it rains in Canada and he smells the wet ground, he is reminded of the day he fled. Movies that are violent are far too upsetting for him to watch, and when he is alone in a crowd without his friends, he worries that he might be attacked.

All of these events in his current life bring back memories that come in the way of flashbacks (actually seeing the event happening again in your mind), during nightmares (terrifying night dreams), and sometimes he can be sitting in class and he finds himself lost in his thoughts or daydreaming (thinking about an event that is not related to what he is doing). Typically a daydream is a positive thought about something good, like a fun party or something good to eat, but in this case it is thinking about an event that is negative in nature.

Nightmares, flashbacks, and daydreams are often accompanied by panic, fear, stress, terror, anger, sadness, or numbness. Many people report that they feel like they are being retraumatized or reharmed by these episodes.

Think about a daydream or a flashback that you might have had recently? What happened? Write it out or put down some words to describe what you saw in your mind. Draw a picture to explain what it was about.

What can you remember about the last nightmare that you had, if you have had one? What happened? Write it out or put down some words to describe the nightmare. Draw a picture to explain what it was about.

In Illustration 8.5, write down any possible triggers you might have for nightmares, daydreams, or flashbacks. If you do not experience these, then leave the arrows blank. If you need to add arrows to any one of the categories, write them in on the diagram.

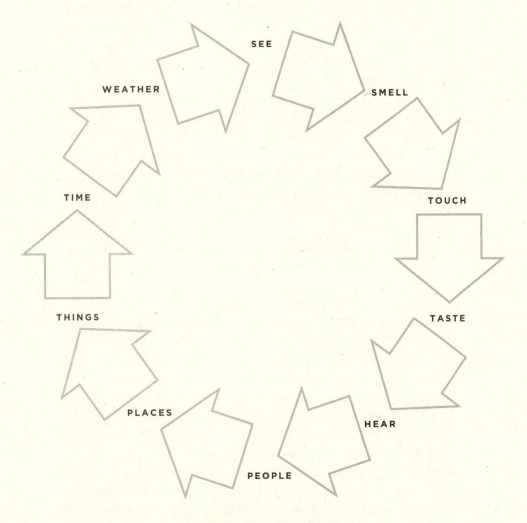

ILLUSTRATION 8.5 *Trigger Factors*

LESSON 18 TRIGGER MANAGEMENT STRATEGIES

Now that you have a better idea of what your triggers are and how these triggers contribute to daydreams, flashbacks, and nightmares, it is important to learn how to manage these triggers so that you remain in control of situations. The purpose of a Trigger Management Strategy is not to experience a trigger; rather, the purpose is to manage it. A trigger will bring with it negative or hard-to-deal-with feelings, which is normal. Your task is to plan effective strategies for managing the trigger and the feelings or symptoms that the trigger evokes.

The following is a list of some strategies that might be helpful in disarming a trigger.

- Do relaxation exercises: Start at the top of your head and practise tensing and relaxing your body muscles. Do one part at a time. Tense up the muscle and then release it. Do this from the top of your head to the bottom of your toes.
- Practise visual imagery: Imagine yourself in a calm and relaxing place. Visualize yourself sitting or laying down in your calm place.
- Try controlled breathing: Breathe in for a count of five and breathe out for a count of five. Try deep abdominal breathing.
- Use positive self-talk: Talk to yourself in your head with a positive message ("You can do it," "I am almost there," "I am safe," "I will be okay").
- Change what you are doing: Choose to distract yourself from your trigger. Change what you are doing, try a different activity.
- Play a sport: Do an activity that you enjoy: Substitute unpleasant feelings with a good feeling by doing an activity that is both good for your body and your mind.
- Play music: Music can help to change your mood. Lively music might help you feel energetic and slower music might help calm you down. Music can help to distract some negative feelings and help you feel positive.

- Do an art activity: You do not have to be an artist to use art to express yourself. Art activities can help to soothe yourself and to reduce stress. Creating something might also bring you enjoyment and personal satisfaction.

Your ideas:

....

....

....

....

....

....

....

....

....

....

TRIGGER MANAGEMENT

Using Illustration 8.6 (on the following page) Start with the first circle at the bottom and write down a trigger that you think would be the easiest to begin with. Write the name of the trigger in the circle and in the space next to it write down a strategy that you will use to help you manage the trigger. Pick a strategy from the list above or use one of your ideas. Fill in the next four circles and the flags in the order of easiest to most difficult.

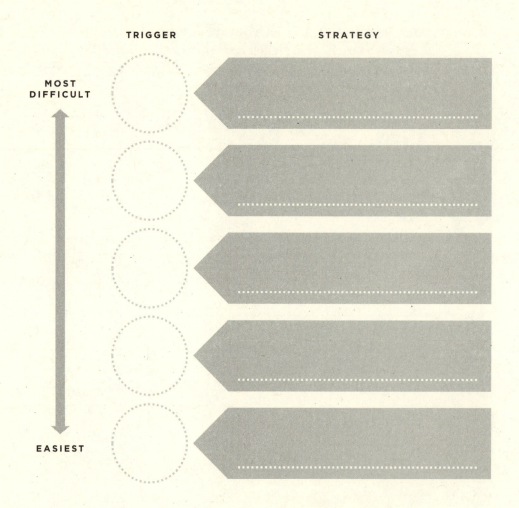

ILLUSTRATION 8.6 *Trigger Management*

LESSON 19 ANGER OR GRIEF COLLAGE

Put together a compilation of music. An iPod or MP3 player works well because you can easily move from one song to another with minimal time lapses in-between.

The purpose of this activity is to create a group collage or group drawing that explores the topic of anger or grief.

This activity can be completed with pastels, paint, pencil crayons, pencils, crayons, or with other art materials such as ribbon, sequins, stickers, yarn, and so on.

Each student is given one piece of poster paper. As the music plays, students draw freely on the poster paper. When the music stops, have the students get up and move to the next drawing. Before each student moves, have a short discussion about what they drew or added to the drawing. Encourage students to discuss the music and the connection they made between the art and music. Discuss similarities and differences between how the music made the students feel.

When the student moves to the next drawing, start the music and have them begin drawing on the next picture. Have each student go around to all of the drawings and then finish back on the piece they started.

At the completion of the drawing session, discuss how certain songs elicited different feelings and types of drawing.

A variation on this activity would be to have students stay on their own piece of paper and change only the music.

Another possibility would be to create one large class mural using craft paper. Students all sit around the one piece of paper and then add to the mural as they move around the piece of paper. Different music selections can be played for the separate drawing sessions.

If separate drawings are created, students could take the piece home that they started to finish it.

Discuss how class members had different styles of art and different emotions or responses to the same music selections. For additional lessons on anger, see *The Anger Workout Book for Teens* (Stewart, 2002).

LESSON 20 YOUR CHOICE

This lesson is adapted from *The Anger Workout Book for Teens* (Stewart, 2002). See this resource for additional lessons and teaching strategies for helping teens cope with anger.

When you are angry, you have a choice about how you will respond.

You can escape by burying your feelings or ignoring/avoiding the situation.

You can express yourself assertively (stand up for your rights) by problem-solving, negotiating, or compromising.

You can explode by venting, blowing up, or being aggressive.

Provide each student with three pieces of coloured paper. Using objects from nature, animals, or plants, draw three different pictures to represent Escape, Express, and Explode.

Once all of the drawings are complete, put them up in three sections of the room. Allow students time to walk from one picture to another and to discuss common elements in the pictures.

Anger can be both harmful or helpful. Anger can make someone stand up for what he or she believes in. Anger might also lead to someone being violent to others or harmful to oneself. Anger is also a warning that something is wrong. How an individual responds to anger is a personal choice. An individual can choose to walk away or engage in a fight. The first step to responding in a helpful way is to be aware of anger and to train your body to respond appropriately to anger.

Using the list in Illustration 8.7, put an *x* over the responses that you typically experience when you are angry. If you have other responses, add them to the list.

Next, how you do generally deal with these responses?

Do you express yourself, escape or avoid anger, or do you explode? Using the open boxes in Illustration 8.8, write a few words or draw a picture to show how people would look or sound if they were to demonstrate each response. Then circle the box that best shows how you respond.

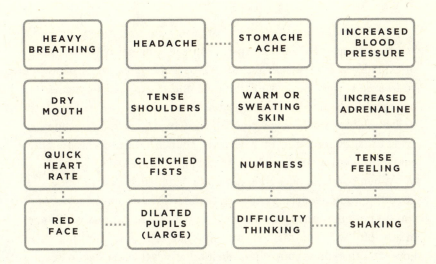

ILLUSTRATION 8.7 *Anger Responses*

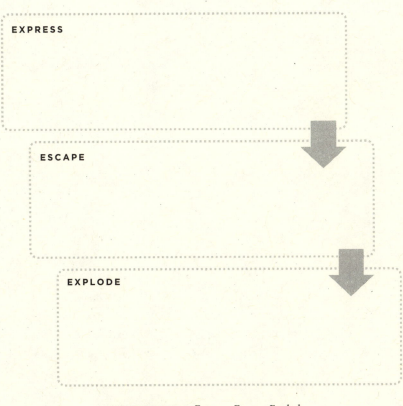

ILLUSTRATION 8.8 *Express, Escape, Explode*

When you feel an angry response, you want to try to express what you are feeling. If you do not express yourself, you may choose to escape or explode, which typically results in harmful behaviour. If you escape, you haven't really dealt with the issue and it can lead to you feeling unhappy or resentful. If you explode, you could hurt yourself or others or you might regret how you reacted. Remember that you can choose to avoid the situation until you have had a chance to think, which is different from avoiding the situation and not responding at all.

When you feel anger creeping up on you, listen to your body. Feel how your body is reacting and then before you behave or act, THINK. If you do not take time to think about how you can express your anger in a helpful way, you may respond in a harmful way. Thinking about how you can express yourself in a helpful way is the first step to dealing with anger.

LESSON 21 FIRST AID FOR ANGER

The *Anger Workout Book for Teens* (Stewart, 2002) outlines four steps to deal with anger:

Step 1: Stop
Step 2: Break
Step 3: Think
Step 4: Respond

This lesson provides a brief overview of how to deal with anger in a helpful way. As the previous lesson explained, it is important to know your personal warning signs for anger. How do you look? How do you feel?

Draw a human figure and show (using objects or drawing) how your body feels when you are angry. Do you have knots in your stomach, is your face on fire, are your legs tense?

NOTE: *If time permits, bring in some old clothing and stuff the figure with clothes. Pin on pictures or write down feelings with a felt pen to show the various warning signs. This is a more concrete activity and can be a lot of fun to do as a group.*

Step 1: STOP

The first step is to notice these signs and STOP. Stop and be aware of your body. Stop everything you are doing, take a deep breath, and experience your feelings. Accept that you are angry.

Step 2: BREAK

Next, take a break. Break the cycle. Physically remove yourself from the situation for a minute, an hour, or more. Go for a walk, exercise, talk to a friend, or anything else that can help you calm down. Some people count backward in their head, some people listen to music, and some people imagine a calm and relaxing place. The important thing to remember is to stop your anger from escalating to the point where you cannot even think about what to do.

Step 3: THINK

Use every bit of your energy to control your mind and think about the best possible way to respond. In your mind, ask yourself, Will this help or will this hurt?

Step 4: RESPOND

This important step encourages you to respond to anger instead of reacting to anger. If you respond, you have thought about the appropriate behaviour. You have considered the consequences of your actions and you have controlled your thinking so that you are able to express yourself in a controlled way.

Stewart (2002) has some general tips for how to respond to someone when you are angry.

Being patient with yourself and others will allow you to communicate most effectively and the Patience Principles will guide you through the steps.

P   Pick a good time and place to talk.
A   Avoid using general words such as *never* and *always*. For example, "You always interrupt."
T   Talk about only one issue at a time.
I   "I" messages work the best. For example, "I feel angry about how you spoke to me."
E   Eliminate exaggeration and criticism.
N   No put-downs or insults.
C   Clarify what you mean to say and what you hear the other person say.
E   Examine and explore other possible points of view and different opinions.
    (Stewart, 2002, p. 60)

*Encourage students to role-play to practise using the Patience Principles.
The following list includes some possible role-play scenarios.*

- A student in one of your classes came up to you and said,
  "Why don't you just go back to your country. We don't want
  you here."
- Two kids from the school are calling you a gang member.
- A friend of yours was accused of stealing something from
  another student's locker. Your friend said to forget about it,
  but you think something should be done.
- Your parent tells you that he or she does not want you hanging around with Canadian kids because he or she thinks
  that you are disrespecting your culture.
- A police officer stops you on the street while you are coming
  home from work. The police officer demands that you empty
  your bag on the street and says that you match the description of someone who just robbed a convenience store.
- Your best friend has betrayed you and lied about something
  very serious.
- A teacher tells you that you will never get a decent job
  because you do not have the academic ability.
- Your boss at work makes you work until 2:00 AM after he
  promised you could go home early because you have an
  exam the next morning.
- The soccer/football team you play with is banned from playing for the rest of the year because students in your school
  badmouthed the referee.
- A teacher accuses you of cheating on an exam and fails you
  in the course.

It is best to encourage students to write their own scenarios and then
role-play the helpful/harmful responses.

LESSON 22 HEALING CEREMONY

Letting Go but Never Forgetting

Consider the customs you have as a way of bringing structure, meaning, and connectivity to your life. How do you celebrate a birthday, wedding, or community event? Pick an event from your culture and explain how the ceremony is conducted.

A healing ceremony is a planned activity that can help students deal with feelings of shame, guilt, or loss. Several students who have come from countries where there has been war reported that they often felt a sense of guilt or shame because they survived and so many others did not. Many refugee children also feel a tremendous amount of guilt because they have left people who continue to live in difficult circumstances. Many students also stated that they have a tremendous sense of responsibility to make a better life for themselves in Canada and to help or support others back home.

Letting go does not mean forgetting events that happened or no longer remembering people you loved. You are entitled to feel shame and guilt, but you do not have to keep it forever. You have a responsibility to heal after what you have experienced.

A healing ceremony is an event that you plan that will help you give purpose or meaning to an unpleasant experience. Some examples of ceremonies include: a candlelight walk, a planting of a tree, or a visit to a memorial. These planned activities help to mark the event and the ritual honours the victims or comforts the survivors. For many, the healing ceremony is a safe and meaningful way to express feelings and emotions. It also marks a particular day when a person or group of people will share grief together and it will also provide an opportunity to put closure on the grief or feelings of shame.

A healing ceremony is a very personal exercise, but there are some guiding steps that might help you plan one out.

YOUR HEALING CEREMONY

The purpose of your ceremony...
....

Date or time of year: ....

Where will the ceremony take place? ....
....

Who will be involved? ....
....

Will there be anyone else at the ceremony?....................................
....

What symbol or object will represent your feelings? Some
examples might include beads, rocks, water, a book, objects from
nature.
Symbol:...

What would you like to do at the ceremony? What will your
actions include?..
....

What would you like to say at the ceremony? What words will
you use?
....
....

Will you create a memory for the healing ceremony? You
might have a healing song, poem, or picture that you use for
future ceremonies.
Memory: ....
....

Draw or illustrate a picture of your healing ceremony.

CHAPTER 9

Lessons on Accomplishments, Resilience, and Support Systems

LESSON 23 CHALLENGES, OBSTACLES, AND BARRIERS

Before you examine all of the positive coping skills you have, it is helpful to take a good look at all of the challenges, obstacles, and barriers you have had to overcome. The model below (identical to the model shown in Figure 4.1 on p. 127) illustrates different levels of challenges that students reported having to cope with after they immigrated to Canada.

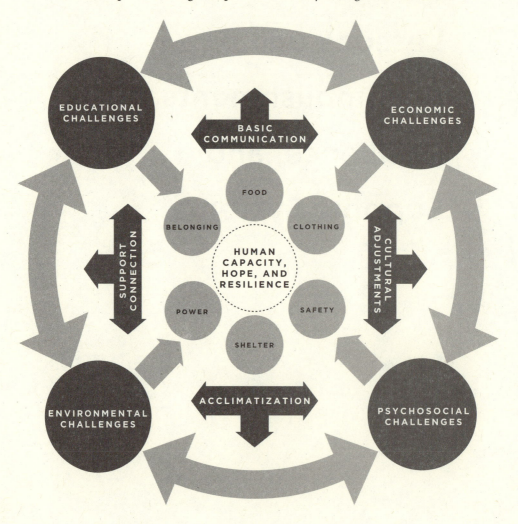

ILLUSTRATION 9.1 *Adjustment Challenges for Refugee Children*

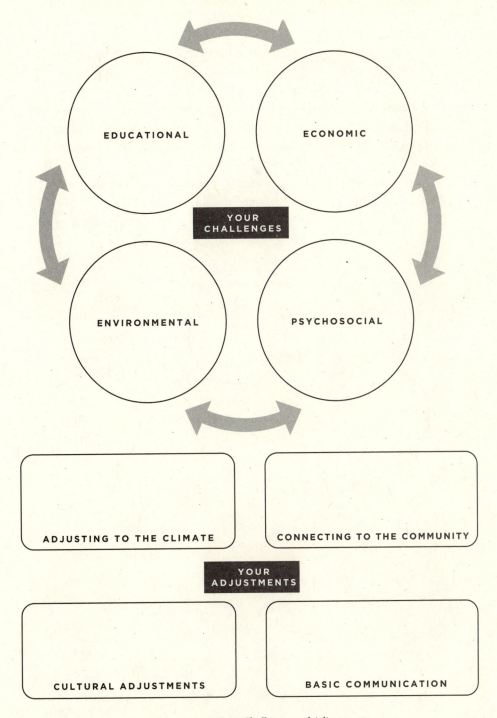

ILLUSTRATION 9.2 *Your Challenges and Adjustments*

Using the spaces in Illustration 9.2 (previous page), take a moment to consider and write down the challenges you have overcome or ones that you continue to struggle with up to this day. The model in Illustrations 9.3 and 9.4 are deconstructed versions of the ones in Illustration 9.2 on the previous page, and space is left for you to write down and record all of your challenges. Sections have been dissected so that it is easier for you to record information.

In each of the spaces in Illustration 9.3, write one example of a need that might have been difficult to acquire. In the part of the circle labeled strengths, write a list of your personal strengths. In the smallest circle, write a word that represents what you hope for in the future.

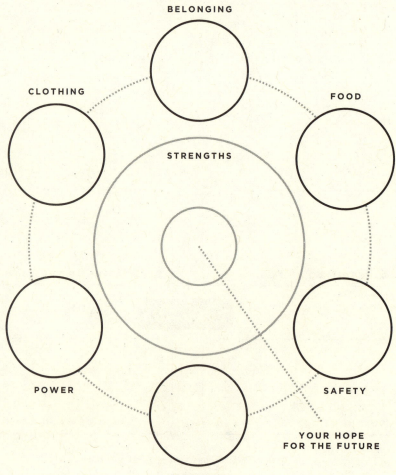

ILLUSTRATION 9.3 *Your Basic Needs*

LESSON 24 HUMAN CAPACITY, HOPE, AND RESILIENCE

Now that we have examined the challenges, adjustments, and changes that refugee students have had to go through, it is time to focus on the individual strengths and the personal capacity that individuals have to help them overcome challenging circumstances. To cope with adversity, a person has certain attributes, characteristics, or strengths. Consider all of your personal strengths. To be a refugee and to have moved to a completely different country already indicates that you have a tremendous amount of resilience. It can be helpful to take a look at all of your strengths and to see that you have many characteristics and traits that can help you work through adversity.

Researchers who study resiliency have identified certain "protective factors." These factors "protect" or support the person when they are dealing with challenges. The more protective factors you have, the more skills or support you have that will assist you with difficult situations.

Resilience is not something you either have or you don't. Resilience is built up over time through experiencing different situations. In fact, dealing with adversity or difficult situations is one way to develop resilience. When an individual has many protective factors, it does not mean that they are resilient and can handle all situations. These people will also feel overwhelmed and insecure when they are faced with adversity. Every situation is different and an individual will also respond differently to each situation.

Before you take a look at your protective factors, try to recall some events in your life that you feel have been both challenging and something you have learned from.

Draw or write about a situation that you believe was challenging, yet in the end helped you to develop positive coping skills.

Protective factors are not the same for everyone; however, there are some factors that are frequently associated with resilience. Each factor in the list of protective factors below is accompanied by a scale of 1 to 10 representing the level of protection if offers you. Circle a number that best reflects your situation. The number 1 represents the least amount of protection you feel that you have and 10 represents the highest possible level.

PROTECTIVE FACTOR	THE LEVEL OF PROTECTION IT OFFERS
1. Being connected to your school	1 2 3 4 5 6 7 8 9 10
2. Being connected to your community	1 2 3 4 5 6 7 8 9 10
3. People who support you	1 2 3 4 5 6 7 8 9 10
4. A person you can go to if you need help	1 2 3 4 5 6 7 8 9 10
5. Feeling good about yourself	1 2 3 4 5 6 7 8 9 10
6. Involvement in school activities	1 2 3 4 5 6 7 8 9 10
7. Playing sports	1 2 3 4 5 6 7 8 9 10
8. Having a sense of hope (optimism)	1 2 3 4 5 6 7 8 9 10
9. A sense of humour (laughing)	1 2 3 4 5 6 7 8 9 10
10. A strong belief system (e.g., spirituality)	1 2 3 4 5 6 7 8 9 10
11. Being flexible (accepting change)	1 2 3 4 5 6 7 8 9 10
12. Able to solve problems	1 2 3 4 5 6 7 8 9 10
13. Ability to learn (e.g., doing well in school)	1 2 3 4 5 6 7 8 9 10
14. Close family relationships	1 2 3 4 5 6 7 8 9 10
15. Close friends	1 2 3 4 5 6 7 8 9 10
16. Money to buy food, clothes, and pay the rent	1 2 3 4 5 6 7 8 9 10
17. A secure place to live	1 2 3 4 5 6 7 8 9 10
18. Skills to handle conflict	1 2 3 4 5 6 7 8 9 10
19. Feeling okay about how you look	1 2 3 4 5 6 7 8 9 10
20. Access to places in community for support	1 2 3 4 5 6 7 8 9 10
Using the same scale, how would you rate your current level of resilience?	1 2 3 4 5 6 7 8 9 10

LESSON 25 BRIDGING THE CONNECTION

The first lesson discussed how sometimes people who are new to a culture feel like they are caught between two worlds. Some people feel like they no longer belong to their home country and, now that they live in Canada, they feel like they have not totally adjusted to life and that there are still many challenges for them to overcome.

It is not necessary for you to forget or to lose the customs and culture of your home country, nor is it necessary for you to adopt all of the Canadian ways of life. Each person will have a very individual plan for how they would like to bridge the two worlds. Each individual will determine what memories they want to keep and the memories they want to forget. They will also decide who will best support them with bridging the two worlds.

A bridge is used to join two pieces of land. Illusration 9.4 (p. 243) shows that there are two sides to the bridge, water underneath it, and a solid structure to keep the bridge up. Try designing your own bridge based on the sample, or use the sample to plan your bridge.

1. On one parcel of land (one side of the bridge), decide what you would most like to remember about your culture, customs, or way of life before you moved to Canada.
2. On the other parcel of land (other side of the bridge), decide what you enjoy or appreciate about the culture, customs, or way of life in Canada.
3. On the metal supports of the bridge structure, list the names of people who will support you in adjusting to life in Canada. Who can you lean on?
4. On top of the bridge, list your personal characteristics that tell what kind of person you are. List activities and events that you enjoy. What kind of personality do you have? What makes you unique?
5. In the sky over the top of the bridge, write down your dreams for yourself. Who do you want to become, what do you want to accomplish? What are some of your goals?

6. Now decide on what memories or events you would like to
   forget. You can also choose to change or discard some of your
   personal characteristics. Put these in the water.

Moving forward and dealing with change does not have to be a
negative experience. You can decide for yourself how you would like
to connect your two experiences. You do not have to feel like you are
stuck in the middle. There is a way, if you work at it, that you can bridge
or connect your experiences so that you remain true to yourself and in
control over your future. Sometimes, just deciding for yourself what
you most like from the two worlds will give you the structure you need
to move forward.

ILLUSTRATION 9.4 *Bridging the Connection*

LESSON 26 SYSTEMS OF SUPPORT

Not everyone experiences the same patterns of adjustment. For some, the process of adjustment is filled with anger, frustration, and sadness. For others, things seem to go their way and the experience of living in a new culture is very positive. When life goes well, people are happy, energetic, and excited about their futures. When individuals have difficulties adjusting, they run the risk of getting sick or emotionally distressed. This can be a difficult time because many people who are new to a country do not know where they can go to get support.

In Canada, there are various places where you can go to get support for yourself. Seeing a counsellor or an adviser is not looked upon negatively. In Canada, people see counsellors for a variety of reasons, sometimes to get advice on where to go to get a job or, for other times, just to talk to someone to get a second opinion. You are not sick because you go to talk to someone; it just means that you are looking after yourself. Some people who are new to a country fear that they will be sent back to their country of origin if they talk about their personal issues. This is not the case in Canada. A counsellor is confidential and will keep information about you private. You have a right to this privacy and you are entitled to ask that your counsellor keep your information to himself or herself. The only time that a counsellor is permitted to share information is when you talk about hurting yourself or someone else. If you are in danger and your safety is a concern, a counsellor will tell someone who will help him or her help you.

If you do not feel comfortable talking to someone, there are other things that you could also try. Consider some of the options that you have in your community or school for where you might get support if you are experiencing difficulties. Who are your supports?

Illustration 9.5 is based on a model that helps you identify the people or places that could help you support yourself. Fill in the diagram on the following page with names, places, and individuals who could support you.

If you know the address, phone number, website, or email address of the person or place, list it as well, so that if you need to go back to your Circles of Support, you have all of the information you need.

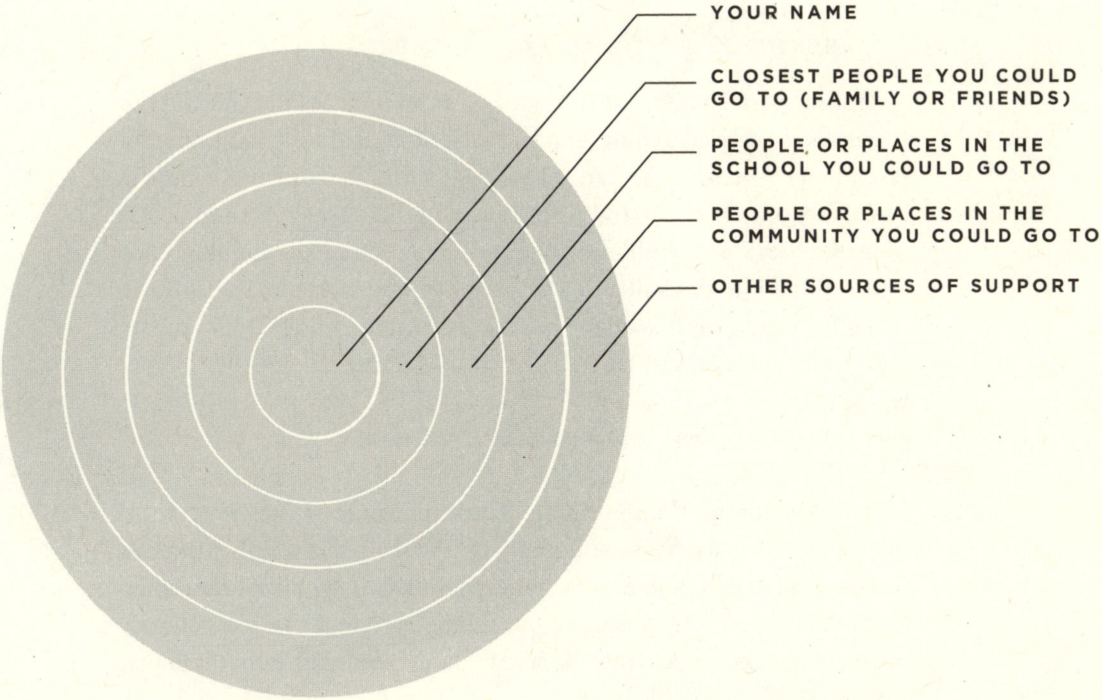

YOUR NAME

CLOSEST PEOPLE YOU COULD
GO TO (FAMILY OR FRIENDS)

PEOPLE OR PLACES IN THE
SCHOOL YOU COULD GO TO

PEOPLE OR PLACES IN THE
COMMUNITY YOU COULD GO TO

OTHER SOURCES OF SUPPORT

ILLUSTRATION 9.5 *Circles of Support*

List the names and contact information of three people you could contact if you were having difficulty.

1..
....
....
2..
....
....
3..
....
....

LESSON 27 IT'S AS EASY AS ABC

It is important to do what you need to do to look after yourself. Long-term stress can lead to illness and other serious medical conditions. You are the only person who can get yourself through a difficult time. You only have one chance to live a healthy and productive life. Your choices now will decide a lot about your future. You have a choice about how you will handle the situations in your life: you can choose helpful or harmful strategies. It is up to you. You can choose to challenge yourself and to do something that will help you lead the kind of life that you dreamed of.

It's as easy as ABC. Attempt. Believe. Celebrate.

ATTEMPT: Attempt doing one thing just for yourself each day. Think of it as a one-a-day feel-good vitamin. Try something new. Pick up a new skill or hobby, join a club, make a new friend, go outside and enjoy nature, do something you enjoy, give someone a hug, tell someone you care about them, take time alone, laugh, do something that will give you a sense of accomplishment.

BELIEVE: You have the power to do anything you set your mind to. There are no boundaries to dreaming. Those who live with regret do so because they had a dream and they never tried to achieve it. Trying and not succeeding still leaves you better off than never trying at all. Believe in yourself and you can overcome the highest obstacles and face the greatest challenges. If you don't believe, you won't achieve.

CELEBRATE: Celebrate every success and every step that you take toward your dreams. Reward yourself with something you enjoy. Go for a walk, read a new book, style your hair differently or get a henna tattoo. Take time to celebrate all of your hard work. Remember to keep track of all of your successes so you always have a record of what you have achieved. Now it is time to put it all to writing. You'll do this by using the calendar in Illustration 9.6. It's easier to stick to a plan when you know what the plan is.

ATTEMPT: Fill in the calendar with something you will attempt to do each day just for yourself. Try to use a different idea for each day of the month. Here are some One-a-Day Ideas:

- Learn a new joke and tell it to someone
- Take a bath
- Sing a song in the shower
- Learn a dance step
- Write a poem
- Sculpt a sculpture
- Make a snowman
- Go for a walk
- Eat a new kind of food
- Learn a new recipe
- Send an email to a friend you haven't talked to in a while
- Set up or change your Facebook site

Try to think of as many One-a-Day Ideas that you can and put them in your calendar. When you attempt one, put a check mark in the box.

MONTH					YEAR	
ONE-A-DAY ATTEMPTS				ATTEMPT, BELIEVE, AND CELEBRATE		
SUNDAY	MONDAY	TUESDAY	WEDNESDAY	THURSDAY	FRIDAY	SATURDAY

ILLUSTRATION 9.6 *ABC Chart*

ILLUSTRATION 9.7 *Believe*

BELIEVE: Write down five things to say in your mind to help you to keep believing in yourself. For example, "I will get through this" or "I am strong and I can handle the situation." Fill in the caption bubbles with positive statements of encouragement.

Now remember to say these things to yourself every day. To help you remember, think about an action you do several times a day. You likely walk through a doorway each day. You eat or drink each day. Pick a time of day to cue yourself to remember to say something positive.

What will be your cue time?..

Every time you do this action each day, say one of your belief statements to yourself. If you do this several times a day, it will keep you thinking positively. When you are being positive, you can't be negative.

ILLUSTRATION 9.8 *Gifts*

CELEBRATE: In illustration 9.8, identify five celebration activites that you can do for yourself to help you celebrate your achievements, attempts, and accomplishments. Remember, trying something and making a mistake allows you to learn, and this is a step in the right direction. Use words or pictures.

LESSON 28 THE TRIPLE-A TEAM

In Canada, a Triple-A hockey team is a group of elite players. To be an elite player takes hours and hours of practice over many years. To be successful at something, it takes a lot of hard work and it is important for you to stay focused on the positive accomplishments you have made. On hard days, it is easy to forget all that you have worked to overcome. This is why it is a good idea to record or keep track of all your accomplishments and successes.

Get a blank journal or workbook and make a three-column list like the one in Illustration 9.9. Label the columns "Attempts," "Achievements," and "Accomplishments." Begin now and fill in all that you have accomplished in the last six months. Transfer this list to your journal and keep it going for as long as possible. You will be amazed at how much you really do and how much you get accomplished.

ATTEMPTS (THINGS I HAVE TRIED)	ACHIEVEMENTS (THINGS I HAVE EARNED)	ACCOMPLISHMENTS (THINGS I HAVE DONE)

ILLUSTRATION 9.9 *Triple A Chart*

LESSON 29 WISH BEADS

I had the opportunity to meet a grandmother in Uganda who makes beads out of recycled paper. She makes necklaces and bracelets to sell, and she earns enough to support eight children who have been orphaned because of war. Living in a poverty-stricken district in Kampala, this grandmother has very little, yet she has created a small business with limited resources as a means to survive.

Strips of paper, approximately ½ to 1 cm wide, are tightly rolled up and then covered in a clear sealant. It is best to use coloured flyers or magazine pages that are all one length to create beads that are similar in size. The beads can be made from a simple piece of paper cut out in the shape of a long thin triangle, rolled up and glued to make a bead. Use a strip of colourful paper about 1 cm wide at bottom, narrower at the top. Roll up the paper starting from the widest part and moving to the narrowest part of the paper (leaving space in the middle of the bead to string thread through later). When the rolling is about two-thirds complete, smear glue on the last third of the paper to seal it, and allow it to dry. Experiment with a few until you are satisfied with the size and shape that you need. The grandmother then strings together the larger beads with smaller spacer beads and affixes a clasp to create a beautiful piece of jewellery.

Beads are a wonderful tool to use as objects of reflection or meditation. If time does not permit, a variety of beads can be bought along with clasps and beading string. Large beads might be symbolic of a wish or a special thought, while smaller beads might be used as spacers. Beads might also be symbolic of a memory or a special event. Bracelets or necklaces could be given as a gift to a special person or worn by the students.

The beads might also be used as a relaxation exercise. Breathing exercises or positive self-talk might be associated with each bead.

Students who have a strong faith or spiritual connection may elect to create prayer beads.

This kind of activity is well suited to a group environment. It helps to break up awkward silences, and conversations develop naturally while students are engaged in this activity. At the end of the exercise, students will have something tangible to take with them after the group or session.

LESSON 30 PATTERNS OF ADJUSTMENT

Chapter 2 discussed the concept of "oscillating patterns of adjustment." In this explanation, the process of adjustment for refugees is said to go up and down, representing both the times when the individual feels like he or she is in harmony with the environment and times when he or she feels the challenges associated with culture shock.

The chart in Illustration 9.10 can help you track these experiences. Plot some of the major events that you have experienced that have contributed to your level of adjustment. The y axis (high or low) represents a level from zero to ten for the level of harmony you felt. The x axis (going right to left) represents the event that occurred in your life. Fill in the chart for six different events labeled *A* through *F*. For example, if event *A* represents "meeting a new friend in Canada" you might chart *A* at a level of eight or nine. Another example for event *B* might be "missing a family member" and you might chart this at a three or four. Fill in the chart for six events and write the event on the bottom of the chart using the space provided. Think about what events have contributed to you either moving closer to, or further away from, harmony with the environment. The higher the number, the more harmony you felt. The lower numbers represent more challenges and difficulty with adjusting.

A...

....

B...

....

C...

....

D...

....

E...

....

F...

EVENTS IN YOUR LIFE

ILLUSTRATION 9.10 *Adjustment scale*

LESSON 31 FOOTSTEPS

Some students do not feel comfortable tracing their feet. If this is the case, students can substitute their hands for their feet. If this, too, is difficult, any shape can be used or a foot can be drawn freehand. Give each student a pencil and a medium-sized piece of paper. Have them trace their feet two times (or only once, depending on time). Cut out the foot shapes. On two of the feet, illustrate and write "Where you have been and what you have accomplished." On the other set of footsteps, write "Where you are going and what you would like to accomplish."

If students feel comfortable displaying their work, create a large mural of a path or road on the wall. Display the footsteps around the room.

LESSON 32 MYSTERY BAG

This activity can be highly emotional. It is best to prepare students for this and to ensure that there is ample time after the activity so that you can debrief with the students. It is also a good idea to bring tissue, just in case.

Have each student bring in three objects that are special to him or her. These objects should be placed in a cloth bag that is not see-through. Ask students to consider why the object is special to them and what this object says about the kind of person they are. Each student is asked to bring their three objects in a bag and to have a turn presenting their objects and their explanations to the rest of the class.

Some possible items might include: photographs, a shirt, a shoe, a jacket, jewellery, figurines, certificates, cards, and so on.

PRESENTATION DAY

Clear away desks, if applicable, and have everyone sit in a circle either on the floor or on chairs. It is important that everyone be at the same level. Ask the students to take a turn when they feel ready. There is no need to go in order around the circle. Remind students that only one person is permitted to talk at once. When students are waiting for their turn, they should put their bags behind them or under their chair. When students present, they can allow questions or not. After they present their three objects, they can pass them around the group if they want. This is not advised for very special objects in case they get damaged. If anyone feels uncomfortable talking, they may want to just show their objects and have students ask questions. This is often easier than talking about what makes something special.

Some students may be presenting objects that are one of a few things they have from their home country. They might also bring in objects that once belonged to family members who have died. Many students fled their homes with only the clothes they were wearing, so bringing objects that they have had for a long time will not be possible and could make students feel uncomfortable. Some students could also draw a picture of a memory that is very important to them; this picture could then be put in the bag.

The option to pass should also be offered to all students as this could be potentially sensitive for many. It can also be an absolutely amazing exercise to do when there is a strong sense of trust in a group. I would not suggest doing this with group members that are fairly new to one another. It is best done with students who have been in a class or a course together for a period of time.

LESSON 33 PERFORMANCE MASKS

Masks are worn throughout the world in many cultures as a means of expression, performance, or spirituality. Normally worn on the face, a mask can protect or conceal the performer or the mask can act as makeup. The use of a mask often denotes power and mystery. In many cultures, the masked performer is the central character and the one who holds the most power. Masks play an important part in theatre performances throughout the world and particularly in non-western cultures. Masks are also used in celebrations such as carnivals, festivals, and ceremonies. It is important to note that in some cultures the use of a mask is used to communicate with spirits.

This lesson must be taught cautiously and only when the teacher discusses the meaning of the mask and how students perceive using the mask in performance. If students are uncomfortable, I suggest making puppets or another appropriate prop.

The purpose is to conceal the performer and to provide a layer of safety between the performer and the audience. Students should be encouraged to make their own mask, but due to time constraints, masks could also be purchased from a store and then used for future years. Taking students to the store to buy the masks is advised.

The following suggestions are possible starters for a skit the students can develop. The end audience for this skit might be fellow classmates, teachers, or community members.

1. Have students work in small groups to explore a topic related to one of the challenges they experienced after coming to Canada. Students are to write a skit or series of vignettes to teach others about the challenges for refugee students.
2. Have students work in small groups to share a success that they have had in Canada or a story about how someone overcame a challenge.
3. Have students tell a folktale or a story from their culture using the masked characters.
4. Have students write a skit about what they have learned in a unit of a class. The skit could be an alternative assessment

strategy for determining the knowledge students have acquired in a particular topic.

5. Have students develop a skit that has a political message or a skit that advocates for a group of people.

6. Have students create a ceremony or festival as a culminating event for a group or a course.

Craft stores sell Styrofoam mask forms that could be decorated by students using various objects (e.g., feathers, ribbons, buttons, yarn, sequins, beads).

LESSON 34 DJEMBES

Djembes and other African drums are musical instruments, ceremonial objects, and tools for communication. The drum can be played many ways to create different sounds and tones. It can also be played softly or loudly. The purpose of this activity is to explore a variety of feelings/emotions using the drum as a tool of expression.

Play a variety of beats and have students talk about what feeling or emotion could be associated with the sound. Alternatively, have a list of feeling words and ask the students to play a sound on the drum that represents the word. Play the drum and have students move their bodies to the sound that they hear (e.g., jumping, running, skipping). Vary the tempo of the movement.

Have students develop a poem either individually or as a group. Play the drum when particular words or sounds appear in the text. Many students have also written their personal stories and adding the drum or other instruments as they read them can be used to create effect.

Words can be associated with a particular type of beat. Words of a story can be repeated in the poem and the students can drum in unison when the text appears. Individual students can be assigned a line of a poem to drum. Encourage students to use different tones, volume, rhythm, and different parts of the hands or body to create different sounds and techniques.

Some students may feel inhibited to do this activity. It might be necessary to separate the students into groups where they feel safe with their peers. Having students move to sound might be a completely different type of exercise, and they may not be ready to do this activity.

CHAPTER 10

Culminating Lessons, Looking Forward, and Promoting Peace

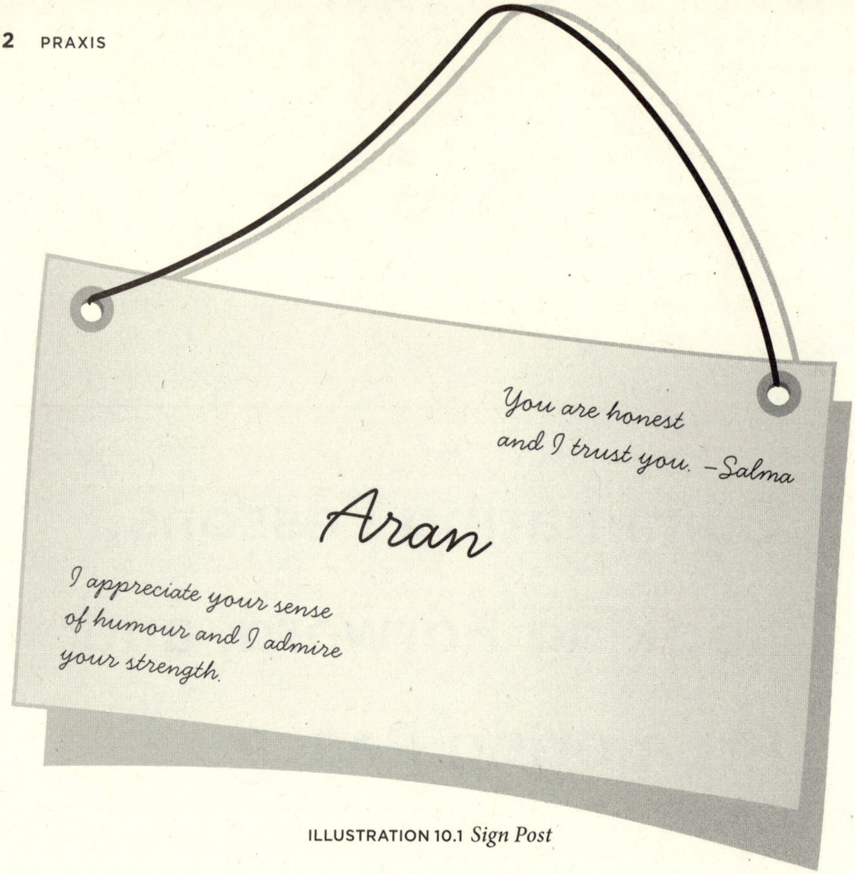

You are honest
and I trust you. —Salma

Aran

I appreciate your sense
of humour and I admire
your strength.

ILLUSTRATION 10.1 *Sign Post*

LESSON 35 SIGN POST

This lesson is best done as a culminating activity to provide closure to a class or a group. The purpose is to provide students with a collection of supporting words or positive memories that they can use as a source of encouragement after the group or class has finished.

Provide each student with a piece of cardstock (photo paper also works) the size of a standard piece of paper and a piece of ribbon. Punch two holes in the cardstock and run the ribbon through so that the student has a hanging sign. Have each student write his or her name in the middle of the card and then hang the card so it displays across the student's back.

Have all of the students walk around and write a word of encouragement on each student's card. This can be anonymous or students can sign their names to their statements.

When everyone has had the opportunity to sign the back of the cards, students can remove the cards and read the signs.

A variation of this activity is to provide index cards to each student. Have students write their name on their set of cards. For example, if there are 15 students in the class, each student would receive 15 index cards and he or she would write their name on all of the cards. Students should write a card to themselves as well. Collect all of the cards and distribute one of each name card to each student. Each student would then have 15 different index cards (one for each student in the class). Each student will then write a note of encouragement or support on the index card. All of the cards can be collected and put into an envelope and either given to the student at the end of the class or mailed to the student after the course is completed.

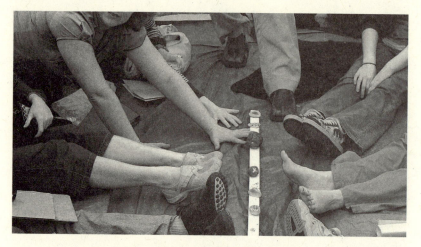

ILLUSTRATION 10.2 *Wish Ceremony*
A wish ceremony with students at the University of Winnipeg as a final exercise in the course Teaching and Assisting Children Affected by War.

LESSON 36 WISH STONES

This lesson has been adapted from an activity in *A Kind of Friendship: Working for and With War Affected Children and Youth* published by the Children as Peacebuilders (CAP) Project.

MATERIALS: One stone per person, non-washable paint and brushes. A wishing well or piece of coloured paper to place the stones on during the ceremony.

Discuss the concept of granting wishes. Each student is to bring a stone (something that would cover the palm of their hand). Students are to create their own wish-granting stone. Some students like to put a word on their stone that represents their wish, while others like to create a design or a symbol. It is important to use non-water-soluble paint. If water-based paint is used, the paint will smudge and run off when it gets wet.

When the group is done, have a wishing ceremony or create a wishing well in the centre of the room. Each student says what his or her wish is and places the stone in the well. The option to pass or not to share should be provided, as this can be a difficult exercise for some students.

LESSON 37 PEACE MANDALAS

A mandala is a circular model that represents wholeness. The word mandala originates in Indian culture. This holistic structure can be used to present or display information while at the same time showing how this information is connected and how one concept intersects with another. This interconnectedness demonstrates how all of the separate parts contribute to the overall structure. The mandala reminds us of our relationship to the world that extends beyond and within our bodies. A mandala represents a sign of change or transformation and it is often associated with the emergence of something new or a new understanding of self (Malchiodi, 2007).

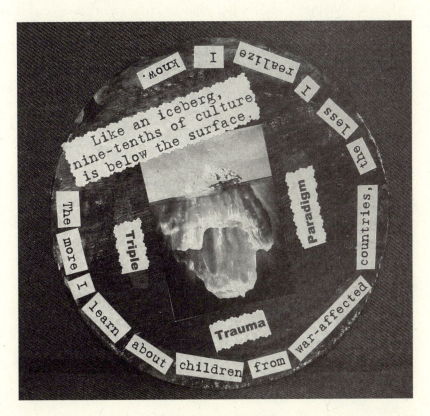

ILLUSTRATION 10.3 *Mandala*

Tibetan monks believe that a mandala consists of five excellencies: The Teacher, The Message, The Audience, The Site, and The Time.

Ask students to think about objects in nature that might represent a concept of wholeness (e.g., sun, moon, flowers, food, shells). Encourage students to examine a variety of objects to investigate how the separate parts contribute to the creation of the entire structure.

Provide each student with a circular piece of paper. As this is a very abstract concept to teach, have students do an online search to see examples of various types of mandalas.

Have each student create a personal mandala that represents the concept of peace and unity (coming together).

A variation on this activity is to cut out two very large circles on paper. Cut up one circle and divide it into as many equal parts as there are students in the class. Give each student a triangle of paper and ask them to create a collage or picture representing the concept of peace. When each student has completed his or her pie piece, have the group collaboratively arrange and glue together the pieces onto the other large circle.

LESSON 38 CANADA'S REPORT CARD

Before looking beyond our borders to investigate conflict, violence, and peace-building initiatives in countries around the world, it is important to examine the role of conflict and violence in Canadian society. How is Canada doing in terms of promoting a culture of peace? What are we doing well? What needs to improve? Gather examples and evidence from numerous sources to support the grades you would give to Canada. How well is Canada working toward a socially just world?

Section 1

Explore a variety of sources before you assign your grades and write your comments. Consider the evidence that you find from your investigation. Is there a culture of peace that is promoted on the source, or is there a culture of violence or conflict that you see? On the chart in Illustration 10.4a, list a grade for each of the outcomes based on evidence from your sources.

- Television Shows
- Websites
- Literature
- Workplaces
- Professional Sports and Youth Sports
- School Culture
- Crime Statistics/Police Reports
- Movies
- Games
- Local and National News
- Newspapers
- Blogs/Twitter

ILLUSTRATION 10.4a *Canada's Report Card*

OUTCOMES	GRADE	EVIDENCE/COMMENTS
Canada's Grade in Promoting Peace		
Canada's Grade for Dealing Effectively with Conflict		
Canada's Grade for Eradicating Violence		
Canada's Grade for Positive International Relations		
(insert your own criteria)		

ILLUSTRATION 10.4b *Canada's Report Card*

PERSONAL AND SOCIAL MANAGEMENT SKILLS	GRADE	EVIDENCE/COMMENTS
Works Independently		
Organization		
Respect for Diversity		
Responsibility and Reliability		
Work Habits and Follow-through		
Cooperation		
Initiative		
Social Responsibility		
Demonstrates Appropriate Behaviour		
Sets, Monitors, and Evaluates Goals		

Section 2

Consider how well you think Canada is performing in terms of personal and social management. On the chart in Illustration 10.4b, assign a grade to each of these using the criteria below.

E = Excellent

G = Good

S = Satisfactory

N = Needs Improvement

ILLUSTRATION 10.4c *Canada's Report Card*

ISSUE	GRADE	EVIDENCE/COMMENTS
Poverty		
Education		
Human Rights		
Sanitation		
Hunger		
Homelessness		
Medical Services		
Child Protection		
Racism		
Discrimination		
Violence		

Section 3

How well is Canada dealing with the following issues related to social justice? On the chart in Illustration 10.4c, assign a grade using the same criteria from the previous section (E, G, S, N).

Issues include:
- Poverty
- Education
- Human Rights
- Sanitation
- Hunger
- Homelessness
- Medical Services
- Child Protection
- Racism
- Discrimination
- Violence

Consider some of Canada's Strengths and Weaknesses and what the country needs to work at in terms of promoting a culture of peace and a more socially just country/world.

Strengths

Weaknesses

Section 4: The Interview

If you were calling in Canada's top leaders from across the country to have an interview to discuss Canada's report card, what would be the most urgent issue that you think would need to be addressed in terms of promoting a culture of peace and social justice?

Write what you would discuss in the following space.

The facilitator can take this a step further and have students role-play this interview with two students representing Canada and two students acting as teachers.

ILLUSTRATION 10.4d *Canada's Report Card*

OUTCOMES	GRADE	EVIDENCE/COMMENTS
My Grade for Promoting Peace		
My Grade for Dealing Effectively with Conflict		
My Grade for Eradicating Violence		
My Grade for Supporting Social Justice Issues		
(insert your own criteria)		
My Strengths		
My Weaknesses/What I Need to Work On		

Section 5: Self-Assessment

Now that you have done an assessment of Canada's role in promoting peace and social justice, consider your role in achieving the same outcomes. How would you assess your progress? What are your strengths and what do you need to work on? Grade yourself on the chart in Illustration 10.4d.

ILLUSTRATION 10.5 *Inukshuk created by Jack Dunlop*

LESSON 39 THE WAY TO PEACE

An inukshuk is an Inuit cultural symbol. It is a landmark or monument (also called a "cairn") built from stone. The Inuit were once nomadic people of Canada, and the inukshuk was erected by the Inuit to point the way for travellers. It might also warn of impending danger, be a mark of respect, or help with hunting animals or catching fish. An inukshuk might also be erected as a memorial. The arms of the inukshuk point the way to food, water, or shelter. In some instances, the long legs of the inukshuk would create a covering where people could camp underneath or where food would be stored out of the weather. Inuksuit (plural for inukshuk) vary in shape and size. Typically, one or two rocks form the head, a larger rock marks the arms, and smaller rocks form the trunk and the legs. The practice of erecting inuksuit along national highways and provincial parks is common across Canada. The Inuit tradition forbids the destruction of inuksuit.

Using Illustration 10.6, create an inukshuk to point the way toward peace. First, consider what attitudes or thoughts you need to promote (the head). Next, what is one thing that you are willing to personally commit to as a means of promoting peace? In other words, what direction will you take going forward? On the trunk section, write what support or help you need to achieve what you are committed to achieving. On the leg rocks, list concrete actions that you will take in order to reach your commitment goal.

Fill in the outline of the inukshuk and then create your own model to leave somewhere as a reminder of your commitment to peace. To create the model, collect rocks to create the figure. It is easiest to use a glue gun to keep the rocks together if you need to move the inukshuk. The inukshuk can be mounted on a piece of foam core (two cardboard pieces with foam in between).

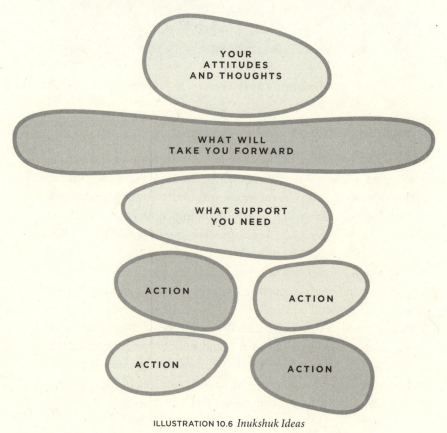

ILLUSTRATION 10.6 *Inukshuk Ideas*

LESSON 40 MICRO AND MACRO MESSAGES OF PEACE AND SOCIAL JUSTICE

A personal vision for peace is a statement of commitment from an individual or group. Decide what issue or advocacy statement you could create to encourage others to work toward a world with peace. Create a micro message to be displayed on a button or a name tag. There are button-maker kits available that can be used to create the micro messages. If this is not available, name tags could be used. A three-word phrase or one-word statement fits the best. Buttons can be worn by the group or individuals to promote a micro message of peace. Words such as HOPE, UNDERSTANDING, TOLERANCE, ACCEPTANCE, or FORGIVENESS are examples of micro messages that may be used. Students can then wear their message at home, at school, or in the community.

A macro message is similar, but it is done on a much larger scale. Bulletin boards, murals, or school signs work well for this activity. Create a group macro message that promotes peace and social justice. The message should be only one sentence, and all students must work collaboratively and cooperatively to reach consensus on the words that will be used. The message can be decorated with pictures from newspapers or magazines, or students may wish to create artwork using paints, felts, crayons, or pencil crayons. Students might sign the macro message as a personal sign of commitment.

ILLUSTRATION 10.7 *Baggage*

LESSON 41 JOURNEY'S END

The following activity is a personal reflection based on the student's personal growth throughout the classes or sessions. I was inspired by one of my university students to create this lesson. As a final project for my course Teaching Children Who Have Been Affected by War, I asked the students to show me what they had learned throughout the course. I asked students to choose a suitable genre or media source that would best represent their learning. A variety of projects were created: videos, songs, poetry, books, scrapbooks, magazines, slide shows, paintings, collages, sculptures, mandalas, storybooks, reader's theatre, and more. Illustration 10.7 is a photograph is from a student who chose to create a collage in a suitcase. Here is how she describes the process:

> I chose the suitcase as my three-dimensional collage object. I know that the onus of my experiences in this class will change day to day. This suitcase physically represents the weight of knowledge I know I will always now carry with me. You and I know a suitcase as an object built to carry things, the object we use to travel. The suitcase is the object we use to carry our belongings while we go on exciting vacations. An individual who is an immigrant to Canada might see a suitcase as an object in which he or she carries a few prize, hand-selected treasures to their new homeland. Individuals who are refugees know a suitcase as a luxury they have never known; they have no opportunity to thoughtfully collect any belongings. They do not know this comfort. As a teacher, I recognize this suitcase, my suitcase, as the baggage I carry with me when I enter a school, a classroom, and the lives of all my students.

> I feel that one of the most impressionable themes of this class has been connection: connection to family, connection to homeland, connection to a world unknown ... famine, fast food, loneliness, community. The web represents my day-to-day life and the world wars that are happening simultaneously. The web I have created in my suitcase represents the connections associated with my own life and war-affected children. I find myself having daily realizations

about how close I have been to several countries at war, about how many of the people I know who would consider themselves war-affected. The web is a visual reminder of this connectivity that can neither be erased nor ignored.

My baggage does not tell any specific story other than my own. I acknowledge that I have grown in this class; I know that I still have much growing and learning to do. I know that the knowledge I carry in this suitcase will belong to me always, I will not ignore it because it will only become a heavier weight on my heart. I do not look at this object as an entirely negative or positive thing. It is a representation of the changes that have, are, and will happen in my world. *Baggage* is a physical representation of the knowledge I carry and responsibility I accept.

—Lacey Jade Collins

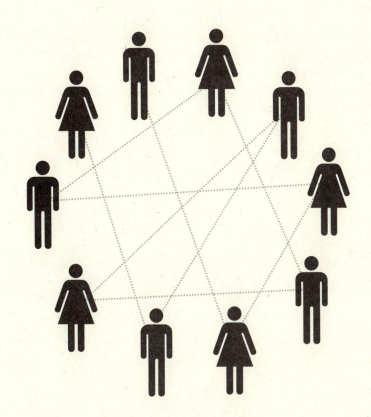

ILLUSTRATION 10.8 *A Web of Connections*

LESSON 42 A WEB OF CONNECTIONS

Have each student think about something meaningful they have discovered about themselves over the time they have been involved with the group/course. Alternatively, students could state something important they have learned from the group.

Each person will have the opportunity to speak when it is his or her turn.

Have all group members sit in a circle on the floor. The facilitator goes first and holds a large ball of yarn. The facilitator begins with a statement and then rolls the ball of yarn to a person across the circle (be sure to hold on to the end of the yarn when you roll it). Each student has a turn when he or she receives the ball of yarn. As each student has a turn, the yarn creates a web of connections (Illustration 10.8). After the last student has spoken, return the ball of yarn to the facilitator. To close the activity, the facilitator thanks the students for their contributions and then ties off the yarn.

CHAPTER 11

Recommendations for Policy and Practice

RECOMMENDATIONS FOR SCHOOL LEADERS

The role of the school leader can greatly influence the overall culture of the school and can also be the driving force behind school reform (Fullan, 2001; Leithwood & Jantzi, 1999; Leithwood, Jantzi, & Steinbach, 1999). There is a need for stronger leadership and for school leaders to take action against issues related to injustice. Moreover, participants from the microsystem most frequently discussed the need for the school to interact and work in partnership with other agencies and programs in the community. As both the literature and the research suggests, the role of the school leader is paramount to the process of guiding change and for creating a socially just system. The focus for the first set of recommendations directly targets what school leaders can do to improve the success of refugee students. Following this, recommendations will be offered for consideration by federal and provincial governments, local school divisions, and community agencies.

School leaders have the ability to articulate a clear stand against war, violence, and the abuse of human rights. Moreover, they are uniquely positioned within the school and the community to address issues of inequity, power, and oppression. Training school leaders through administrator preparation programs, annual meetings, professional development seminars, conference proceedings, and journal articles are all means with which to create school leaders who are more committed to issues of social justice. School leaders can facilitate the transformation of the school culture, curriculum, and pedagogical practices to more appropriately meet the needs of refugee children.

The Interstate School Leaders Licensure Consortium (ISLLC) developed six standards that were intended to improve the quality and integrity of school leaders (Council of Chief State School Officers, 1996). Joseph Murphy, who is a leading scholar in the field of educational administration, chaired the consortium, which was originally comprised of 24 member states. Presented in 1996, 40 states have now either adapted or adopted the ISLLC framework (Murphy, 2005). The most notable use of the standards is to form the basis of assessment and licensing of school leaders (Murphy, 2005). For the purpose of this discussion, the ISLLC standards provide the most comprehensive and solid platform on which to base the following recommendations and subsequent discussion.

Recognizing that the social fabric of society has changed, and will continue to change, the perspective of the consortium was to "focus on the heart and soul of effective leadership" and the "creation of powerful learning environments" (Council of Chief State School Officers, 1996, p. 8). While all six standards are relevant to the development of effective school leaders, the last three are of particular interest to this study and are stated as follows:

> STANDARD 4: A school administrator is an educational leader who promotes the success of all students by collaborating with families and community members, responding to diverse community interests and needs, and mobilizing community resources.

STANDARD 5: A school administrator is an educational leader who promotes the success of all students by acting with integrity, fairness, and in an ethical manner.

STANDARD 6: A school administrator is an educational leader who promotes the success of all students by understanding, responding to, and influencing the larger political, social, economic, legal, and cultural context.

Standard 4 articulates the importance of creating and maintaining strong interactions within the various systems. The lack of interaction between the various systems and the school was the most frequently occurring theme discussed by members of the microsystem. Schools are an integral part of the larger community and the school is a fundamental system in students' lives. That said, the school leader should facilitate the activities and processes that link the various systems that influence students. It is advised that school leaders collaborate with parents and community groups by: (1) providing welcoming information (print, video, computer-based) in multiple languages represented in the community, (2) providing translation services to help parents and students who are not proficient in English, and (3) encouraging parents to attend school functions by eliminating barriers (language, work schedules, child care) that prohibit their involvement.

School leaders must also establish partnerships with refugee community groups and businesses to support the following: (1) mentoring and tutoring programs, (2) school-community liaison workers, and (3) increased opportunities for students to take part in sport and recreation activities. School leaders should also implement a school-based plan to encourage collaboration and to develop networks of support amongst the school staff in an effort to decrease feelings of isolation.

Before responding to the community's needs and interests, the school leader must first actively engage in dialogue with community members to learn about the prevailing issues. To assess the needs of the community, the following four recommendations are advanced: (1) school leaders should document specific demographic data pertaining to marginalized students and their achievement in school,

(2) achievement data should be recorded throughout the year and there should be greater accountability for the achievement of all students, (3) school leaders should also collect data on the number of students accessing mental health services within the school community, and (4) school leaders should also engage in continuing conversations with the staff and students on issues related to social justice.

As Standard 5 states, the school leader must promote justice and equality. School administrators should exemplify the characteristics of ethical and moral behaviour, and they should be the advocates for the children, their families, and the communities they serve. It is essential for the school leader to set an example for the staff and the community by promoting equality, fairness, and respect. If the school leader does not exemplify these characteristics, the participants suggested that the overall tone and culture within the school will be adversely affected. When school leaders are committed to eradicating inequality and injustice, they will be able to recognize how the school system continues to marginalize and oppress certain groups of children. Moreover, they will be more apt to make changes to transform the system to better meet the needs of all students. Promoting justice requires reducing misunderstandings.

To promote the success of all students, school leaders should develop and implement pedagogical practices that strengthen the school culture. Theoharis's (2007) study found that schools that provided separate programs maintained the marginalization of particular students because students were provided inferior instruction. Over a span of four years, six out of the seven schools in his study eliminated segregated programs and all of these schools reported an increase in passing grades on local and state reading test achievement data for the English-language learners. The school is a primary source of socialization and when ethnically diverse students are not integrated, issues related to misunderstandings and misinterpretations between ethnic groups increase. Programs such as sports or after-school drop-in clubs increase integration and contribute to greater cultural understanding and acceptance. Supporting these structures and programs will benefit all students, particularly those who have been marginalized. The practice of segregated English as an Additional Language programs should be reviewed to determine whether this is the most appropriate educational environment for refugee children.

Promoting fairness equates to treating people equally. Although some would dispute this notion and suggest that it is impossible to treat people absolutely equally (Allison, 2005), it is a desirable goal and one that administrators should strive to achieve. School administrators should understand and utilize the legal system to protect the rights of all students and to serve as an advocate when students' rights are not respected.

Standard 6 suggests that the administrator understands global issues that affect teaching and learning. School leaders should be knowledgeable about the issues concerning refugee children and they should use this knowledge to influence policy makers at the federal, provincial, and school division levels. School leaders should also provide opportunities for staff to learn about the political, social, and cultural issues that influence students and the school community. School leaders must facilitate learning for all staff in the area of best practices for teaching English-language learners. Issues related to teachers' attitudes and behaviours were one of the top 10 most frequently occurring themes in the interviews with the school staff. The attitudes and behaviours that were discussed by the participants included: racism, discrimination, unfair treatment, exclusionary actions, and disrespectful comments. Most of the adult participants suggested that a lack of information about refugee students, combined with inadequate support for the staff, was what contributed to these counterproductive attitudes. That said, if these attitudes do exist and refugee students are treated in such a manner, then a comprehensive educational program is needed for all staff.

There is also a need for leaders to articulate a vision and direction for the school, to be a role model for moral and ethical behaviour, and to respond to the diverse needs of the school community. Using the aforementioned standards as the overarching framework to improve the capacity of school administrators will promote the kind of leadership that is needed to respond to the changing needs of society. Implementing the stated recommendations will promote the success of all students, including those who have come from countries of conflict.

RECOMMENDATIONS FOR FEDERAL AND PROVINCIAL GOVERNMENT DEPARTMENTS

The following recommendations are addressed to federal and provincial government departments. One of the major barriers influencing student learning was financial difficulty. Current federal government funding for newcomers expires after a period of one year, which is an inadequate length of time to support all of the challenges associated with post-migration. Students who engage in full-time studies should be provided with financial support to keep them in school. The following two recommendations are advanced: (1) the financial commitment from the federal government must extend until the student completes secondary school, (2) the repayment of the government loan to pay for the airfare to come to Canada should be waived for all refugees.

Federal and provincial governments need to engage coherently in the discourse on social justice. The school system is not the only system that influences the lives of students. Changes that contribute to the liberation of marginalized individuals must occur at all levels of the ecological system. Underachieving or disengaged students are the responsibility of governments, communities, families, and schools. That said, policies, programs, structures, and systems to support refugee students must be derived from meaningful and collaborative discussions and planning at the federal, provincial, and local levels in concert with newcomers to Canada as well as refugee workers, refugee council and refugee advocacy organizations.

Racism and discrimination were referenced by most, if not all, of the members of the various ecological systems. Racism and discrimination was an overarching challenge for refugee students living in Canada. Citizenship and Immigration Canada should develop and implement an educational program for all citizens to promote the benefits of receiving newcomers. Anti-racism and sensitivity training should be taught to all government agencies (e.g., justice system, child welfare, education), as well as to the general public and the business sectors. It is imperative that the public opinion regarding the acceptance of refugees remains positive. Preventative and proactive programs must be in place to counteract any negative or anti-refugee discourse.

Mediation and conflict resolution programs must be implemented in Canadian schools to address the conflict between various cultures. In particular, the existing conflict between the Aboriginal students and the immigrant students in Manitoba requires immediate attention. In collaboration with Citizenship and Immigration Canada, provincial education departments should establish a campaign to promote diversity and to combat racism and discrimination in all Canadian schools.

The provincial and federal governments should provide funding to establish a locally based Refugee Studies Centre to conduct research and to collect and disseminate information related to refugee issues. Similar to the Refugee Studies Centre in Oxford, England, this centre could be attached to a university and run under its existing structure of governance. The Refugee Studies Centre would conduct the following: (1) academic research related to refugee issues, (2) international advocacy projects related to refugees, (3) education related to international development and global conflict, and (4) education and training for those who work with refugee children and their families. Because education and the roles of the people within the school community figured so prominently in the lives of the students, the centre would best be aligned with a faculty of education. Courses related to teaching children affected by war must be incorporated into the training programs for undergraduate and post-graduate teachers, counsellors, and administrators.

RECOMMENDATIONS FOR LOCAL SCHOOL DIVISIONS

The local school divisions should develop a team of experts who are knowledgeable on the issues related to the educational and psychosocial needs of refugee children. This team should consist of psychologists, trauma workers, counsellors, community liaison workers, resource teachers, school leaders, and other support agencies. This team of support people could be divisionally based and be accessed by schools to assist children. Post-conflict and non-westernized models of psychosocial support must be available to all refugees. Evidence from this study clearly delineated issues related to the staff members feeling overwhelmed by the issues concerning refugee students. Moreover, staff members frequently indicated that they felt "unprepared" or "unable" to adequately meet the psychosocial needs of the students. Having a divisionally based support team of people who are knowledgeable and skilled in the area of supporting refugee students is needed to both provide assistance to the students and to support the school staff.

There should be a designated staff member in each school to be the case manager or support person for refugee children. These people would work with the transition support teams and other social agencies. Refugee support teachers would be based in each school where refugee students are enrolled. The percentage of time allocated for this position would vary depending on the number of refugee students in the school. The school division would need to ensure that staff is trained to assume these roles within the various schools.

It is recommended that school divisions consider offering courses outside of the typical school day or week to accommodate students and parents/caregivers who work. Weekend school programs or intensive newcomer support classes should be offered as an alternative to individuals who want to take additional courses or who need to upgrade. Many students were desperate to improve their education. It is essential that school divisions accommodate the needs expressed by these students. The federal government should allocate funding to the province so that alternative education programs are more accessible to newcomers.

School divisions must also provide psychosocial support to students and their families, particularly for issues related to loss, the separation of family members, violence exposure, gang awareness, and trauma. Most of the educational programming for newcomers is currently focused on acquiring language and numeracy skills. It is recommended that school divisions make provisions for ensuring that local schools can offer appropriate psychosocial support to students. Support groups, individual counselling, and classroom-based programs need to be implemented by qualified individuals who understand issues related to refugee students.

It is imperative that school divisions develop policy for the provision of English as an Additional Language programs. There must also be a serious commitment from local school divisions in the form of financial support and professional development to improve the outcomes for English-language learners.

RECOMMENDATIONS FOR COMMUNITY AGENCIES

Centralized reception centres for refugees must be able to provide long-term support to newcomers. Evidence from this study suggests that additional services are needed to mediate many of the continuing challenges for newcomers. Increasing services would necessitate the commitment of additional resources from the aforementioned funding sources.

The proposed centre would initially assist families and their children with settling into a school and the community and then it would also extend services to long-term post-migration assistance. A reception centre should include the following services: legal assistance, psychosocial counselling, family mediation, personal health and nutrition counselling, advocacy assistance, parenting classes, English-language support for parents and children, preschool programs, technology education, career development courses, and information on the rights and responsibilities of Canadians. Individuals within these aforementioned agencies would benefit from taking part in continuing discussions for the purpose of improving collaborative relationships and more interactive networks to support newcomers in the community.

Many of the students felt disappointed that their lives in Canada were not what they had imagined. It is advised that the services of the agencies that sponsor refugees as well as the services in the aforementioned reception centre extend to include pre-migration and trans-migration education and counselling for refugees. All refugees should be knowledgeable about what to expect before they immigrate to Canada.

RECOMMENDATIONS FOR TEACHERS

The advice generated from the students clearly outlined several suggestions that teachers could do to support refugee children. The evidence also demonstrated that there are numerous teachers in schools who are working tirelessly to do whatever is in their means to support children. The job that these people are doing is commendable, and the school system needs to do everything possible to support the work these people do.

The teachers in this study assumed various roles as counsellors, advocates, mentors, community liaisons, activists, and caregivers. Having said this, there are also many teachers who could do a lot more to support refugee children and for whatever reason they have either chosen not to or they were not sure what they could do to support these children.

The following recommendations are intended to provide teachers with some basic suggestions for supporting the adjustment of refugee students, for involving refugee children in school activities, and for being a culturally responsive teacher who creates a safe and accepting environment for all students.

INCREASE UNDERSTANDING OF INTERNATIONAL ISSUES: Many students arriving in Canadian schools originate from countries that are in tremendous conflict. Educators should be knowledgeable of the various conflicts in the world, so that they are better able to understand the unique needs of their students. Read online newspapers from countries where your students have originated so that you are able to discuss current events and learn about issues that are unique to the specific country. Keep up to date on environmental, political, and social events occurring in parts of the world.

ENHANCE ADULT AND STUDENT RELATIONSHIPS: Engage in activities, events, and programs that bring youths and adults together in a collaborative working relationship. Provide refugee youth with the opportunity to take part in leadership activities. Foster the development of their assets and unique skills and gifts.

DISPLAY CULTURALLY DIVERSE MATERIALS AND RESOURCES: Several books and posters are available that represent stories of refugees or pictures of culturally diverse people. Have these materials available for all students to access and incorporate the resources into your daily teaching lessons.

EDUCATE CANADIAN STUDENTS ABOUT THE IMPORTANCE OF DIVERSITY: Provide Canadian students with knowledge of cultures, human rights, and the personal stories of refugees. Highlight the strengths of refugee people and celebrate achievements they have made.

ADDRESS ISSUES OF RACISM AND DISCRIMINATION: When issues of racism, discrimination, stereotyping, racial profiling, or prejudiced attitudes arise, deal with it immediately. Take these actions seriously and use the behaviour as a means to educate students about human rights, diversity, the Charter of Rights and Freedoms, and other topics related to citizenship and social justice. Encourage students to talk about issues together in an open and safe environment.

ENCOURAGE ADVOCACY: Encourage students to use their experiences to advocate for change either in schools or in their community. When they see injustice, engage them in critical discussions and encourage them to stand for issues they believe in. Engaging youth in their own acts of liberation is essential to promoting a socially just environment.

UNDERSTAND CULTURE SHOCK: Refugee children will experience culture shock to a greater extent than many other students because of the magnitude of differences between their country of origin and Canada. Creating a "survival skills" lesson might be one strategy to provide intensive knowledge about westernized ways of life (e.g., opening a locker, talking to teachers, using the bathroom, reading a timetable). A suggestion would be to have former newcomer students write the "survival skills" for future newcomers.

SUPPORT THE INTEGRATION OF REFUGEE STUDENTS: Help refugee students integrate into the school community. Offer activities or clubs so students can engage with diverse groups of students. Encourage students to change their seating in a class, but only if it is safe to do so. Sports teams offer an excellent opportunity for students from diverse cultures to play and work together, particularly if students have difficulty with language. Assist with developing activities or workshops where the refugee students teach Canadian students about diversity or human rights issues.

LISTEN, ENCOURAGE, AND CARE: Students will share personal information with people they trust. In most cases, students do not like to be asked or probed about where they came from and what they have experienced. While you should never not ask, there is a difference between interest in their life and pressure to tell their story. When students do share about their past, listen. Listen actively and give them your undivided attention, paraphrase what you hear them say, ask for clarification if needed. Thank students for sharing their stories or personal experiences with you and keep them confidential unless safety is a concern. Reassure students, support them, and ensure that they feel understood.

TEACH COPING SKILLS AND STRATEGIES: This book offers a variety of coping skills and strategies to foster self-expression and understanding. Help students find appropriate ways to express themselves; if you don't, they will often resort to harmful behaviours to help them cope with events in their lives. Once these behaviours are adopted, it is far more difficult to break the cycle of harmful behaviour and introduce positive coping mechanisms.

KNOW WHEN TO REFER: When there are issues of safety, make a referral to a qualified individual (e.g., counsellor or psychologist) or to an agency that is better equipped to deal with psychosocial issues. If you see a change in behaviour or the student's behaviour is deteriorating (e.g., involvement with drugs or alcohol, criminal activity, physical violence,) refer the student to someone who is trained to counsel or provide therapy. If you have a "gut feeling" that something is wrong with a student, talk to him or her. If you get a sense that things are just not right, refer the student to a trained professional. If it ends up not being serious, you will still know (and so will the student) that you did this because you cared. If you act in the best interest of the student, you will know that you are following the correct path. The student may not know it at the time, but they will realize this later.

INVOLVE THE PARENTS OR GUARDIANS AS MUCH AS POSSIBLE: It is difficult for some refugee parents to get to the school because of younger children to look after or because they work, in many cases, two or more jobs. In some instances, parents will not know the (English or French) language and this will make it very difficult for them to come to talk to teachers. In many cultures, parents consider it a sign of disrespect to engage with the school. Nonetheless, make it easy for parents to come to talk to you. Get someone to look after children during parent meetings, offer translation services, provide print materials in the parent's language of origin. Keep attempting to involve the parents as much as possible; don't give up.

FOSTER AND ENCOURAGE THE LANGUAGE OF ORIGIN: Refugee students should be encouraged to maintain their language of origin. Their first language is an integral part of who they are and keeping this language alive is imperative. Encourage dual-language projects and support the sharing of languages amongst cultures. Celebrate diversity and encourage multiculturalism.

MAINTAIN HIGH EXPECTATIONS: Refugee children must not be viewed as victims or as traumatized students. Teachers must not assume that refugee children are at a disadvantage; rather, it is the teacher's challenge to uncover the various strengths, gifts, and talents of each individual. High expectations coupled with a supportive attitude will encourage students to strive for what they have set their mind on achieving. High aspirations create strong-willed individuals who are focused on a goal. Adversity is a strong motivator. Achieving goals for the refugee student might look different from the typical path of a Canadian student; nonetheless, the refugee student must be encouraged and supported to achieve the highest of expectations they set to accomplish. Although the refugee student will have challenges that a Canadian student will not have, evidence clearly supports that the majority of refugee students have a tremendous work ethic and a drive to create a successful life in Canada.

KNOW YOURSELF: Be aware of your own culture and belief system. Understand your role in Canadian society and culture and be aware of how your values, morals, and judgments will inform your teaching practices.

PURSUE PROFESSIONAL DEVELOPMENT OPPORTUNITIES: Know what you need to learn more about. Develop skill and competencies to better teach refugee children. Be open to learning more about teaching refugee children on such topics as: adjustment issues, psychosocial support, differentiated instruction, alternative assessment strategies, second-language instruction, and curriculum development.

The recommendations are not limited to those in the field of education. The issues revealed in this study and discussed in this book extend beyond the educational setting to the broader sociological, political, and ideological foundations of the culture in which we live. Canada has made a commitment to the international community through *The Responsibility to Protect* document (International Commission on Intervention and State Sovereignty, 2001), which makes every state responsible for protecting the basic human rights of all of its citizens. "The responsibility to protect implies the responsibility not just to prevent and react but to follow through and rebuild" (International Commission on Intervention and State Sovereignty, 2001, p. 39).

As a country, Canada needs to begin by taking a closer look at its responsibility to protect citizens within its own national boundaries. Canada's responsibility to protect must expand in scope to include its role to react, prevent, and to help rebuild the lives of refugee children and their families after they have immigrated to Canada. Coordinated support services are urgently needed to facilitate the positive transition of these children into Canadian society. Moreover, it is imperative that the people in the educational system acquire more knowledge about the experiences of refugee children to facilitate and foster a positive and productive learning environment for these students. Canada has agreed to welcome refugees into the country; as such, it is necessary to articulate what will be done to help these people be successful and productive members of society. This book reveals that many of these individuals are poised for achievement and success if the barriers that have been imposed are recognized and removed.

SUMMARY AND CONCLUSION

With the commitment of individuals who are willing to address the plight of children who have been affected by war with a sense of urgency and expediency, there is hope that these children will receive the basic entitlements and the appropriate education that they deserve.

Bronfenbrenner's bioecological model (2001) helped to reveal that a multi-ecological and coordinated program to support refugee children would likely ameliorate many of the challenges that they experience. Instead of working with children as isolated individuals, there needs to be more culturally appropriate and contextually inclusive approaches that focus on children who are part of a much larger ecological system. The centrality of a key member from the microsystem who created a much smaller and more intimate network of support for the student mediated many of their adjustment challenges. The emergence of a nanosystem was revealed when closely examining how the various systems functioned, how they interacted with one another, and how they supported the student. The addition of the nanosystem does not contradict the propositions set forth by Bronfenbrenner; rather, it illustrates the power of the proximal processes and the resulting networks that are created to support students who are in need.

As a country, Canada has a responsibility to protect refugee children, which includes the implementation of specific recommendations to help rebuild and reconstruct their lives post-migration. There should be a genuine and sincere commitment from the Canadian government, the provincial governments, the local school divisions, and the school communities to ensure that children who have been affected by war will be protected and supported after they immigrate to Canada.

Definitions of Terms

Acculturation

The process of cultural change and adaptation that occurs when an individual comes into contact with a different culture.

Adjustment

Adjustment is a life-long process whereby the individual changes his or her behaviour in order to create a more harmonious relationship with the environment. The term denotes a multidimensional and reciprocal process of change made by the individual who interacts with his or her physical and social environment. The environment must also adjust to meet the needs of the individual. Adjustment relates to a balance between an individual's needs and his or her level of satisfaction as well as the needs of the social environment.

Assimilation

Assimilation refers to the merging of cultural traits from a previously distinct cultural group to another culture that is usually more dominant. The process whereby a minority individual gradually adopts the customs and attitudes of another culture is referred to as cultural assimilation.

Asylum-Seeker

Is a person who has applied for refugee status in a foreign country.

Child

For the purposes of this book, the definition of *child* will be consistent with the definition adopted in the Convention on the Rights of the Child (1989), which states, "A child means every human being below the age of 18 years unless, under the law applicable to the child, majority is attained earlier" (Office of the High Commissioner for Human Rights, 1989). The discussion will centre on children who are at the high school level, ranging from the ages of 15 to 19. For the purposes of consistency, each adult fitting into this category will be referred to as a child.

Children Affected by War

With more than 30 wars worldwide occurring at the present time (War Strategy, 2006), and the unique circumstances surrounding these conflicts, this book will limit the scope of the discussion to children originating from Afghanistan and the sub-Saharan African regions, including: Sierra Leone, Uganda, Burundi, Rwanda, Liberia, and Sudan. The continent of Africa has, for the most part, been most seriously affected by major civil wars since 1960. Although the historical, political, and economic factors of these various countries differ and generalizations cannot be made amongst the cultural groups, the particular countries from Africa and Afghanistan share some commonalities, to be discussed more thoroughly in various chapters.

At the present, the term *war-affected children* is commonly used in literature to discuss children who have come from countries where there has been conflict. I believe it is important to refer to the child first and then discuss how he or she has been affected by war. I feel strongly that the term *war-affected child* encourages labelling and the homogenization of children who have experienced far too much adversity already. Instead, I would like to first discuss the child for who he or she is and then discuss to what extent he or she has been affected by conflict. While labels and terms are often necessary to encourage discussion and to further the understanding of an issue, we must be careful not to assume that just because a child is a refugee, he or she has been traumatized or has been adversely affected by war. If there is one overarching message that I wish to convey in this book, it is the diversity of circumstances that children have experienced and the multiplicity and range of personal responses children will have to any given experience. Despite trying to find common experiences and ways to support children who have encountered similar circumstances, there is no tested program or set of lessons that a teacher can implement that will solve the complexity of issues concerning children who have lived through war. Instead, I offer some ideas and strategies that might be useful in supporting some children and I will provide explanations of some programs that have been developed and implemented within schools that have been successful in connecting children and youth to school systems, to individual teachers, and to community organizations.

Child Soldiers/Children Associated with Armed Groups

Children who have lost their parents through death or displacement are more vulnerable than those living with their families, and more at risk of being recruited into armed forces or groups. Children may be forcibly abducted from their families and forced to take part in serious acts of violence, often against family members or friends. These children are referred to as *child soldiers* and serve many peripheral functions in zones of conflict. The *Cape Town Principles* defined a child soldier as:

> Any person under 18 years of age who is part of any kind of regular or irregular armed force in any capacity, including but not limited to cooks, porters, messengers, and those accompanying such groups, other than purely as family members. Girls recruited for sexual purposes and forced marriages are included in this definition. It does not, therefore, only refer to a child who is carrying or has carried arms. (UNICEF, 1999, p. 1)

Three well-known armed opposition groups are the Lord's Resistance Army (LRA), which is located in northern Uganda, the Revolutionary United Front (RUF) in Sierra Leone, and the Liberation Tigers of Tamil Eelam (LTTE), also known as the Tamil Tigers, in Sri Lanka. These forces recruit children, the majority between 12 and 16, and are noted for extreme violence and brutality. Acts of sexual abuse, physical and mental torture, unlawful arrest and detention, disfigurement and mutilation, and forced cannibalism are common among these militant groups. New abductees are often forced to kill family members or neighbours and, if they do not comply, they are killed.

Youth are attractive to many military commanders throughout the world because they can be easily trained to carry out the most repulsive orders, they are able to tote most of today's lightweight weapons, and they can be found in abundance when adult males become scarce (Briggs, 2005). This is carried out in the countries where children, poverty, and violence are in abundance. Although some suggest that children voluntarily choose to join rebel forces to increase their power and prestige, a child is not able to fully comprehend the extent of the risks of conflict and, in some cases, the child's only means of survival (e.g., money for food) is with the rebel armies. *Joining voluntarily* may not be the most appropriate term to describe the realities of this situation. Although efforts have been undertaken by various international organizations for the disarmament, demobilization, and reintegration (DDR) of child combatants, a strategy to stop the use of child soldiers is imperative (UNICEF, 2003).

Immigrant

An immigrant is a person who becomes a permanent resident of another country that is not his or her native land. A refugee may be considered an immigrant, but the term *immigrant* does not necessarily mean that the person is also a refugee. One can be an immigrant but not be considered a refugee. Broadly defined, an immigrant is often referred to as someone who moves for economic reasons and the refugee is considered to be someone who flees for political reasons (McBrien, 2005).

Internally Displaced Person

Is a person who has had to leave his or her home, but remains within the boundary of the home country. These people are forced to leave because of armed conflict, war, general violence, environmental disasters or man-made disasters, or because of generalized violence. It is estimated that there are approximately 26 million internally displaced people and out of this population children make up 43 per cent of the internally displaced (UNHCR, 2009).

Psychosocial Effects of War

Studies conducted in the field of child and adolescent psychology and psychiatry were particularly useful for reviewing the literature related to the psychological and social effects of war on children. The term *psychosocial* notes the relationship between both the psychological and the social effects that influence each other. Machel (2001) refers to the psychological effects as those that affect emotion, behaviour, thoughts, memory, learning ability, perceptions, and understanding. Relationships altered by death, separation, estrangement and other losses, family and community breakdown, damage to social values and customary practices, and the destruction of social facilities and services are all considered to be social effects. The economic capacity of the family that has been affected by war is also considered to be a social effect.

Refugee

Although I will often conflate the terms *war-affected* and *refugee*, the terms are not synonymous. As the following definition describes, the term *refugee* is a much broader term that encompasses people who must leave their country of origin because of circumstances including, but not limited to, conflict or war.

The United Nations High Commissioner for Refugees (UNHCR) is an international agency committed to the protection and assistance of the refugee population. The 1951 Convention Relating to the Status of Refugees defines a refugee as follows:

> Someone with a well-founded fear of being persecuted for reasons of race, religion, nationality, membership of a particular social group

or political opinion, is outside the country of his nationality and is
unable or owing to such fear, is unwilling to avail himself of the protection of that country; or who, not having a nationality and being
outside the country of his former habitual residence as a result of
such events, is unable or, owing to such fear, unwilling to return to
it. (UNHCR, 1951 p. 16)

The term *refugee* has evolved since it was first defined and it now encompasses children who have fled conflict and who are seeking asylum.
Asylum-seekers are people who have crossed an international border
for reasons of securing their personal safety. While not all refugees have
been affected by war, a refugee may have been forced to relocate due to
environmental issues, political issues, or for reasons of personal safety.

Too often, the term *immigrant* is used to discuss issues related to
a refugee. I argue strongly that these two terms are distinct and must
not be used interchangeably. A refugee has been forced to relocate due
the reasons mentioned above. An immigrant chooses to leave his or her
country most often for issues related to work and economical factors. A
refugee is compelled to leave his or her country of origin for reasons of
asylum, safety, or fear of persecution.

Annotated Bibliography

AUTOBIOGRAPHIES, MEMOIRS, AND STORIES OF CHILDREN AND WAR

Ali, N. (2010). *I am Nujood, age 10 and divorced*. New York: Three Rivers Press. This is the story of the forced marriage and abuse of ten-year-old Nujood. Her defiance of her family and customs have inspired other girls to challenge their marriages and advocate for their basic human rights.

Bashir, H. (2008). *Tears of the desert: A memoir of survival in Darfur*. New York: Random House. The story of Halima and the atrocities and losses she endured living in Darfur. Despite her suffering, this tragedy is a story of hope.

Beah, I. (2007). *A long way gone*. Vancouver, BC: Douglas and McIntyre. The autobiography of a child soldier from Sierra Leone who eventually came to New York. Includes a chronology of events in recent Sierra Leone history.

Bixler, M. (2006). *The lost boys of Sudan*. Athens, GA: University of Georgia Press. The personal stories of four Lost Boys of Sudan who came to America after being on the run in Sudan, Kenya, and Ethiopia. The boys were orphaned or separated from their families and caught in the brutality of Sudan's civil war.

Bok, F. (2003). *Escape from slavery*. New York: St. Martin's Press. The story of a seven-year-old boy who was taken to the north of Sudan to be a slave to Muslim farmers. He escapes after 10 years and moves from prisons to refugee camps and then is granted relocation in America.

Bul Dau, J., & Sweeney, M. (2007). *God grew tired of us*. Washington, DC: National Geographic Society. John Bul Dau became a Lost Boy of Sudan at age 12. This autobiography explores the brutality of his experiences but also provides a rich glimpse into African culture and a message of inspiration for future generations.

Cleave, C. (2009). *Little Bee*. Toronto, ON: Doubleday. A fictional story about a young girl from Nigeria, her escape to England, and her life in a detention centre. After escaping from the centre, Little Bee finds a woman in England whom she encountered on the beach in Nigeria. The two lives of the women are intertwined to tell a compelling story about racism, war, children, and the treatment of refugees.

De Temmerman, E. (2001). *Aboke girls: Children abducted in northern Uganda*. Kampala: Fountain Publishers. A journalist reconstructs the journey of two Aboke girls who managed to escape from the Lord's Resistance Army in northern Uganda.

Deng, B., Deng, A., Ajak, B., & Bernstein, J.A. (2005). *They poured fire on us from the sky: The true story of three lost boys from Sudan*. New York: Publicaffairs. The personal accounts of three boys who were forced from their homes and trekked alone across Africa's largest country to make it to safety and eventually come to the United States.

Eggers, D. (2006). *What is the what*. San Francisco: McSweeney's. The true memoirs of a Sudanese lost boy. His journey began in Sudan with the start of the civil war and took him across thousands of miles to camps in both Ethiopia and Kenya. He ultimately ended up in the United States, where he faced further struggles.

Filipovic, Z. (2006). *Zlata's diary.* New York: Penguin. The story of 11-year-old Zlata, who wrote her diary from 1991 to 1993 during the Bosnian War. The diary includes many descriptions of war through the eyes of a child who is struggling to understand religious and cultural differences in her city.

Gourevitch, P. (1998). *We wish to inform you that tomorrow we will be killed with our families: Stories from Rwanda.* New York: Picador. A story of the genocide in Rwanda and a story of survival.

Grennan, C. (2010). *Little princes.* NY: HarperCollins. A book about an American volunteer, Conor Grennan who volunteered at Princes Children's Home in Nepal. A story about child trafficking and civil war in Nepal.

Hatzfeld, J. (2005). *Into the quick of life.* London: Serpent's Tail. (English translation, originally published in French, 2000.) The horrifying accounts from 14 individuals, ranging from teens to adults, who survived the Rwandan Genocide.

Iweala, U. (2005). *Beasts of no nation.* New York: HarperCollins. This recent novel is the dark coming-of-age tale of a young boy turned child soldier in an unnamed West African country. His search for normalcy draws him into an eerily close relationship with his commander and fellow soldiers.

Joya, M. (2009). *A woman among warlords.* New York: Scribner. Malalai Joya is a remarkable woman who was raised in refugee camps in Pakistan and Iran. She became a teacher in a secret school and contributed to establishing a free medical clinic and orphanage. *Time* magazine named her one of the 100 Most Influential People of 2010.

Kamara, M., & McClelland, S. (2008). *The bite of the mango.* New York: Annick Press. The story of Mariatu Kamara, who was a child in Sierra Leone and who is now a student in Canada and a UNICEF Special Representative for Children and Armed Conflict.

London, C. (2007). *One day the soldiers came.* New York: HarperCollins. Former research associate with Refugees International, Charles London tells the remarkable stories of refugee children and children affected by war and violence.

Nazer, M., & Lewis, D. (2004). *Slave*. London: Virago Press. The story of a 12-year-old girl from Sudan and how she was kidnapped and sold into slavery and who eventually escaped.

Nemat, M. (2007). *Prisoner of Tehran*. Toronto, ON: Viking. The story of Marina Nemat, a woman from Tehran. Arrested on false charges, she was sent to Evin prison, where she was tortured. She was freed after suffering harrowing atrocities in prison and only when she agreed to convert to Islam and be married.

Oron, J. *Cry of the giraffe*. Toronto, ON: Annick. Based on real events, this book tells the story of Wuditu and her family as they flee Ethiopia for Sudan because of persecution for their Jewish faith.

Phan, Z. (2009). *Little daughter: A memoir of survival in Burma and the West*. Toronto, ON: Penguin. A true story of a Burmese woman and her life as a refugee in Thailand, her escape to Bangkok, and her life after she claimed asylum in the United Kingdom.

Rusesabagina, P. (2006). *An ordinary man*. New York: Penguin. The story of Paul Rusesabagina, who was the owner of a hotel in Rwanda during the genocide in 1994. He helped shelter 1,268 Rwandans and is now internationally renowned for his efforts.

Salbi, Z. (2006). *The other side of war*. Washington: National Geographic Society. The stories of war told by women survivors and a collection of stunning photographs that add rich contextual background to the beautifully written stories.

Scroggins, D. (2004). *Emma's war*. London: Harper Perennial. The story of Emma McCune, who married a rebel leader in Sudan. The story is an account of the struggles of violence and conflict during the civil war in southern Sudan.

Wiesel, E. (1958). *Night*. New York: Hill and Wang. A story of the terrifying memories of Elie Wiesel's life in the Auschwitz concentration camp and Buchenwald.

REPORTS AND BACKGROUND
ON CHILDREN AND WAR

Allen, T. (2006). *Trial justice: The international criminal court and the Lord's Resistance Army*. London: Zed Books. Through an in-depth exploration of the conflict in Uganda, this book examines hostility toward the newly established ICC (International Criminal Court), the global impacts of international criminal justice, and their future implications for amnesties and peace talks.

Boyden, J., & de Berry, J. (2004). *Children and youth on the front line: Ethnography, armed conflict and displacement.* New York: Berghahn Books. This book is about the experiences of children and adolescents who have grown up in conflict situations. This book also discusses the blurred lines between casualty and combatant.

Briggs, J. (2005). *Innocents lost: When child soldiers go to war.* New York: Basic Books. An eye-opening report on the reasons why children become soldiers and what the world can do to end this situation. A journalist travels to various countries and reports on his experiences and contacts with youth in conflict.

Dallaire, R. (2010). *They fight like soldiers, they die like children.* Toronto, ON: Random House. Background to the issue of child soldiers and a discussion on initiatives to eradicate this global problem.

Dunson, D.H. (2005). *No room at the table: Earth's most vulnerable children.* New York: Orbis Books. A broad introduction to issues surrounding global suffering on the part of children. The author tells the stories of several real children in each chapter and highlights issues such as conflict, poverty, hunger and sexual exploitation.

Lewis, S. (2005). *Race against time.* Toronto, ON: House of Anansi Press. A collection of the 2005 CBC Massey Lectures Series by Stephen Lewis. Internationally recognized prolific speaker Stephen Lewis eloquently explores issues surrounding the developing state of many of the world's countries. The main focus is on the state of Africa and the HIV/AIDS epidemic.

Machel, G. (2001). *The Impact of war on children.* London: C. Hurst and Co. This comprehensive UN report examines the realities of children in conflict and focuses on issues including child soldiers, health, sexual violence, weapons, landmines, child protection, and media. It also puts forth a children's agenda for peace and security.

Office of the United Nations High Commissioner for Refugees. (2006). *The state of the world's refugees: Human displacement in the new*

millennium. Oxford: Oxford University Press: UNHCR. A primarily statistical report, this book provides factual information about
the refugee experience, analyzes policy issues, and underscores
the struggle to implement a durable international solution to displacement. Four additional editions of this resource include other
topics and challenges, including: *Humanitarian Action* (2000), *A
Humanitarian Agenda* (1997), *In Search of Solutions* (1995), and *The
Challenge of Protection* (1993).

University of Alberta. (2006). *Children and war: Impacts, protection
and rehabilitation (Phase Two: Protection).* Los Angeles: Dr. W.
Andy Knight (research director). This is part of a research project
through the University of Alberta. It offers some excellent articles
regarding the protection of child soldiers both from a local and
international perspective.

Wessells, M. (2006). *Child soldiers: From violence to protection.*
Cambridge, MA: Harvard University Press. Based on participatory
research and interviews with child soldiers, this book illuminates
the enormity of youth involvement in global conflict.

Additional resources are included in the reference list.

REFUGEE CHILDREN AND POST-MIGRATION EXPERIENCES

Asgedom, M. (2002). *Of beetles and angels.* New York: Little, Brown
and Company. The story of a young boy whose journey took him
from civil war in east Africa to a refugee camp, to an American
suburb, and then onto Harvard University.

Berry, J.W., Phinney, J.S., Sam, D.L., & Vedder, P. (Eds.). (2006).
*Immigrant youth in cultural transition: Acculturation, identity
and adaptation across national contexts.* Mahwah, NJ: Lawrence
Erlbaum Associates. Using data from more than 7,000 immigrant
youth, this volume includes four distinct patterns of adolescent
acculturation: integration, ethnic, natural, and diffuse.

Eisikovits, R. (2008). *Immigrant youth who excel.* Charlotte, NC:
Information Age. This book focuses on the successes and

achievements of immigrant youth. The authors question many of the assumptions and goals of educational systems.

Portes, A., & Rumbaut, R.G. (Eds.). (2001). *Ethnicities: Children of immigrants in America*. Berkeley: Russell Sage Foundation. A collection of scholarly essays that explore the issues faced by the children of immigrants in "western" societies. See *Legacies*.

Portes, A., & Rumbaut, R.G. (Eds.). (2001). *Legacies: The story of the immigrant second generation*. Berkeley: Russell Sage Foundation. A collection of scholarly essays that explore the issues faced by second generation immigrants in "western" societies. A companion to *Ethnicities*. Both collections are based on the Children of Immigrants Longitudinal Study (CILS) involving more than 5,000 youth from across the United States. An essential read to understanding immigration studies.

Rutter, J. (2003). *Supporting refugee children in 21st century Britain: A compendium of essential information*. Staffordshire: Trentham Books. This British guide to working with refugee children is divided into three sections: being a refugee in the United Kingdom (including policies, rights, and integration issues); refugees in schools (including an overview of the EAL experience, racism, policies, and bridging the gap between school and family); refugee groups in the United Kingdom (including statistics and brief background information on the countries where refugees originate). Most of the contents are relevant to the Canadian context.

RESOURCES FOR EDUCATORS

Bergman, C. (Ed.). (2003). *Another day in paradise*. New York: Orbis Books. The stories of war as told from humanitarian workers from around the world.

British Columbia Curriculum Supplement. (2008). *Making space: Teaching for diversity and social justice throughout the K-12 curriculum*. British Columbia: Library and Archives Canada Cataloguing in Publication. This government publication is a curriculum supplement that aims to help teachers integrate refugee perspectives into their teaching. It is divided by grade and takes a cross-curricular approach. Also available online.

Children as Peacebuilders (CAP) Project. (2003). *A kind of friendship: Working for and with war affected children and youth.* Ottawa: Cultural Connections. This is a resource manual for teachers and other educators who want to provide or adapt programming for war affected children. It gives an overview of some war-affected issues, suggests guidelines for programmers, and then provides ideas for a wide range of activities, projects, and issues to be explored with war-affected youth. A very readable and hands-on guide.

Dallaire, R. (2003). *Shake hands with the devil: The failure of humanity in Rwanda.* New York: Carroll & Graff. The riveting story of Lt. Gen. Roméo Dallaire and his United Nations Mission in Rwanda during the 1994 genocide.

Figley, C.R. (Ed.). (2002). *Treating compassion fatigue.* New York: Routledge. A collection of research on the topic of secondary traumatic stress. Sections of the book include assessment, treatment, and prevention strategies on the topic of compassion fatigue.

Fong, R. (Ed.). (2004). *Culturally competent practice with immigrant and refugee children and families.* New York: Guilford Press. This compilation of resources provides a philosophical framework, background information, and effective approaches for dealing sensitively with the needs of refugee children and their families. Written by a variety of experts, it covers the experiences of refugees from 14 different countries in detail.

Goldhagen, D.J. (2009). *Worse than war.* New York: Public Affairs. A provocative book about the investigation of genocide. The author provides substantial evidence to help readers understand the concepts of genocide and eliminationism and he puts forth a compelling argument for individuals, institutions, and governments to end the scourge on humanity.

Hamilton, R., & Moore, D. (2004). *Educational interventions for refugee children: Theoretical perspectives and implementing best practice.* New York: RoutledgeFalmer. Drawing on international research (New Zealand), its focus is quite broad and it highlights topics ranging from support services to intervention to the need for schools to identify and prepare for the arrival of refugee students.

Jones, C., & Rutter, J. (Eds.). (2001). *Refugee education: Mapping the field*. Staffordshire: Trentham Books. A compilation of scholarly articles that explore the complexities of the relationship between war affected children and the "western" school system.

Marten, J. (Ed.). (2002). *Children and war*. New York: New York University Press. An historical examination of war and how children have been affected by war.

Mortenson, G., & Relin, D.O. (2007). *Three cups of tea: One man's missino to promote peace one school at a time*. New York: Penguin. After a failed attempt at climbing Pakistan's K2, Greg Mortenson provides a compelling and extraordinary story of how he worked to build a school and provide an education to children—especially girls in Pakistan and Afghanistan (also available in a young reader's edition).

Mortenson, G. (2009). *Stones into schools*. New York: Viking. A follow-up book to Mortenson's *Three Cups of Tea*. The book describes how Mortenson and his manager established the schools in Afghanistan. His non-profit agency, Central Asia Institute, has established more than 130 schools in Pakistan and Afghanistan and has greatly benefited women and girls throughout the two countries.

Nolen, S. (2007). *28 stories of AIDS in Africa*. Toronto, ON: Vintage Canada. The stories of the African AIDS pandemic and the personal stories of the men, women, and children involved.

Osler, A. (Ed.). (2005). *Teachers, human rights and diversity*. Staffordshire: Trentham Books. This anthology of essays from the United Kingdom and the United States explores the pertinent question of how to educate citizens in multicultural societies. Intended as a guide for educators in any capacity, it provides tools for using the principles of human rights in resolving and overcoming cultural differences.

Pearce, S. (2005). *You wouldn't understand: White teachers in multiethnic classrooms*. Staffordshire: Trentham Books. This volume illuminates the attitudes of white teachers toward ethnic diversity.

It suggests that whiteness is not so much a biological as a social way of being. It challenges educators to examine their ingrained perspectives and to acknowledge that to teach is a significant and political activity.

Rothschild, B. (2006). *Help for the helper.* New York: W.W. Norton. A resource book for therapists who work with traumatized clients. An overview of research on the neurobiology of empathy and a comprehensive discussion on vicarious trauma and compassion fatigue.

Rutter, J. (1998). *Refugees: A resource book for primary schools.* London: The Refugee Council. This volume contains stories, cartoons, activities, and background information for teachers to use with their elementary school classes. The language is simple, but the issues are powerful.

Rutter, J. (2004). *Refugees: We left because we had to: A citizenship teaching resource for 11-18 year olds.* London: Refugee Council. A companion to the previous book, this volume provides a wealth of information, stories, activities, and images to help older students engage with the realities of world conflict and immigration. A very well-put-together resource.

Sen, A. (2006). *Identity and violence: The illusion of destiny.* New York: Norton. This book by a Nobel Prize–winning author is a philosophical critique of the causes behind our world's brutality. It explores concepts of identity and race as well as what is really meant by multiculturalism and the historical divide between "west" and "east." A good theoretical foundation for thinking about war-affected children.

Weber, C. (2006). *Nurturing the peacemakers in our students: A guide to writing and speaking out against war and peace.* Portsmouth, NH: Heinemann. Peter Elbow and other famous writing teachers provide strategies for teaching peace to students.

PSYCHOSOCIAL NEEDS OF WAR-AFFECTED CHILDREN

Ahearn, F.L. (Ed.). (2000). *Psychosocial wellness of refugees.* New York: Berghahn Books. A collection of qualitative and quantitative research on the psychosocial wellness of refugees.

Apfel, R., & Simon, B. (Eds.). (1996). *Minefields in their hearts.* London: Yale University Press. A collection of papers by leading experts in the field of mental health pertaining to children in war zones and communal violence.

Bracken, P.J., & Petty, C. (Eds.). (1998). *Rethinking the trauma of war.* New York: Free Association Books. This book suggests that treating war-affected individuals for PTSD (either in their own countries or after their arrival as refugees in new countries) may not be culturally sensitive. It asks the reader to consider the possibility that western therapy is not appropriate in all cases and critiques the popular discourse on trauma.

De Jong, J. (Ed.). (2002). *Trauma, war and violence: Public mental health in socio-cultural context.* New York: Springer. This book offers information about mental health programs that have been established in poverty-stricken and war-torn countries. Its information is extensive, but its primary focus is on adults.

Eyber, C., & Loughry, M. (2003). *Psychosocial concepts in humanitarian work with children.* Washington: The National Academies Press. A resource on the topic of refugee children and mental health. After a brief overview of refugee issues (such as stress, resilience, and trauma), it provides a 100-page annotated bibliography. Although the bibliography deals primarily with psychosocial concerns, the scope of resources is very broad.

Kline, M., & Levine, P. (2007). *Trauma through a child's eyes: Awakening the ordinary miracle of healing.* Berkeley: North Atlantic Books. This is a sequel to *Waking the Tiger* (below). It further examines the physiological basis of trauma with an emphasis on resilience.

Kohli, R.K.S., & Mitchell, F. (2007). *Working with unaccompanied asylum seeking children.* New York: Palgrave. This book can be used to help asylum-seeking children who are either orphaned or unaccompanied. It is designed to aid post-migration victims.

Levine, P.A., & Frederick, A. (1997). *Waking the tiger: Healing trauma.* Berkeley: North Atlantic Books. This book provides an approach to dealing with trauma that focuses on the physiological.

Malchiodi, C. (2008). *Creative interventions with traumatized children.* New York: Guilford Press. A resource that includes creative interventions to help children deal with a variety of traumatic

experiences. Some topics include children who have been mal-
treated, accident survivors, and students who have been affected
by bullying.

Rothschild, B. (2000). *The body remembers: The psychophysiology
of trauma and trauma treatment*. New York: W.W. Norton and
Company. An exploration of the physiological impacts of trauma.

Wilson, J.P., & Drozdek, B. (2004). *Broken spirits*. New York: Brunner-
Routledge. A handbook on the impact of dislocation, trauma, and
loss. Based on empirical research and clinical and social experience, the authors offer a comprehensive account on the mental
health of traumatized asylum-seekers, refugees, and war and torture victims.

Williams, M.B., Poijula, S. (2002). *The PTSD workbook*. Oakland: New
Harbinger. This book provides simple, effective techniques for
overcoming traumatic stress syndrome symptoms.

COMMUNITY BUILDING AND ALTERNATIVE THERAPY RESOURCES

Darley, S., & Heath, W. (2008). *The expressive arts activity book: A
resource for professionals*. Philadelphia: Jessica Kingsley Publishers.
This book informs the reader about the various ways an individual
can use different art forms to express feelings and perceptions.
This book also discusses how various forms of art can be used as
therapy.

Jones, A. (1998). *104 activities that build*. Richland, Washington: Rec
Room Publishing. This book aims to build community, confidence,
self-esteem, and cooperation.

Jones, A. (1999). *Team-building activities for every group*. Richland, WA:
Rec Room Publishing. This text includes 100+ games and activities
to help build teamwork and group interaction skills.

Kaduson, H., & Schaefer, C. (Eds.). (1997). *101 favorite play techniques*.
New York: Rowman and Littlefield. This book provides simple
ideas for helping students to gain confidence and work through
their feelings using play.

Liebmann, M. (1986). *Art therapy for groups: A handbook of themes, games and exercises.* Brookline, MA: Brookline Books. This is a practical guide to activities, lessons, and games that teachers can use to promote art therapy for groups.

Malchiodi, C.A. (1998). *Understanding children's drawings.* New York: Gilford Press. An overview of the multidimensional aspects of children's drawings. A resource for therapists and counsellors.

Malchiodi, C.A. (2007). *The art therapy sourcebook.* New York: McGraw Hill. This is a step-by-step guide with instructions on how to use art therapy to help students recover from pain or trauma.

Simmons, L. (2006). *Interactive art therapy: "No talent required" projects.* New York: Routledge, Taylor and Francis. A collection of instructions and projects for all levels to help students work through major events and/or issues in their lives.

Williams, M.B., & Poijula, S. (2002). *The PTSD workbook.* Oakland, CA: New Harbinger. A collection of techniques and interventions to help trauma survivors. Workbook format.

BOOKS FOR CHILDREN AND YOUNG ADULTS

Ahmed, S.S. (2007). *Qayb libaax. The lion's share.* Minneapolis, MN: Minnesota Humanities Commission. Appropriate for grades 4–8. A folktale teaching children not to take more than they need.

Askar, S., & Munsch, R. (2007). *From far away.* Vancouver, BC: Annick Press. A young girl's first-person account of moving to Canada as a refugee. Appropriate for early years.

Candappa, M., & Rutter, J. (Eds.). (1998). *Why do they have to fight?: Refugee children's stories from Bosnia, Kurdistan, Somalia and Sri Lanka.* London: The Refugee Council. Stories, resources, photographs, and interactive activities for children to learn about refugees. Appropriate for grades 4–8.

Davies, H., & Rutter, J. (2001). *Kosovan journeys: Refugee children tell their stories.* London: The Refugee Council. An oversized book that tells the stories of refugee children in their own words. Early years.

Dalton, D. (2006). *Living as a refugee in America: Carbino's story.* Milwaukee: World Almanac Library. Part of the Children in Crisis series, this book tells the story of a Sudanese refugee. Suitable for middle years.

Ellis, D. (2000). *Breadwinner.* Toronto, ON: House of Anansi Press. A story of life in Afghanistan as told through 11-year-old Parvana.

Ellis, D. (2002). *Parvana's journey.* Toronto, ON: House of Anansi Press. This, the second book in the fictional *Breadwinner* trilogy, tells the story of Parvana's quest to be reunited with her family and her courageous efforts to deal with adversity. Her encounters with people and her daily experiences of life in Afghanistan help the reader understand the lives of children who live amidst war.

Ellis, D. (2003). *Mud city.* Toronto, ON: House of Anansi Press. In this, book three in the *Breadwinner* trilogy, Shauzia, Parvana's best friend, has left Afghanistan in search of a better life. She must fend for herself in Pakistan.

Gallo, D.R. (Ed.). (2004). *First crossing.* Cambridge, MA: Candlewick Press. A collection of 10 stories written by teenagers who have emigrated from war-affected countries and are now living in the United States.

Goode, K. (2003). *Jumping to heaven: Stories about refugee children.* Kent Town, South Australia: Wakefield Press. A collection of short stories based on the true experiences of refugee children. Appropriate for grades 5–8.

Hassan, M. (2007). *Dhegdheer: A scary Somali folktale.* Minneapolis, MN: Minnesota Humanities Commission. A dual-language folktale about the message of good and evil. Suitable for middle years.

HimRights and Watch List. (n.d.). *Farewell to firearms: A pictorial report.* Lalitpur, Nepal: Children in armed conflict in Nepal. This book about conflict was written and illustrated by children living in conflict in Nepal.

Howard, H. (2006). *Living as a refugee in America: Mohammed's story.* Milwaukee: World Almanac Library. Part of the Children in Crisis series, this book tells the story of an Afghani refugee. Suitable for middle years.

Khan, R. & Himler, R. (1998). *The roses in my carpets.* Toronto, ON: Stoddart Kids. A story about a young boy who lives in Afghanistan and who finds refuge in weaving carpets. After being tormented by nightmares of war, he must now cope with the tragic news of his little sister being hit by a car. As she recovers in the hospital we learn about the close familial bond and the hope for a better future. Suitable for Grades 3–6.

Levine, K. (2002). *Hana's suitcase.* Toronto, ON: Second Story Press. This book tells a true story that became an international bestseller. Imprisoned by the German Nazis, Hana Brady was later killed in the gas chambers in Auschwitz. When Hana's suitcase was sent to the Tokyo Holocaust Education Resource Centre, it became an artifact that would help children understand the effects of war.

Milway, K.S. (2008). *One hen: How one small loan made a big difference.* Toronto, ON: Kids Can Press. *One Hen* is a story of how reaching out to someone with a small loan can have a big impact. The main character, Kojo, is based on a real person, Kwabena Darko, who changed a community in Ghana. Suitable for grades 3–8.

Mohammed, K., & Williams, K.L. (2007). *Four feet, two sandals.* Grand Rapids, MI: Eerdmans Books for Young Readers. The touching story of two young girls who become friends in a refugee camp. Appropriate for grades 3–5.

Mortenson, G., & Relin, D.O. (2009). *Three cups of tea* (Young readers ed.). New York: Puffin. This adaption of Greg Mortenson's story, intended for young readers, tells about his work building more than 60 schools in Pakistan and Afghanistan.

Mortenson, G., & Roth, S.L. (2009). *Listen to the wind: The story of Dr. Greg & three cups of tea.* New York: Penguin. A story about Greg Mortenson and how he was inspired to build schools in remote regions of Pakistan and Afghanistan. An early years book based on the bestselling book *Three Cups of Tea: One Man's Mission to Promote Peace One School at a Time.* Best for early years. A young reader's edition is also available.

Naidoo, B. (Ed.). (2004). *Making it home.* New York: Puffin. A collection of stories of children who have been forced to flee their homes and become refugees because of war and violence. The stories include maps and brief histories of each country and picture of the child authors. Suitable for early and middle years.

Radunsky, V. (2004). *What does peace feel like?* New York: Atheneum Books for Young Readers. A brightly illustrated book that teaches young children about peace.

Scholes, K. (1989). *Peace begins with you.* San Francisco: Sierra Club Books. A book about peace and a call for social justice. This book encourages children to think about how they can contribute to peace in the world. Appropriate for grades 4–6.

Seuss, Dr. (1973). *Did I ever tell you how lucky you are?* New York: Random House. An old man narrates the book and tells the young creature it is really quite lucky compared to creatures from other places. Suitable for all ages.

Seuss, Dr. (1984). *The butter battle book.* New York: Random House. This rhyming classic exposes the ridiculousness of war. Best suited to middle years. Despite being Dr. Seuss, some of the content would be too advanced for early readers.

Seuss, Dr. (1996). *My many coloured days.* New York: Knopf. Good for all ages. A picture book about colours and mood.

Smith, D.J. (2002). *If the world were a village.* Toronto, ON: Kids Can Press. A beautifully illustrated book about the makeup of the world's people. Chapters are organized into categories such as, ages, languages, food, air and water, schooling, and several others to help children be more globally aware of the people around the world.

Stratton, A. (2004). *Chanda's secrets.* Toronto: Annick Press. A fictional and gripping personal story of a young woman and her family living in sub-Saharan Africa.

Strauss, R. (2007). *One well: The story of water on earth.* Toronto, ON: Kids Can Press. A rich and beautifully illustrated book about water resources around the world. Helps children imagine that there is only one well in the world and to think about limited drinking water resources.

Winter, J. (2008). *Wangari's trees of peace.* New York: Harcourt. The true story of Kenyan environmentalist Wangari Maathai. Wangari was awarded the Nobel Peace Prize in 2004 because of her contribution to world peace through the Green Belt Movement. Suitable for all grades.

References

Ahearn, F. (Ed.). (2000). *Psychosocial wellness of refugees*. Oxford: Berghahn.

Allison, D.J. (2005, May). A *brief indictment of social justice in education administration*. Paper presented at the Canadian Association for the Study of Educational Administration, Winnipeg, MB.

Anderson, A., Hamilton, R., Moore, D., Loewen, S., & Frater-Mathieson, K. (2004). Education of refugee children: Theoretical perspectives and best practice. In R. Hamilton & D. Moore (Eds.), *Educational interventions for refugee children* (pp. 1–12). New York: RoutledgeFalmer.

Ashcroft, B., & Ahluwalia, P. (1999). *Edward Said* (2nd Ed.). New York: Routledge.

Bhabha, H.K. (1994). *The location of culture*. London: Routledge.

Boothby, N., Strang, A., & Wessells, M. (Eds.). (2006). *A world turned upside down: Social ecological approaches to children in war zones.* Bloomfield, CT: Kumarian.

Boyden, J., & de Berry, J. (Eds.). (2004). *Children and youth on the front line.* Oxford: Berghahn Books.

Bregman, G., & Killen, M. (1999). Adolescents' and young adults' reasoning about career choice and the role of parental influence. *Journal of Research on Adolescence, 9*(3), 253–75.

Briggs, J. (2005). *Innocents lost: When child soldiers go to war.* New York: Perseus.

Bronfenbrenner, U. (1977). In U. Bronfenbrenner (Ed.), *Making human beings: Human: Bioecological perspectives on human development* (pp. 41–49). Thousand Oaks, CA: Sage Publications.

Bronfenbrenner, U. (1979). *The ecology of human development.* Cambridge, MA: Harvard University Press.

Bronfenbrenner, U. (1992). Ecological systems theory. In R. Vasta (Ed.), *Six theories of child development: Revised formulations and current issues* (pp. 187–249). London: Jessica Kingsley Publishers.

Bronfenbrenner, U. (1994). Ecological models of human development. In T. Husen & T.N. Postlethwaite (Eds.), *International encyclopedia of education* (2nd Ed., Vol. 3, pp. 1643–47). Oxford: Pergamon.

Bronfenbrenner, U. (1999). Environments in developmental perspective: Theoretical and operational models. In S. Friedman, T. Wachs (Eds.), *Measuring environment across the life span: Emerging methods and concepts* (pp. 3–28). Washington, DC: American Psychological Association.

Bronfenbrenner, U. (2001). The bioecological theory of human development. In N. Smelser & P.B. Baltes (Eds.), *International encyclopedia of the social and behavioral sciences* (Vol. 10, pp. 6963–70). New York: Elsevier.

Bronfenbrenner, U. (Ed.). (2005). *Making human beings human: Bioecological perspectives on human development.* Thousand Oaks, CA: Sage Publications.

Bronfenbrenner, U., & Morris, P. (1999). The ecology of the developmental process. In W. Damon & R. Lerner (Eds.), *Handbook of Child Psychology* (5th Ed. pp. 793–828). New York: John Wiley & Sons.

Brydon, D. (ed). 2000. *Postcolonialism: Critical concepts in literary and cultural studies* (5 vols.). London & New York: Routledge.)

Canadian International Development Agency. (2005). *CIDA's action plan on child protection: Promoting the rights of children who need special protection measures.* [Electronic version]. Retrieved October 2, 2005, from www.acdi-cida.gc.ca/childprotection.

Castle, G. (Ed.). (2001). *Postcolonial discourses: An anthology.* Oxford: Blackwell.

Children as Peacebuilders (CAP) Project. (2003). *A kind of friendship: Working for and with war affected children and youth.* Unpublished resource manual. Ottawa, ON: Cultural Connections.

Council of Chief State School Officers. (1996). *Interstate School Leaders Licensure Consortium: Standards for school leaders.* Retrieved March 29, 2006, from www.ccsso.org/content/pdf/isllcstd.pdf.

Crawley, H. (2006) *Child first, migrant second: Ensuring that every child matters.* London: Immigration Law Practitioners' Association.

Crawley, H., & Lester, T. (2005). *No place for a child.* London: Save the Children, UK.

Delgado, R., & Stefancic, R. (Eds.). (2000). *Critical race theory: The cutting edge.* Philadelphia: Temple University.

Dixson, A.D., & Rousseau, C.K. (2005). And we are still not saved: Critical race theory in education ten years later. *Race Ethnicity and Education, 8*(1), 7–27.

Freire, P. (1970). *Pedagogy of the oppressed.* New York: Continuum.

Fullan, M. (2001). *Leading in a culture of change.* San Francisco: Jossey-Bass.

Gandhi, L. (1998). *Postcolonial theory: A critical introduction.* New York: Columbia University Press.

Garbarino, J., & Zurenda, L. (2008). Long term effects of war on children. In L.R. Kurtz (Ed.). *Encyclopedia of violence, peace, and conflict* (pp. 1154–67). Amsterdam: Elsevier.

Gibson, M.A. (1998). Promoting academic success among immigrant students: Is acculturation the issue? *Educational Policy, 12*(6), 615–33.

Goldhagen, D.G. (2009). *Worse than war: Genocide, eliminationism, and the ongoing assault on humanity.* New York: Public Affairs.

Green, A. (2006, November 22). A blunder for which we'll all pay the price. *Daily Mail*, p. 9.

Hamilton, R., & Moore, D. (Eds.). (2004). *Educational Interventions for refugee children*. New York: RoutledgeFalmer.

Harding, K., & Walton, D. (2007, February 24). Canada's hottest new import? Employees. *The Globe and Mail*, p. A14.

Hiddleston, J. (2009). *Understanding postcolonialism*. Stocksfield, UK: Acumen.

Hirschman, C. (2001). The educational enrolment of immigrant youth: A test of the segmented-assimilation hypothesis. *Demography, 38*(3), 317–35.

International Bureau for Children's Rights. (2010). *Children and armed conflict: A guide to international and humanitarian human rights law*. Montreal, QC: Author.

International Commission on Intervention and State Sovereignty. (2001). *The responsibility to protect*. Ottawa, ON: International Development Research Centre.

Knudson, K. (2004). *Winning the war against antipersonnel mines: Biggest challenges still ahead*. [Electronic Version]. Retrieved February 8, 2006, from www.icbl.org/news/lm_2004.

Ladson-Billings, G. (1998). Just what is critical race theory and what's it doing in a nice field like education? *Qualitative Studies in Education, 11*(1), 7–24.

Ladson-Billings, G., & Tate, W.F. (1995). Toward a critical race theory of education. *Teachers College Record, 97*(1), 47–68.

Leithwood, K., & Jantzi, D. (1999). The effects of transformational leadership on organizational conditions and student engagement with school. *Journal of Education Administration 38* (2), 112–29.

Leithwood, K., Jantzi, D., & Steinbach, R. (1999). *Changing leadership for changing times*. Buckingham, UK: Open University Press.

Lunga, V.B. (2008). Postcolonial theory: A language for a critique on globalization? *Perspectives on global development and technology (7)*, 191–99.

Machel, G. (2001). *The impact of war on children*. London: Hurst & Company.

MacKay, T., & Tavares, T. (2005, October 20). *Building hope: Appropriate programming for adolescent and young adult newcomers of war-affected backgrounds and Manitoba schools.* Winnipeg, MB: Manitoba Education, Citizenship and Youth.

Malchiodi, C. (1998). *The art therapy source book.* New York. McGraw-Hill.

Malchiodi, C. (2008). *Creative interventions with traumatized children.* New York: Guilford Press.

Manitoba High School Athletics Association. (2005) *FAQs and Eligibility.* [Electronic version]. Retrieved on May 18, 2007, from www.mhsaa.mb. ca/ pages/faqs/eligibility.php.

McBrien, J.L. (2004). *Discrimination and academic motivation in adolescent refugee girls.* (Doctoral dissertation, Emory University, 2004). Dissertation Abstracts International, A 66/05.

McBrien, J.L. (2005). Educational needs and barriers for refugee students in the United States: A review of the literature. *Review of Educational Research, 75*(3), 329–64.

McBrien, J.L. (2009). Beyond survival: School-related experiences of adolescent refugee girls in the United States and their relationship to motivation and academic success. In G.A. Wiggan & C.B. Hutchison (Eds.). *Global issues in education: Pedagogy, policy and the minority experience* (pp. 294–330). Lanham, MD: Rowman & Littlefield.

Middleton, E.B., & Loughead, T.A. (1993). Parental influence on career development: An integrative framework for adolescent career counselling, *Journal of Career Development, 19*(3), 161–72.

Memmi, A. (1967). *The colonizer and the colonised.* Boston: Beacon Press.

Miles, M.B., & Huberman, A.M. (1994). *Qualitative data analysis* (2nd Ed.). Thousand Oaks, CA: Sage.

Murphy, J. (2005). Unpacking the foundations of ISLLC standards and addressing concerns in the academic community. *Educational Administration Quarterly, 41*(1), 154–91.

Nunez, A. (2004). Using segmented assimilation theory to enhance conceptualization of college participation. *InterActions: UCLA Journal of Education and Information Studies, 1*(1), 1–21.

Office of the High Commissioner for Human Rights. (November 20, 1989). *Convention on the rights of the child.* [Electronic version]. Retrieved August 31, 2006, from www.unhchr.ch/html/menu3/b/k2crc.htm.

Papageorgiou, V., Frangou-Garunovic, A., Iordanidou, R., Yule, W., Smith, P., & Vostanis, P. (2000). War trauma and psychopathology in Bosnian refugee children. *European Child & Adolescent Psychiatry, 9,* 84–90.

Parker, L. (1998). "Race is ... race ain't": An exploration of the utility of critical race theory in qualitative research in education. *Qualitative Studies in Education, 11*(1), 43–55.

Portes, A., Fernandez-Kelly, P., & Haller, W. (2005). Segmented assimilation on the ground: The new second generation in early adulthood. *Ethnic and Racial Studies, 28*(6), 1000–40.

Portes, A., & Rumbaut, R. (2001). *Legacies: The story of the immigrant second generation.* Los Angeles: University of California Press.

Portes, A., & Zhou, M. (1993). The new second generation: Segmented assimilation and its variants. *Annals of the American Academy of Political and Social Science, 530,* 74–96.

Rieff, D. (2007, April 15). Battle over the Banlieues. *The New York Times Magazine,* pp. 52–57.

Rumbaut, R., & Portes, A. (2001). *Ethnicities: Children of immigrants in America.* Los Angeles: University of California Press.

Rutter, J. (2003). *Supporting refugee children in 21st century Britain.* Stoke on Trent, UK: Trentham Books.

Rutter, J. (2006). *Refugee children in the UK.* Berkshire, UK: Open University Press.

Rutter, J., & Jones, C. (Eds.). (1998). *Refugee education: Mapping the field.* Stoke on Trent, UK: Trentham Books.

Sadoway, G. (2001). Canada's treatment of separated refugee children. *European Journal of Migration and Law, 3,* 347–81.

Said, E.W. (1978). *Orientalism.* New York: Random House.

Said, E.W. (1993). *Culture and imperialism.* New York: Random House.

Santrock, J. (2001). *Educational psychology.* Boston: McGraw-Hill.

Scott, F. (2006, November 23). *The £400,000 cost of asylum seekers to city council taxpayers.* [Electronic version]. Retrieved November 24, 2006, from http://iccoventry.icnetwork.co.uk.

Sebald, H. (1989). Adolescents' peer orientation: Changes in the support system during the past three decades. *Adolescence, 24*, 937–46.

Slack, J. (2006, November 22). Migration: The shocking figures. *Daily Mail*, p. 8.

Spivak, G.C. (1985). "Can the subaltern speak? Speculations on window sacrifice." *Wedge 7/8*, 120–30.

Statistics Canada. (2007, March 13). Portrait of the Canadian population in 2006: *National Portrait.* Retrieved April 8, 2007, from www12.statcan.ca/english/census06 /analysis/popdwell/ NatlPortrait1.cfm.

Stewart, J. (1998). *The STARS program (Steps to achieving real-life skills).* Toronto, ON: University of Toronto Press.

Stewart, J. (2000). *The tough stuff series: Immediate guidance for troubled students, middle/senior school* (13 books). Carson, CA: Jalmar Press.

Stewart, J. (2002). *The anger workout book for teens.* Carson, CA: Jalmar Press.

Stewart, J. (2004). *The STARS program* (7 books). Torrance, CA: Hunter House.

Stewart, J. (2007). *Children affected by war: A bioecological investigation into their psychosocial and educational needs.* Unpublished doctoral dissertation, University of Manitoba, Winnipeg, MB, Canada.

Stovall, D. (2005). A challenge to traditional theory: Critical race theory, African-American community organizers, and education. *Discourse: Studies in the Cultural Politics of Education, 26*(1), 95–108.

Stovall, D. (2006). Forging community in race and class: Critical race theory and the quest for social justice in education. *Race Ethnicity and Education, 9*(3), 243–59.

Theoharis, G. (2007). Social justice educational leaders and resistance: Toward a theory of social justice leadership. *Educational Administration Quarterly, 43*(2), 221–58.

Travis, A., & Taylor, M. (2006, November 30). Riot squad fights to regain control of immigration detention centre. *The Guardian*, p. 10.

Trusty, J., Watts, R.E., & Crawford, R. (1996). Career information resources for parents of public school seniors: Findings from a national study. *Journal of Career Development, 22*(4), 227–38.

United Nations General Assembly. (2008, August). *Promotion and protection of the rights of children.* [Electronic version]. Retrieved February 20, 2009 from http://www.iom.int/jahia/webdav/shared/shared/mainsite/policy_and_research/un/63/A_63_227.pdf63 session.

United Nations High Commission for Refugees (UNHCR). (1951). *Convention and protocol relating to the status of refugees.* New York: Author.

UNHCR. (2009, June) *2008 Global trends: refugees, asylum-seekers, returnees, internally displaced and stateless persons.* [Electronic version]. Retrieved February 20, 2009, from www.unhcr.org/4a375c426.html.

United Nations International Children's Fund (UNICEF). (1999). *Cape Town Principles.* Cape Town, South Africa: Author.

UNICEF. (2003). *Convention on the rights of the child.* [Electronic version]. Retrieved January 10, 2006, from www.unicef.org/crc/.

UNICEF. (2004). *Children and landmines: A deadly legacy.* [Electronic version]. Retrieved March 2, 2006, from www.unicef.org/media/media_24360.html.

UNICEF. (2007). *Progress for children.* [Electronic version]. Retrieved February 2010 from www.UNICEF.org/protection /files/ Progress_for_Children-No.8_EN_081309(1).pdf.

UNICEF. (2009). *Machel study 10-year strategic review. Children in conflict in a changing world.* [Electronic version]. Retrieved March 2, 2009 from http://www.un.org/children/conflict/_documents/machel/ExecutivesummaryMachel07.pdf

United Nations Security Council. (2009). *Security Council Resolution 1882, Children and armed conflict.* [Electronic version]. Retrieved February 8, 2009, from www.un.org/Docs/sc/unsc_resolutions09.htm.

United Nations Security Council. (2010). *Security Council Resolutions.* [Electronic version]. Retrieved January 2011 from http://www. un.org/documents/scres.htm.

War Strategy. (2006). *Wars update.* [Electronic version]. Retrieved September 2, 2006, from www.strategypage.com/qnd/wars/ articles/20050923.aspx.

Webb, E., & Davies, M. (2003). Refugee children: Don't replace one form of severe adversity with another. *Archives of Diseases in Childhood, 88,* 365–66.

White, E. (2006, November 23). Refugees moved from Hartshead. *Tameside Advertiser,* p. 1.

Whitehead, T. (2006, November 22). The welfare bill is £60m and it will grow and grow. *Daily Express,* pp. 1, 6.

Whitehead, T., & Drake, M. (2006, November 30). Illegal immigrants to be freed after riot at detention centre. *Daily Express,* p. 17.

Williams, P., & Chrisman, L. (1994). *Colonial discourse and post-colonial theory.* New York: Columbia University Press.

Young, R.J.C. (2001). *Postcolonialsim: An historical introduction.* Malden, MA: Blackwell.

Zhou, M. (1997). Segmented assimilation: Issues, controversies, and recent research on the new second generation. *International Migration Review 31*(4), 975–1008.

Index

politicization of wearing the hijab, 176

mediation and conflict resolution programs for Canadian schools, 287

medical checkups, 45, 111

memories, 31–32, 98–99. *See also* daydreams; flashbacks; nightmares

mental health issues, 192
    seizures and visions, people talking in own mind, 96–97
    stigma attached to, 101
    suicide attempts, 96, 98, 100
    westernized checklists for, 101

mental health of parents, 105–8

mental health practitioners, 10

mental safety, 12

mentoring and tutoring programs, 283

mentors, 121. *See also* advocates

mesosystem, 17, 19, 151, 162–64
    deficiencies in, 121, 164

micro messages of peace (lesson), 275

microsystem, 17, 19, 135–36, 151–62, 205

military use of children, 4–5. *See also* child soldiers

mosque, 161

multiculturalism, 4, 12, 293

multidimensional and comprehensive framework, 17

multi-ethnic cities and countries
    responsibilities of citizens in, 167, 177

multisectoral approach to protection of children, 6

multitiered federal, provincial, and local approach, 93

murder, 4, 43, 52. *See also* violence

Murphy, Joseph, 282

music, 192–93

music therapy, 193

musical storytelling (lesson), 208

Muslim girls, 176

Muslim students, 132, 134

My Many Coloured Days (Seuss), 204

my world (lesson), 198

mystery bag (lesson), 255

nanosystems, 136, 138–41, 162, 165, 205, 295
    close, interpersonal relationship or network, 50, 135, 193
    created by support person, 134
    help students adjust to school, 140

narrative, 11, 27. *See also* storytelling, techniques of

National Asylum Support Service, 174

negative attitudes toward refugees, 173, 176, 187
    preventative and proactive programs to counteract, 286

negative influences coming from the community, 160

neighbours, 19

newcomer support classes, 288

newcomers
    need education on rights in Canada, 167, 175, 177

nightmares, 220–21

No Place for a Child (Crawley and Lester), 170

non-westernized models of psychosocial support, 287

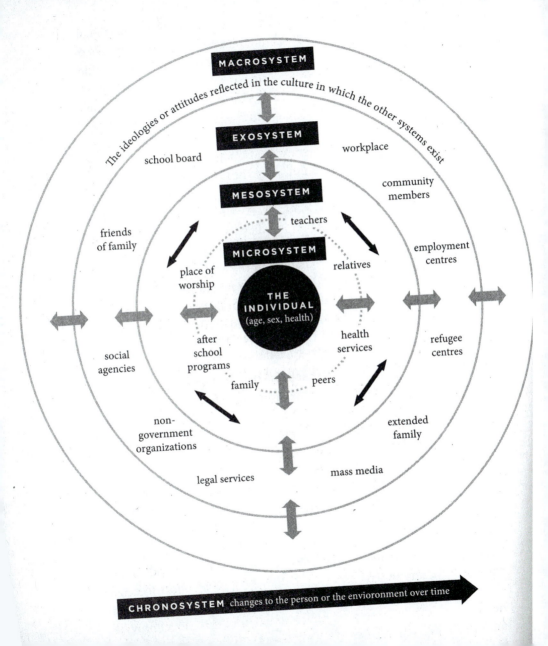